*John Dewey and the Philosophy
and Practice of Hope*

John Dewey and the Philosophy and Practice of Hope

Stephen M. Fishman
&
Lucille McCarthy

University of Illinois Press
Urbana and Chicago

An earlier version of chapter 2 appeared
in *Philosophy Today*, 49.2 (2005).

An earlier version of chapter 4 appeared
in *Transactions of the Charles S. Peirce Society*
XLI.3 (2005).

Library of Congress Cataloging-in-Publication Data
Fishman, Stephen M.
John Dewey and the philosophy and practice of hope
/ Stephen M. Fishman and Lucille McCarthy.
p.   cm.
Includes bibliographical references (p.) and index.
ISBN=13 978-0-252-03200-4 (cloth : alk. paper)
ISBN=10 0-252-03200-4 (cloth : alk. paper)
1. Dewey, John, 1859–1952. 2. Hope.
I. McCarthy, Lucille Parkinson, 1944–   II. Title.
B945.D44F48   2007
191—dc22   2007005069

For our families,
Berrye, Aleisa, Daniel, Susan, and Riley
Ed, Gavin, and Aubin

The good [of doing philosophy] is that you climb mountains . . . [in order to] see other mountains to climb.

—John Dewey, quoted by Max Otto

The best way of honoring Dewey is to work on Dewey's problems—to reconstruct his insights, to see, if need be, farther than Dewey saw. If it may be given to us to see farther, it will be largely because he pointed out to us where to look.

—John Herman Randall Jr.

CONTENTS

ACKNOWLEDGMENTS

Steve Fishman thanks his longtime colleague Michael Eldridge for the warm friendship that colors their countless and always fruitful exchanges about Dewey. In addition, we thank Thomas Alexander, Joseph Betz, Raymond Boisvert, Elizabeth Cooke, Jim Garrison, David Hansen, Sam Keen, John McDermott, Bruce Novak, James Pawelski, Steven Rockefeller, Ira Shor, and Robert Westbrook for their encouragement and for their generosity in commenting on our study at various stages of its development. We also thank the students in Fishman's Philosophy and Practice of Hope class for their willingness to explore their experiences with us. Finally, we are grateful to Angela Burton, Kerry Callahan, Joan Catapano, and Cope Cumpston of the University of Illinois Press for their support for this project.

ABBREVIATIONS

The following sources by Paulo Freire, Gabriel Marcel, and C. R. Snyder are abbreviated in the text as indicated; full bibliographic information is provided in the "Works Cited." In addition, throughout this book, we use the definitive edition of Dewey's works, *The Collected Works of John Dewey*, edited by JoAnn Boydston and published by Southern Illinois University Press between 1969 and 1990 in three sets titled *Early Works (EW)*, *Middle Works (MW)*, and *Later Works (LW)*.

WORKS BY PAULO FREIRE

CWL	"Conscientizing as a Way of Liberating"
ECC	*Education for Critical Consciousness*
EDL	"Education: Domestication or Liberation?"
ELC	"Education, Liberation, and the Church"
ERC	"The Educational Role of Churches in Latin America"
LNAT	"Letter to North American Teachers"
PF	*Pedagogy of Freedom: Ethics, Democracy, and Civic Courage*
PHEART	*Pedagogy of the Heart*
PHOPE	*Pedagogy of Hope*
PO	*Pedagogy of the Oppressed*
PPL	"The Process of Political Literacy"
RES	"Response"
TWT	"The Third World and Theology"

WORKS BY GABRIEL MARCEL

BH	*Being and Having: An Existentialist Diary*
DH	"Desire and Hope"
HV	*Homo Viator: Introduction to a Metaphysic of Hope*

MAH	*Man against Humanity*
MJ	*The Metaphysical Journal*
OM	"Concrete Approaches to Investigating the Ontological Mystery"
OMM	"On the Ontological Mystery"
SK	"Sketch of a Phenomenology and a Metaphysic of Hope"

WORKS BY C. R. SNYDER

HT	"Hope Theory: Rainbows in the Mind"
PH	*The Psychology of Hope*
PPFH	"The Past and Possible Futures of Hope"
DIV	"Development and Initial Validation of the Domain Specific Hope Scale" (with Susie C. Sympson)
FPP	"The Future of Positive Psychology" (with Shane J. Lopez)
HIM	"Hope: An Individual Motive for Social Commerce" (with Jennifer Cheavens and Susie C. Sympson)
SOR	"Somewhere over the Rainbow: Hope Theory Weathers Its First Decade" (with Hal S. Shorey, Kevin L. Rand, Jill R. Hockenmeyer, and David B. Feldman)

PROLOGUE

Steve Fishman and Lucille McCarthy

Hope has come on hard times these days. Richard Rorty tells us that the prophecies of the two great utopian dreams—those represented by the New Testament and *The Communist Manifesto*—are no longer tenable. Both future visions—Christ's Second Coming followed by a millennium of peace and the triumph of the proletariat ushering in a classless society—have been, in Rorty's words, "ludicrous flops." Unfortunately, he concludes, we have no comparable literature, free of the false predictions of the New Testament and *The Manifesto*, to give to our children to support inspiration and hope. Similarly, Robert Westbrook paints a dark picture of another foundation of Western hope, namely, education and its ability to help bring about democratic social reform. This vision of education goes back at least as far as Jefferson. However, Westbrook argues, education for democracy has never been well thought out in American public schools. Even more depressing, he claims that if we were able to develop a sound program to hone the skills necessary for active and informed citizenship, students trained in this way would have, in America's current political climate, no place in which to exercise them.[1]

Historian Christopher Lasch goes one step further than Rorty and Westbrook. He argues that the Anglo-American liberal tradition and its conception of progress, the idea that the opportunity to live a fulfilling life can be extended to all people, is basically flawed. According to Lasch, the terrible calamities of the twentieth century show that the liberal desire for continuing improvement is not only untenable but also inadequate to stimulate the sort of commitment to the well-being of others that the arduous task of social reconstruction requires. He warns that the liberal dedication to extending to all people the opportunity for a fulfilling life is so beyond human capability, given the earth's population, its resources, and human understanding, that it "invites retribution." That is, it is a form of hubris that is bound to provoke "the corrective, compensatory force of nemesis" that exists in the world.[2]

Looking at more popular literature, Amy Chua's *New York Times* bestseller, *World on Fire*, paints a dismal picture of the prospects for just societies around the world, societies that bring about human emancipation and material well-being for all. According to Chua, post–World War II expectations that the widespread development of capitalism, when combined with democratic elections, would result in economic and social equality have been disappointed. She produces overwhelming evidence that free-market economies and democracy do not, in fact, work together for the common good but are, to the contrary, often in fundamental contradiction.[3]

These unhappy prospects for our hope for a more just and equitable society are especially difficult to accept in a country such as ours, one whose charter documents and national story conceive its history as a noble experiment in democratic life. As several commentators have pointed out, the success of democracy depends upon the hope by its citizens that the rapid changes and permeability of democratic societies will ultimately lead to better, rather than worse, conditions.[4]

Why I Was Drawn to Write about Hope

Steve Fishman

My own despair surprises me. For the first time, I tell myself a sad narrative about my country and its current legacy to the world's future. All those Founding Father principles and Progressive Era ideals—equal opportunity, freedom of speech and assembly, government by the people and for the people, cultural pluralism—now seem little more than public relations sound bites. This sad story I tell myself about the world and my country is radically different from the one I wrote during my earliest school years. My 1940s and 1950s were underlined with post–World War II promise. I, a Hungarian immigrant's grandson, had opportunities that were totally beyond the reach of my parents and grandparents. In the working-class neighborhood where I grew up in the Bronx, New York, the title of one of Harry Golden's books, *Only in America* (1958), was not just another product of a clever wordsmith. In my neighborhood, it was the "amen" that concluded every report of every local child's success. The fact that I could attend graduate school and teach at an American university confirmed for me, my family, and my neighbors the continued vitality of our country's historic promise.

Events in the 1960s and '70s fit comfortably into the hopeful grand narrative I had constructed (with the help of my teachers and parents) as a young schoolboy. In the 1960s and '70s, the United States continued to seem earnest about making good on its charter pledge to put justice, freedom, and equality at the center of its mission. There were the dramatic successes of the civil rights and women's movements, the broad-based positive response to John F. Kennedy's civic zeal, and the powerful role of student activism in ending the Vietnam War.

The civic republicanism of Kennedy, the courage of Martin Luther King Jr., and the effective role of student activism now seem far away. Such moral idealism appears to have lost its energizing, rallying-cry force in an era in which the so-called end of ideology has made capitalism and the quest for personal pecuniary profit the summum bonum of U.S. life. Given the culture of industrial imperialism and ethnic belligerence in which I live, I ask myself, why go on teaching? Sure, I may be a positive influence on a few students, and, sure, some of them may be a positive influence on their classmates and me. However, given the enormity of my country's and the world's problems, my work in the classroom seems a futile gesture. It is as if the world is in flames and I go about my business—teaching my typical philosophy courses—as if nothing unusual is going on.

This study, written with my longtime co-researcher, Lucille McCarthy, is my attempt to do something about the "unusual" that is going on. It reflects my efforts to find within philosophy—in particular, within the work of John Dewey—reasons to continue my life's work as a teacher despite its limited efficacy. It reflects my efforts to use my classroom to find ways to resist the hopelessness and despair that the present situation fosters in me.

WHY I TURN TO DEWEY

The first reason I turn to Dewey is personal: I have a relationship with him, so to speak. That is, I have written about him before. In the past, he has helped me understand the difficulties I encountered in my own education, and he has also helped me transform my teaching practices.[5] Buoyed by the insights I have gained by reading and writing about Dewey on earlier occasions, it makes sense to me to turn to him for advice once again.

Second, Dewey's writing seems undergirded by a confidence that our efforts to improve things are always worthwhile. This confidence is all the more impressive because I also hear in Dewey a deep appreciation for the difficult challenges that life presents. It is his sensitivity to the "darkness and despair" and the "trouble and defeat" of life, his sensitivity to the feebleness of our individual efforts and to the precariousness of the human situation, that leads me back to him again and again (*LW* 9:11, 5:272).[6] Yet despite Dewey's recognition of life's perils, despite his recognition that his own era was one in which the mood of "hope" and "progress" that marked the Victorian Age had been shattered, he never surrendered his ameliorist's vision that things can get better (*MW* 5:277–78). Although he was disappointed in the outcomes of some of his public crusades—his failure to change the main thrust of American education, his inability to succeed with the "Outlawry of War" movement after World War I, and his failure to develop a viable third political party in America—Dewey's hopefulness about social progress never waned. This hopefulness was also forged in the context of devastating personal losses, including the deaths of two young sons, Morris, at two years of age, of diphtheria, and Gordon, at eight, of typhoid fever. Thus, I believe that a better understanding of what enabled Dewey to soldier on through his personal and public crises can be a valuable aid in helping me soldier on through the present dark times.

Dewey's confidence that life, despite its perils, always offers us opportunities for personal growth and chances to make things better is epitomized for me in a conversation Dewey had near the end of his life, a few words of which we highlight in one of the epigraphs to this book. This conversation was reported by Dewey's friend, the philosopher Max Otto, at Dewey's memorial service in 1952 at the Communitarian Church of New York. Otto recounted,

> One evening several months before his ninetieth birthday, John Dewey was discussing cultural trends with some dinner guests. Suddenly a young doctor of medicine blurted out his low opinion of philosophy. "What's the good of such clap-trap?" he asked. "Where does it get you?"
>
> The great philosopher settled quietly back into his chair and smiled in appreciation of the young man's frankness. "You want to know what's the good of it all?" he asked. "The good of it is that you climb mountains."
>
> "Climb mountains!" retorted the youth, unimpressed. "And what's the use of doing that?"
>
> "You see other mountains to climb," was the reply. "You come down, climb the next mountain, and see still others to climb." Then, putting his hand ever so gently on the young man's knee, he said, "When you are no longer interested in climbing mountains to see the other mountains to climb, life is over."[7]

What I hear in Max Otto's story about Dewey is not only Dewey's confidence that life's challenges are opportunities for growth but also Dewey's respect for creativity. In particular, I hear his appreciation of the joy of taking on a new problem—a new mountain to climb—and experiencing the exhilarating journey from felt trouble and uncertainty to resolution and better understanding. I also hear in Otto's story Dewey's confidence that creativity and growth are at the center of life and help take some of the sting from death. They help us generate an answer to life's most fundamental question: Why go on?

CONSTRUCTING A THEORY OF HOPE FOR DEWEY

Anyone turning to Dewey for a theory of hope faces a serious challenge because, despite his voluminous work, he never focuses on hope as a topic of sustained exploration.[8] However, he does mention hope at various points and gives substantial clues about his views of hope in passages scattered throughout his work. Thus, constructing a theory of hope for Dewey, attempting to say for him what he would have said about hope had he given it his full attention, requires patient sifting.

The image of someone developing a theory of hope for Dewey that comes to my mind is that of a gold miner sifting through pebbles at Sutter's Creek. You can miss Dewey's nuggets about hope the first and second times you read him, but if the student of Dewey is patient, and if he or she keeps on sifting, during the third or fourth time a golden nugget will appear, a nugget that repays all previous effort. The reader will see me doing this sifting in Part I of this book and me and my undergraduate students doing this sifting in Lucille McCarthy's account of my course on hope in Part II.

In addition to wanting to find in Dewey ways to remain hopeful about my efforts as a teacher, there is another reason for my attempt to construct a theory of hope for Dewey. Given Dewey's paramount position in America's intellectual history, I believe this effort serves as a contribution to Dewey scholarship. That is, Dewey, at the present time, is of interest to a large number of scholars and practitioners worldwide. In philosophy, Richard Rorty's work, begun in the 1970s, has stimulated a resurgence of Dewey scholarship, with studies by Alan Ryan, Robert Westbrook, and Steven Rockefeller among the most noteworthy.[9] In the field of education, there are countless theorists and teachers who see Dewey not only as an important figure in the history of educational reform but also as a fruitful source of ideas and inspiration for present reform.[10] In view of this broad and substantial ongoing exploration of Dewey's work, I believe my efforts to construct a theory of hope for him, and McCarthy's efforts to study undergraduates attempting to do the same in my classroom, can add a new dimension to our understanding of Dewey. These efforts can, if successful, shine a light on a previously unexplored way of reading and profiting from his work.

WHY TEACH ABOUT HOPE?

As much as I believe it is useful to help Dewey scholars see his work in a different way, namely, through the lenses of hope, I want to do more than this. That is, I take Dewey seriously when he tells us that it is ridiculous for philosophers to sit in their rooms arguing with one another about the significance of their introspections while, outside, "burly sinners" rule the world (*MW* 12:192). Although I may be unable to do much in any direct way to stop the "burly sinners," I am in total agreement with Dewey's worry that philosophers may end up talking to themselves. I worry with Dewey that we may waste a lot of good brainpower and energy with very little practical effect.

So what can I, as a philosopher, do that has immediate practical consequences? If I were a public intellectual of the stature of Dewey, I could try to use my exploration of hope in the political arena or try to influence public opinion at large. But I have no public stature of that sort; my primary social role is classroom teacher. Thus, the way that I can affect the world directly, the way I can make philosophy hit the ground and throw my "puny strength" into "the moving unbalanced balance of things," to use Dewey's terms, is to teach a course about hope (*LW* 1:314). Exploring this topic with students so they might better understand and enhance their levels of hope would give me a chance to make a difference in at least a few people's lives. It would allow me, albeit in a very modest way, to avoid being the sort of armchair philosopher that Dewey cautions against, the scholar who talks only to other scholars while doing little to ameliorate real-world problems. Indeed, as McCarthy will describe in Part II of this book, I was able to teach an undergraduate course in the spring of 2005 titled The Philosophy and Practice of Hope. In the next section, she reports on her role in this project and the conflicts and forces that underlie her participation.

Why Study Steve Fishman's Course on Hope?
Lucille McCarthy

Four years ago, when Steve Fishman and I finished our third book, we had been working together for thirteen years, and, frankly, I was tired. During this time, we had coauthored numerous two-part studies in which Steve was responsible for explicating philosophic or educational theory and I then tested or illustrated that theory in Steve's teaching practice. Thus, I had, during this period, returned to Steve's classroom again and again, using it as a laboratory in which to answer a variety of pedagogical questions. I had watched him teach innumerable classes, both in person and on videotape, seen him labor over his responses to countless student essays, and sympathized as he pulled his hair about students whose commitments to their jobs and social lives seemed to trump—can you imagine?—their commitment to his philosophy courses. So when we finished our third book and Steve asked me to join him in studying Dewey and hope, I declined. I told him I thought it was time to go our separate ways.

However, I found that opting out of our collaboration was not, as I had anticipated, a relief. To the contrary, having no classroom inquiry in progress for the first time in many years left me feeling useless, at sea, and, in ways that were relevant, ironically, to the very research topic I had backed away from, somewhat hopeless. This was the last thing I needed, since, like Steve in recent years, I have found myself shorter on hope than ever before. In ways similar to him, I am concerned with the world situation. In particular, I despair about the ecological suicide that we humans are engaged in committing, the ever increasing gaps between rich and poor, and a seemingly endless procession of ethnic and national conflicts, fueled in part by my own country's greed and reliance on force to settle disputes rather than on more intelligent, democratic, and peaceful negotiation.

In addition to these broad social reasons for reduced hope, I have personal ones. I have just turned sixty, and this means that projects that were important to me in the past and gave meaning to my life no longer do so. For example, my children have left home and are shaping their own lives and, thus, no longer need me. My husband and I, as well as my friends and I, who once shared carpools, watched lacrosse games, and chaired PTA meetings, must, therefore, struggle to create new projects. Similarly, as an English teacher for nearly forty years, in classrooms ranging from ninth grade to graduate level, I find myself challenged, at each new semester's start, asking, "How will I manage to teach these courses again? Where is the energy, the excitement? I've been here so many times before; maybe it's time to call it a day." In addition, like Steve, I wonder about the morality of preparing college students to enter the workforce and take their place in the capitalist system of which I am so often critical. Yet I do not want to retire from teaching. Not only do I still hope, with my teaching, to make some positive contribution to social reform. I also fear that if I retreat from the classroom I might fall prey to the same feelings of uselessness I experienced when I tried to retire from research.

So as Steve and I talked further about my joining him to study Dewey and hope, I realized that a central question for me—in my public and private lives, in my teaching and research careers—concerned hope. I realized that I needed to understand it better, how it is generated, its consequences, and what it looks and feels like in particular settings. So I signed on. I agreed to join Steve once more in studying his teaching and his students' learning, believing that if I could understand the theory and practice of hope in his classroom, I might do better in my own. I also wanted to figure out how to bolster hope in my personal life, how to find the sort of engagement and purpose my children once provided. Finally, from this study, I wanted the experience that first attracted me to classroom research twenty years ago. I wanted to hear students tell me their stories, get inside their heads and hearts as they shared their accounts of their classroom experiences and, in this project, their narratives of hope and despair.

Organization of the Book

PART I: THE PHILOSOPHY OF HOPE
(Steve Fishman)

In Part I of this book, the part in which I construct a theory of hope for Dewey, I might have organized my discussion around four or five of the main features of his theory, devoting a chapter to each one. These chapters would have included ones on wholeheartedness, the method of intelligence, a sense of belonging and obligation to nature and the world, and experiences of engrossment and intense living. However, a great deal has been written about these aspects of Dewey's thought, and, although I would have approached them with a different primary interest, that is, hope, I believed it would be repetitive and less fruitful than the comparative approach I do take. As the reader will see, after presenting in Chapter 1 the theory of hope I construct for Dewey, I engage Dewey in dialogue with three quite different theorists, other voices of the twentieth century who, unlike Dewey, discuss hope explicitly: French existential philosopher Gabriel Marcel, Brazilian educational philosopher Paulo Freire, and contemporary U.S. psychologist C. R. Snyder. Engaging Dewey in conversations with Marcel, Freire, and Snyder enables me to look at Deweyan theory from a variety of angles and offers an advantage that, I believe, straight exposition of Dewey's ideas does not permit. This advantage is that Dewey's voice becomes clearer and more resonant when it is heard in dialogue with these other voices, ones that are also powerful but different from Dewey's.

More specifically, in Chapter 2, "Dewey in Dialogue with Gabriel Marcel: Hope with and without God," I show that there are stark differences between Dewey, the non-theist, and Marcel, the theist. However, I also show that, in some surprising and revealing ways, Dewey's and Marcel's theories of hope coincide.

In Chapter 3, "Dewey in Dialogue with Paulo Freire: Hope, Education, and Democracy," I take up and develop a number of threads from earlier chapters. Freire, like Marcel, focuses on the importance for hope of *caritas* love, I-thou relations, and authentic being. However, in Freire, these themes take on new significance because they are shaped by Freire's commitments to Marxism and neocolonial critique. In addition, by bringing Dewey and Freire into conversation, I find that the object of their ultimate hope is similar: the extension of democracy in continual social reconstruction. I also discover that both Dewey and Freire, despite their diverse intellectual and social contexts, view reform in education as an important means to their hopes for change. Exploring Dewey's and Freire's ideas about how education might be used to promote democratic living helps assuage some of the doubts that I have expressed about the efficacy of my teaching in what I consider dark times.

After comparing Dewey's and Freire's approaches to hope, I continue in Chapter 4 to contextualize the theory of hope I construct for Dewey by engaging him in conversation with psychologist C. R. Snyder. I do this because in the past two decades psychologists have given unprecedented attention to hope research, and Snyder has been a leading figure in this effort. This research played an important role in the establishment of the so-called positive psychology movement in the late 1990s. However, unlike Dewey and the other two philosophers, Marcel and Freire, with whom I compare Dewey in preceding chapters, Snyder, like most members of the positive psychology community, does not discuss the consequences for others of the things we choose as the objects of our hope. As a result, in Chapter 4, the moral and political dimensions of hope come into relief when I bring C. R. Snyder and positive psychology into dialogue with John Dewey.

Finally, in Chapter 5, I conclude Part I with a brief summary of what I consider the highlights of the theory of hope that I construct for Dewey.

PART II: THE PRACTICE OF HOPE
(Lucille McCarthy)

I begin Part II of our book in Chapter 6, "Teaching a Course on Hope," by describing the undergraduate philosophy course that Steve Fishman taught in the spring of 2005. My aim in this chapter is to help teachers who might want to offer such a course. After presenting biographical information about Fishman and his ten students, I describe Steve's general pedagogical approach. I then provide details about his reading and writing assignments and how various students responded to them. I conclude by "rolling the tape" of one class discussion, the day in mid-February when students talked about the first chapter of Dewey's *Common Faith*, so readers can get a sense of the group interaction in this particular classroom.

In Chapter 7, "Undergraduates in a Course on Hope," I report my answers to my central research questions: What ideas from the literature on hope, if any, did students find personally useful? How did they apply these ideas to their lives, and what, if any, difference did this application make in their levels of hope? I answer these questions for all ten students, and, in doing so, I divide them into two groups according to their reasons for enrolling in the course. Five of the ten students told me they enrolled in Fishman's class because they "needed more hope," whereas the other five said they signed up for reasons unrelated to hope. Although the impact of the course varied widely among the ten students, I suggest that students' needs regarding hope when they entered played an important role in determining what they took from the course.

In Chapter 8, "Highlights of the Classroom Study," I conclude Part II with a summary of the research findings that stand out for me from my semester-long inquiry in this undergraduate course. In "Final Reflections," Steve and I revisit the motives and aspirations that led him to initiate this project and me to eventually accept his invitation to join him. In this final section, each of us discusses the ways in which our joint study has satisfied—or failed to satisfy—our desire to increase our levels of hope.

PART I

The Philosophy of Hope

ONE

Constructing a Deweyan Theory of Hope

Steve Fishman

> [Human] birth is the eternal reminder of the possibility of a new and different world; and though as time goes by the hope is frustrated and the tragedy of dissipation . . . recurs, yet the promise constantly returns. A new life, a life as yet one of potentiality, will signify to man the possibility of a different world until all hope dies from the human breast.
>
> —John Dewey, "A Key to the New World" (*LW* 2:227)

Before presenting the Deweyan theory of hope that I have constructed, I open this chapter with some comments about what stands out for me from this study. What strikes me most about the various hints and clues that Dewey offers about hope is that they reflect his sense of life as dogged by suffering and uncertainty. Not only is Dewey sensitive to life's suffering and uncertainty, he is also very much aware of life's brevity. As he puts it, "Time is the tooth that gnaws; it is the destroyer; we are born only to die and every day brings us one day nearer death" (*LW* 14:98). This stands out for me because I too have been gifted or cursed, I am not always sure which, with a strong sensitivity to the hardships and anxieties that all living creatures endure. Further, Dewey is unable to invoke divine intervention or an all-powerful, transcendent God to rekindle hope in the midst of our suffering. In this regard, I am also one with Dewey. However, in the face of "frustration" and "tragedy," Dewey, as evidenced by the quote I use as the epigraph for this chapter, does not cry Cassandra and dry wash his hands as I myself am often wont to do. Rather, he offers advice about how to resist the temptation to despair. He gives us reasons to continue to pursue our most important hopes even when these hopes seem dashed and beyond repair.

What also stands out for me is that, although Dewey talks about particular hopes, like hoping for a successful interview with a potential employer (*LW* 10:49–50), his overriding concern—a concern he shares with Gabriel Marcel and Paulo Freire, the philosophers with whom I compare him in Chapters 2 and 3—is with what I call "ultimate hope" and "living in hope."[1] By living in hope, I mean having an ultimate hope or goal toward which one works that gives one's life significance in relation to nature and the human community. Living in hope means that one has a sense of belonging, purpose, faith in one's ideals, and unification. When I say that Dewey focuses more on helping us live in hope than on helping us achieve particular hopes, I do not mean that he denies the importance of realizing particular goals as we pursue our ultimate hope. Nor does he deny the energy generated by particular achievements. In fact, as students of Dewey's work know, he devotes considerable attention to systematizing the sort of effective problem solving that helps us achieve particular goals (*LW* 8:105–352). However, Dewey—unlike C. R. Snyder, the psychologist of hope with whom I compare him in Chapter 4—puts more emphasis on ultimate hope and living in hope than on particular goals because he understands that people can achieve many particular hopes and still feel that their lives do not add up to much. Conversely, people can fail at numerous specific goals and still live in hope if they are working toward their ultimate goals, engaging, that is, in activities that make them feel that life is significant and purposeful.

I use the phrase "living in hope" to describe Dewey's focus despite its religious overtones. Whereas "living in hope" usually suggests that one's life is undergirded by an expectation of eternal existence in an otherworldly heaven, Dewey's idea of living in hope is that one's life is undergirded by faith in an ultimate hope for this-worldly social reform. Devotion to an ultimate hope of this latter sort, according to Dewey, can give one the sense of belonging, purpose, and unification that belief in God provides for many others.

In what follows, as I construct a theory of hope for Dewey, I focus on the conditions that he believes promote living in hope. The three that stand out for me, ones I call Dewey's keys to living in hope, are gratitude, intelligent wholeheartedness, and enriched present experience. As the reader will note in my discussion of these keys, Dewey directs his comments to people who are tempted by despair. This is not surprising given that he is sensitive to the fact that life is dogged by failure and disappointment. It is also not surprising given his awareness that those who work toward achieving his sort of ultimate hope—earthly reform—find that their accomplishments are largely outside their control. In thus addressing people who have faced up to life's limitations, Dewey joins philosophers like Marcel and Freire who believe that to truly live in hope is to have experienced despair and found the wherewithal to overcome it.

Three Keys to Deweyan Hope: Gratitude, Intelligent Wholeheartedness, and Enriched Present Experience

KEY #1 TO LIVING IN HOPE: GRATITUDE AS A SOURCE OF BELONGING AND PURPOSE

Dewey's first key to living in hope is gratitude toward our ancestors and toward nature. This gratitude not only gives us a sense of belonging in the world; it also provides us with purpose: to preserve and enhance the goods we have inherited from our predecessors and nature. These feelings of belonging and purposefulness are important for everyone but especially for those who have social reform as their ultimate hope, people who, as I have said, may despair about their limited ability to make progress toward their ultimate goal. Dewey explains the importance of gratitude in the following quote:

> There is sound sense in the old pagan notion that gratitude is the root of all virtue. Loyalty to whatever in the established environment makes a life of excellence possible is the beginning of all progress. The best we can accomplish for posterity is to transmit unimpaired and with some increment of meaning the environment that makes it possible to maintain the habits of decent and refined life. Our individual habits are links in forming the endless chain of humanity. Their significance depends upon the environment inherited from our forerunners, and it is enhanced as we foresee the fruits of our labors in the world in which our successors live. (*MW* 14:19)

It is not for our existence that Dewey wants us to be grateful but, rather, for what is excellent in our existence. He wants us to recognize the sacrifices that our predecessors have made to bring about the goods that are available to us, and he wants us to honor an implicit contract with these predecessors to maintain and further these goods. In addition, Dewey believes that just as we are linked to a long chain of predecessors, so we are connected to a long line of successors. That is, the implicit contract to preserve and extend what is excellent is not only with those who preceded us but also with those who follow us. Thus, he wants us to recognize the infinite implications and, thereby, the gravity and importance of everything we do. Although our lives and actions are "flickering" (*MW* 14:227), they have consequences beyond anything we can fully imagine or know. He writes,

> In a genuine sense every act is already possessed of infinite import. The little part of the scheme of affairs which is modifiable by our efforts is continuous with the rest of the world. The boundaries of our garden plot join it to the world of our neighbors and our neighbors' neighbors. That small effort which we can put forth is in turn connected with an infinity of events that sustain and support it. . . . When a sense of the infinite reach of an act physically occurring in a small point of space and occupying a petty instant of time comes home to us, the *meaning* of a present act is seen to be vast, immeasurable, unthinkable. (*MW* 14:180)

The gratitude that Dewey speaks of toward the past and the responsibility it implies to the future involve the acceptance of an obligation that no one demands of us but that he believes we should freely, and joyfully, accept. This focus on gratitude is one of Dewey's most powerful attempts to counteract the frequent sense that human life is absurd in a world that so often defeats us and in which our own death and the deaths of our loved ones are inevitable. Gratitude to our ancestors and responsibilities to our progeny, he believes, can provide the willpower to go on, the sense of belonging and purpose that often leave us in the presence of grinding poverty, injustice, and mortality.[2]

Another way to understand Dewey's conception of gratitude is that it is a reflection of his deep piety toward nature, including our ancestors and progeny. In effect, Dewey's first key to living in hope urges revision of the worldview of those of us who might see our efforts to achieve our ultimate hope for earthly reform as futile. Instead of viewing ourselves as alone in an indifferent universe, he would ask us to see ourselves and our ultimate hope as part of nature. Dewey acknowledges that when our plans are foiled, we are tempted to feel alienated from nature and to "hug our ideals" to our bosom as if our ideals were strangers in the world (*LW* 1:313). However, Dewey reminds us that, no matter how frustrated we are, our ultimate hope is also part of the world. Both we and our aspirations are the result of an evolutionary chain that goes far back into nature. We are links, as he says, in a long human line, a line toward which we should feel reverence and piety. No matter how much our lives are uniquely our own, we remain fundamentally interconnected with others. Just as Buddhists see the sun and rain and earth in the oranges they peel, Dewey wants us to see the Jefferson, Frederick Douglass, and immigrant grandmother in ourselves and others. When we succeed, we have taken the first step toward living in hope. We have taken the first step toward developing gratitude and the motivation to pass on to future generations in better and more accessible form what we find excellent in our culture.

I thus see gratitude as the social gospel side of the theory of hope that I construct for Dewey, and this social gospel side can be heard in several moving passages in his work.[3] It is the refrain with which he ends both the first chapter of *Human Nature and Conduct* and the final chapter of *A Common Faith* (*MW* 14:20; *LW* 9:58). It can also be heard in the words that, fittingly, appear on the stone that marks Dewey's grave site at the University of Vermont. I quote from the ending paragraph of *A Common Faith:*

> The things in civilization we most prize are not of ourselves. They exist by grace of the doings and sufferings of the continuous human community in which we are a link. Ours is the responsibility of conserving, transmitting, rectifying and expanding the heritage of values we have received that those who come after us may receive it more solid and secure, more widely accessible and more generously shared than we have received it. Here are all the elements for a religious faith that shall not be confined to sect, class, or race. Such a faith has always been implicitly the common faith of mankind. It remains to make it explicit and militant.

In sum, Dewey's feelings of deep connection and gratitude to nature and the human community—his natural and social piety—suggest that, as links in a long evolutionary chain, the decision we make about whether to abandon or maintain ultimate hope is not fully our own. It also belongs to a long line of human and animal life stretching into the infinite past and an indefinite future. To decide to cease our efforts to ameliorate our social problems is, then, to betray nature and those who have given us the luxury and responsibility of this decision.

Relating gratitude to my own life, I suspect that I make it the first key to Deweyan hope because it resonates so powerfully with my personal history. I have gratitude and reverence for many people but especially for my maternal grandfather. He was an old man when I was born, and he hardly knew me since I was the youngest of his many grandchildren. However, I recall one Sabbath afternoon when I was four that is crucial to my life narrative. My grandfather took down an old book from a shelf in his immigrant's walk-up apartment on the Lower East Side of New York, put me on his knee, and then slowly turned the pages, pointing to and saying aloud the letters of the

Hebrew alphabet. He could not know it, but many years later I realized that we had made an implicit contract, one that neither of us wrote up or signed, that I would devote myself to trying to pass on in better and more accessible form what he had given to me. What happened that afternoon when I was four, the contract we made that I would care for the young, that I would try to pass on a love of literacy and the importance of the book, has helped me in those times of darkness when I have felt alone and with little zest to continue my work. In those times, I usually do not go too far down the dark road of despair before returning to that scene, before remembering my grandfather's gift and deciding, once again, that I will honor our contract, that I will not betray him.

In addition, in my lowest moments, times when I am saddened by the inevitability of my own death and the deaths of my loved ones, I take Dewey's account of gratitude as a kind of pep talk. I take him to be saying to me, "Look, Fishman, you and your loved ones will die, and you might as well add that the sun may go out and civilization disappear without a trace, but moping over these things does no one, including yourself, any good. Although there are no guarantees that you can make things better for others, and there are no guarantees that anyone will take up your work after you are gone, there is always a chance that your efforts will make a difference. After all, if a small act by your grandfather could have such a deep impact on you, your own similar acts have the potential to have such effects upon others. But one thing you can be sure of: if you let your focus on death lead you to despair and inaction, you will lose the only chance you have to make your life meaningful by making life better and more fulfilling for someone else." This Deweyan pep talk helps me pull up my socks. Obviously, I have not had an actual exchange with Dewey, but, given his own recognition of human suffering, I feel as if he sensitively honors my own anxieties about life. In this context, one in which Dewey and I have managed to step at least partially into one another's shoes, I find that he gives me good reasons for going on with my work, reasons that do not rely on a supernatural world or false hopes about immortality.[4]

KEY #2 TO LIVING IN HOPE: INTELLIGENT WHOLEHEARTEDNESS AS A SOURCE OF FAITH IN OUR IDEALS

Whereas Dewey believes gratitude offers the belonging and purposefulness we need to continually keep reconstructing what is good in the world, his second key to living in hope, intelligent wholeheartedness, offers the faith or reassurance that our goals are worthwhile and that we are doing our best to reach them. Intelligent wholeheartedness helps us focus more on what we can control (our planning, action, and critical reflection) and less on what we cannot control (the consequences of our reformist efforts). By redirecting our attention in this way, intelligent wholeheartedness, like gratitude, helps reduce the temptation to despair and increases our chances of living in hope.

What is intelligent wholeheartedness? For Dewey, it is a way of making choices and acting on those choices. It is a way of claiming and being claimed by an ideal and working to realize that ideal (*LW* 9:17). By choosing goals and ideals intelligently and wholeheartedly, we give ourselves fully to them (*MW* 5:363; *LW* 8:137). We are able to carry on despite the obstacles, the threats to hope, that we inevitably encounter. Unfortunately, we can never be certain that our choices and ideals are truly worthy. Thus, we need faith that in using our intelligence and our wholeheartedness we have chosen well (*LW* 9:17).

In the passage in Dewey's work that I consider the most important for constructing a theory of hope for him, he advises us to cling to ideals we have intelligently chosen even though we may meet with defeat as we attempt to realize them. He urges us not to give up and withdraw but, rather, to continue taking small steps toward our end-in-view, trusting that our "puny" efforts are not for naught, trusting that "our lot is one with whatever is good in existence." He writes,

> Fidelity to the nature to which we belong, as parts however weak, demands that we cherish our desires and ideals till we have converted them into intelligence, revised them in terms of the ways and means which nature makes possible. When we have used our thought to its utmost and have thrown into the moving unbalanced balance of things our puny strength, we know that though the universe slay us still we may trust, for our lot is one with whatever is good in existence. We know that such thought and effort is one condition of the coming into existence of the better. As far as we are concerned it is the only condition, for it alone is in our power. To ask more than this is childish; but to ask less is a recreance no less egotistic, involving no less a cutting of ourselves from the universe than does the expectation that it meet and satisfy our every wish. (*LW* 1:314)

Although Dewey does not use the word "hope" in this passage, I hear him trying to bolster people's confidence that their efforts to reform and add to what is good in society are important because, although there are no guarantees about the outcome, reform will not come without such efforts. These efforts are, as he says, "one condition of the coming into existence of the better." This is one reason for maintaining a life of hope—a pragmatic reason—that Dewey presents in this passage. It gets people to take action that they might not otherwise undertake. A second reason in this passage for maintaining hope is a moral one: Dewey's idea that "fidelity" to the nature to which we belong "demands" that we maintain hope that our intelligently chosen activities—those that pass the test of critical, sensitive, and imaginative reflection—are worthwhile. In other words, if we abandon our intelligently chosen hopes, we fail to fulfill an obligation that our own nature imposes upon us.

Relating Dewey's idea of intelligent wholeheartedness to my own life, I confess that I am often disappointed about the consequences of my activities. I have been someone who has asked for "more than this," for guarantees that my efforts would succeed, and I have been led to despair because, as Dewey says, no such guarantees are possible. Instead, he teaches me that the most I can do is use "thought to its utmost" and throw my "puny strength" into the uncertain world that I inhabit, into "the moving unbalanced balance" of life. The power of Dewey's message for me is that it enables me to feel that, when I have done the best I can, when I have directed my efforts in intelligent, wholehearted ways, I can then let go and not be plagued by my inability to guarantee or control the outcome of my actions. By letting go of control of the outcome, I am better able to appreciate the opportunities to use the sensitivity, imagination, and creativity that the world gives me. Dewey also says that to "ask less" than this sort of intelligent effort of myself also robs me of hope. If I ask less, I live halfheartedly or downheartedly. I bypass my chances to be fully alive, to be the "live creature" who is fully engrossed, who experiences the "intensest," most hope-nurturing moments of life no matter their ultimate outcome (*LW* 10:22).

Put differently, given my own limitations and the world's entrenched social, political, and environmental problems, my efforts do, indeed, to borrow Dewey's word, seem "puny." However, Dewey's second key to living in hope helps me when I remember to ask myself if I am wholehearted about my goals. For example, am I fully devoted to writing this book about Dewey and hope? Am I fully devoted to teaching The Philosophy and Practice of Hope course? Are these goals at the core of who I am? Are they consonant with the work, ideals, and communities of purpose I claim and most respect? When I can answer yes to these questions, I can better appreciate the opportunity to give "my utmost" to this work and the ideals underlying it. The upshot is that testing my endeavors for their Deweyan intelligent wholeheartedness helps me live in hope. It helps me better tolerate, accept, and even, at times, treasure my frequent failures and disappointments.

KEY #3 TO LIVING IN HOPE: ENRICHED PRESENT
EXPERIENCE AS A SOURCE OF UNIFICATION

Enriched present experience means getting the most we can out of our day-to-day encounters. Dewey writes, "We always live at the time we live and not at some other time, and only by extracting at each present time the full meaning of each present experience are we prepared for doing the same thing in the future. This is the only preparation which in the long run amounts to anything" (*LW* 13:29–30). An important way to do this, according to Dewey, is to integrate the past, present, and future by being sensitive to both the consummatory and the instrumental aspects of experience, the ways in which the present is both a fulfillment of yesterday and a preparation for tomorrow (*MW* 9:61). When our present experience is enriched in this way, we feel the engagement and unification that mark living in hope.

A second way to enrich experience is to integrate our failures and successes, to see that learning from failure is vital to success and that success inevitably leads to new problems or failures. However, the unification that characterizes hopeful living does not come just from temporal integration and the integration of loss and gain. It is also engendered by the first two keys of Deweyan hope. Gratitude unifies us with our ancestors and nature. Intelligent wholeheartedness unifies our particular goals under the umbrella of a well-chosen ultimate hope. In this way, the first two keys supplement the third in promoting enriched present experience.

In the following sections, I first discuss temporal integration, and then I explore the integration of failure and success: two ways to enrich present experience and promote unification.

Integrating the Past, Present, and Future   Dewey underlines the benefits of unifying the past and present when he tells us that the importance of the past is to help "increase present alertness" (*LW* 10:24). In other words, the past should not long remain a source of regret for lost opportunities or actions we wish undone. Instead, when the past functions properly it informs the present.

Likewise, the function of future goals and hopes is to help us be interested and alert right now. That is, what Dewey calls our end-in-view should constitute pointers that help us determine what to attend to in present experience.[5] If future goals fail to point back to the present, they only encourage us to ignore the present. They teach us to focus on some future moment, a moment when our goals are reached and we believe, erroneously, that life will truly begin. Unfortunately, according to Dewey, the deposit of disvaluing the present is simply more future moments that, when they become present, are discounted as mere means, as having only instrumental value. We then find ourselves in endless daydreams about happy tomorrows that lead us to put our todays on hold.[6]

Of course, Dewey's emphasis on the present should not be taken to mean that, for him, the past and future are unimportant. As I have explained, the present becomes engrossing and worthy of full exploration only when seen as a fulfillment of past events and a powerful influence on future ones. Dewey writes, "To the being fully alive, the future is not ominous but a promise; it surrounds the present as a halo. It consists of possibilities that are felt as a possession of what is now and here. . . . Art celebrates with peculiar intensity the moments in which the past reenforces the present and in which the future is a quickening of what now is" (*LW* 10:24). Thus, for Dewey, when we integrate present, past, and future, present experience is enriched. We are fully alive in the sense of being totally involved in present activity. When this happens, ends become means—have instrumental value—because they direct present activity. Similarly, means become ends—have intrinsic value—because we experience present activity as fulfillment. Put differently, when we integrate past, present, and future, we are mindful rather than distracted. Our mind, body, and emotions work together, so much so that we are no longer self-conscious about our actions, and, according to Dewey, we lose ourselves to find ourselves (*MW* 9:133). Present experience is so enriched that we experience unity and increase our chances of living in hope.

Integrating Failure and Success   Dewey believes that another impediment to enriched present experience is too much regret about past failures and too much anxiety about future ones. He tells us, "Only when the past ceases to trouble and anticipations of the future are not perturbing is a being wholly united with his environment and therefore fully alive" (*LW* 10:24). Likewise, too much focus on past successes and overanticipation of future ones also limit engagement in the present. As a way of avoiding these distractions from present activity, Dewey suggests altering our worldview, recognizing that failure is an opportunity for future gain and that successes cannot endure indefinitely. As he puts it, "Any attempt to perpetuate beyond its term the enjoyment attending the time of fulfillment and harmony constitutes withdrawal from the world. Hence it marks the lowering and loss of vitality" (*LW* 10:23).

Accepting that our successes and failures are intimately related and of limited duration allows us to focus better on what is most within our control:

the activities in which we are engaged in the present moment. This is not to say that successes and failures are not important but that they function best, as do the past and the future in general, when they help us determine what we want to attend to in the present. Dewey tells us that people who are fully engrossed in the present "can make friends with even [their] stupidities, using them as warnings that increase present wariness. Instead of trying to live upon whatever may have been achieved in the past, [they] use past successes to inform the present" (*LW* 10:23). In short, for Dewey, we help unify our lives when we bring together our past and our future, our failures and successes, in ways that enrich our present experience. It is the sort of unification of experience that is, for Dewey, an important mark of living in hope.

To summarize, Dewey's three keys to living in hope involve using gratitude to maintain our motivation to act in the world, using intelligent wholeheartedness to choose and sustain faith in our choice of ultimate hopes, and using enriched present experience to unify our lives. Gratitude, intelligent wholeheartedness, and enriched experience can give us, according to Dewey, the sense of belonging, purpose, faith, and unity that characterize hopeful living. They can help us live in hope, Dewey tells us, even if in the pursuit of our ideals, the universe "slay" us.[7]

Deweyan Responses to Five Questions about Hope

Having offered an account of what I consider three keys to understanding Deweyan hope, I now present more details about the theory that I construct for him. I organize these details around five questions that help me relate a Deweyan theory to some classic philosophic conceptions of hope. These are (1) What is the nature of hope? (2) What is disciplined hope? (3) What is moral or "reasonable" hope? (4) What is the object of ultimate hope? and (5) Are we justified in hoping for more than temporary, this-worldly fulfillment?

Although I treat each of these questions separately, my answers, on occasion, overlap. For example, it is difficult to discuss the nature of hope without also discussing the objects of hope. Likewise, it is difficult to distinguish disciplined hope from moral hope without also discussing ultimate hope. Nevertheless, I find that these questions are an effective way to fill out the theory of hope I construct for Dewey.

(1) What Is the Nature of Hope for Dewey?

HOPE AS STATES OF BEING

Philosophers have traditionally used the word "hope" to refer to various states of being or dispositions. For example, hope has been characterized as an emotion (Aquinas, Hume), an estimate or expectation (Aquinas, Hume, Day), a habit (Shade), and a virtue (Aquinas, Pieper).[8] Dewey, I believe, would accept all of these characterizations. First, regarding hope as an emotion, I say Dewey would agree because he describes life as a constant movement into and out of harmony with our surroundings. This in-and-out rhythm is, according to Dewey, always colored by emotion, including the emotion of hope (*LW* 10:48).

Second, I believe Dewey would agree that hope is often intertwined with expectation. It gains or loses strength as a person's expectations or estimates of success rise and fall. Dewey gives an example of this when he describes a hypothetical interview in which a job candidate's hopes go up and down as the candidate assesses the trajectory of the interview and the degree of rapport being established with the interviewer. Dewey writes, "The primary emotions on the part of the applicant may be at the beginning hope or despair, and elation or disappointment at the close" (*LW* 10:49). In other words, by the end of the interview, according to Dewey, the applicant's hopes may have been realized, and, thus, he or she experiences joy or elation. By contrast, if the applicant's hopes have not been realized, he or she will experience sadness or disappointment. Hope and despair are, thus, according to Dewey, the primary emotions that accompany the applicant's calculation of his or her chances of being hired, and these emotions wax and wane throughout the interview. Dewey concludes, "It is even possible for each attitude and gesture, each sentence, almost every word, to produce more than a fluctuation in the intensity of the basic emotion; to produce, that is, a change of shade and tint in its quality" (*LW* 10:50). Thus, like Aquinas and Hume, Dewey sometimes describes hope as an emotion intertwined with calculations of success.

Regarding the third characterization of hope as a state of being—namely, a habit—I believe Dewey would also agree. Given his view that habit plays a major role in human conduct, it would follow that our disposition to hope is no exception. When hope becomes a stable part of our character, it becomes a habit. Finally, I believe Dewey would accept that insofar as our habit of hope is intelligent and wholehearted in the promotion of collective goods, it is, indeed, a virtue (*MW* 5:371).

HOPE AS A DESIRE TO ACHIEVE AN OVERARCHING GOAL

In addition to characterizing hope as a state of being or disposition, philosophers have also employed the word "hope" to refer to our desire to reach an overarching goal. For example, Aquinas, besides speaking of hope as an emotion and an expectation, also speaks of hope as a goal. He says that we often hope for something that is arduous or difficult to achieve. Dewey also, on occasion, uses "hope" to refer to the objects we seek or desire. For example, he uses the word "hope" to mean a set of ultimate objectives when he speaks about "the objects of faith and hope," "our hopes and ambitions," and our "hopes and purposes" (*MW* 13:321; *LW* 2:226, 10:34).

DEWEY'S CONTRIBUTION: HOPE AS A NATIVE IMPULSE

Although Dewey is in line with other philosophers, using the word "hope" to refer to states of being and ultimate goals, he adds to the discussion of hope when he claims that it is originally an impulse or instinct (*MW* 14:200). He says that hope is among the native activities that "carry [us] on" regardless of calculations about future achievements:

> Man continues to live because he is a living creature not because reason convinces him of the certainty or probability of future satisfactions and achievements. He is instinct with activities that carry him on. Individuals here and there cave in, and most individuals sag, withdraw and seek refuge at this and that point. But man as man still has the dumb pluck of the animal. He has endurance, hope, curiosity, eagerness, love of action. These traits belong to him by structure, not by taking thought. (*MW* 14:199–200)

In other words, according to Dewey, we are born with eagerness, endurance, love of action, and hope. Humans have a native sense that their activities will yield positive rather than negative results. Dewey's claim that hope is a native impulse does not, however, mean that, for him, hope is self-sustaining. In fact, as I have noted, Dewey repeatedly acknowledges that hope can be frustrated and, at times, very difficult to maintain.

Although Dewey assents to traditional philosophic views of hope as states of being and goals, his recognition of hope as a native impulse provides an interesting dimension to the ongoing discussion. Whereas classic definitions generally view hope as requiring intellectual elements, namely, conscious objectives and estimates of the likelihood of achieving them, Dewey suggests that hope in a very primitive form can be present without any intellectual component. It is, rather, part of our human makeup, an impulse of our animal nature. This approach is very much in keeping with Dewey's view that human behavior is continuous with the life of lower organisms (*LW* 10:30). It follows that, for Dewey, hope is all around us in animal life. It is present where birds build their nests, beavers construct their dams, and hawks seek their mates. That is, hope, according to Dewey, is not an extraordinary phenomenon (*LW* 10:31).[9]

Dewey's view of hope as part of our animal nature has some interesting consequences. First, it can change the way we see the challenge of recovering hope when we despair. Recovering hope for Dewey means opening to our continuities with nature rather than, as for many classic philosophers, reaffirming our ties with a supernatural or divine source. By contrast, Dewey would say that when we are caught in low hope, it is because we have lost our animal sensitivity to nature, our sense that we are nature's product, and, with it, our faith that nature will often sustain us.[10]

A second consequence of Dewey's view that hope in its most primitive form is part of our animal "pluck" is that it can reinforce or remind us of our deep continuities with animal life and nature. We are not only in our environment, according to Dewey. Our environment is also in us. The world in which we live "belongs" to us, just as we "belong" to it (*MW* 14:226–27). More specifically, we are creatures who have evolved from eons of transactions among organic and inorganic material. Thus, it is not poetic license that leads Dewey to speak about our "animal pluck." It is not poetic license that leads him to speak about humans as live "creatures" and to quote approvingly Keats's claim that the glint in an animal's eye as it hunts in the field is like the glint in a human's eye as he or she heads to work along a London street (*LW* 10:39).[11]

Further, according to Dewey, not only do we learn a great deal from animal life about the nature of hope, but animal life also teaches us about hope's objects. No matter the specific content of our hopes—be they ultimate or particular—our most basic goal is harmony among our impulses and our environment. We want moments when we feel our needs have been satisfied, when we feel peace within ourselves and in our relation to the universe. This view of the object of hope explains Dewey's claim that the memory of an underlying harmony "haunts life like the sense of being founded on a rock" (*LW* 10:23). That is, like the impulse to hope, the object of our hope in the most general terms—peace, satisfaction, and security—is deeply rooted in our ancestral nature. This view of harmony as the most general object of hope also accounts for Dewey's claim that the moments of passage from disequilibrium to equilibrium are among those when we are most alive and engaged, the moments of "intensest life" (*LW* 10:22). However, I quickly point out that, for Dewey, our desire for harmony is more complicated than it is for animals.

According to Dewey, our successes lead us to want more sophisticated and more expansive harmonies. We would become bored with a life that is static or routine. In other words, we want our harmonies to also be moments of growth, and we would be frustrated by an equilibrium that lasted indefinitely and without being interrupted by new challenges.

Another way to approach Dewey's view of humans' perpetual efforts to move from disequilibrium to harmony is in terms of his concepts of adjustment, accommodation, and adaptation (*MW* 6:359–61, 364–66, 12:128; *LW* 9:12–13). Dewey calls the process of reestablishing harmony with our environment "adjustment," a state that we can achieve in two ways. First, we can regain harmony by "accommodating" to our physical and social surroundings. This happens when the troubling conditions that we encounter cannot be changed. When adjustment occurs under these conditions, we are passive, and the result is, for Dewey, mere "equilibrium" (*MW* 6:365). By contrast, a second way to achieve adjustment to painful circumstances is through the more active process of "adaptation." This happens when we are able to "adapt," or shape, our physical and social surroundings in ways that help us regain harmony and achieve our desires. When adjustment occurs via adaptation, there results what Dewey calls "growth" or "progress" (*MW* 6:365).

Given the fundamental place that our hope for expanding harmonies occupies in Dewey's view of the human situation, I believe it is fair to claim that Dewey's philosophy is very much a philosophy of hope. His entire corpus of professional writing and social activism can be seen as focused on understanding the conditions that make possible the creative resolution of disequilibrium. That is, his work is always, at its core, an exploration of how to best use our material conditions to achieve better and better harmonies of impulse and nature. This is why, as I will explain later in this chapter, Dewey chooses democracy as his ultimate hope. In his view, democracy is the social arrangement that affords the richest opportunities for the greatest number to develop their abilities to achieve fulfilling harmonies (*LW* 13:18). It is also why Dewey celebrates art, calling it humanity's greatest achievement. In his view, art is a conscious effort to improve upon and deepen what animals do instinctively: work to satisfy their hope for harmony and unification (*LW* 10:31).

In sum, Dewey's view of hope as a native impulse contributes to hope theory and practice by changing the way we understand the task of recovering hope. Instead of seeing this task as an act of defiance in a world that saps our hope, Dewey urges us to see hope everywhere in the animal world that surrounds us. In addition, if I am right about Dewey's idea of hope as the native impulse toward growth and ever expanding harmonies with nature, then we can see his entire professional endeavor as helping us understand and realize our hopes. In this way, constructing a theory of hope for Dewey can shed new light on both his lifework and the energy that drove it.

(2) What Is Disciplined Hope for Dewey?

Disciplined hope, for Dewey, is our primitive, native impulse to hope plus careful planning. Without such planning, the native impulse can turn into mere pie-in-the-sky thinking. In fact, Dewey explicitly cautions us about this sort of impotent hope, what he terms "burning hope" and "wishful hope" (*MW* 14:175, 177). His point is that no matter how much we may desire the achievement of some objective, wishing will not make it so. What is required to fulfill our goals is discipline, and this includes, for Dewey, observation, foresight, and imagination. That is, despite the fact that, for Dewey, hope is ours "by structure rather than thought," native impulse, if it is to be practical, must be integrated with thought. To succeed in achieving what we hope for means careful deliberation about what is required to reach our objectives.

By making this distinction between hope as native impulse and disciplined hope, Dewey anticipates C. R. Snyder, the contemporary psychologist and researcher of hope with whom I further compare Dewey in Chapter 4. Specifically, Dewey foreshadows Snyder in suggesting that it makes sense to hope for something only when we have planned carefully. Dewey also notes the importance of clarifying our objectives, working to achieve what he calls an "adequate" perception of our goals. He writes, "The question is . . . how far the work of thought has been done, how adequate is its perception of its directing objective. For the moving force may be a shadowy presentiment constructed by a wishful hope rather than by study of conditions: it may be an emotional indulgence rather than a solid plan built upon the rocks of actuality discovered by accurate inquiries" (*MW* 14:176–77). In sum, disciplined hope, for Dewey, involves both careful planning, that is, careful consideration of possible routes to our goals, and continual refinement of our objectives.

(3) What Is Moral or "Reasonable" Hope for Dewey?

As I have just explained, disciplined hope, for Dewey, is distinguished from wishful hopes by the clarity of people's goals and the planning that lies behind their efforts to achieve them. That is, disciplined hope requires that people figure out how to get from point A to point B. However, to turn a disciplined hope into a moral hope involves something more. In addition to clarity of goals and careful planning, moral or "reasonable" hope, for Dewey, is marked by characteristics like wholeheartedness, persistence, and a willingness to make personal sacrifice (*MW* 5:363, 371). He tells us that hope is moral when people have full interest in their goals, when they so completely identify with their goals that pursuit of them is central to their being. He also tells us that hoping is moral when people face up to the uncertainties of life, recognize the risks involved, and move ahead despite the personal dangers. Dewey describes the power of moral hopes to keep us believing in and pursuing our ideals in the face of all obstacles and personal risks: "Hope and aspiration, belief in the supremacy of good in spite of all evil, belief in the realizability of good in spite of all obstacles, are necessary inspirations in the life of virtue. The good can never be demonstrated to the sense, nor be proved by calculations of personal profit. It involves a radical venture of the will in the interest of what is unseen and prudentially incalculable" (*MW* 5:371). As reflected in this quote, moral hope, for Dewey, involves faith that the good will win out although darkness and trouble always dog our actions. It involves faith that human intelligence and wholeheartedness can be trusted. It also requires, as Dewey says, "a radical venture of the will in the interest of what is unseen and prudentially incalculable." In other words, moral hope involves a surrender of ourselves—our will—to our objective or ideal. We allow our ideal, that which is part of "the unseen and prudentially incalculable," to claim and direct our will without regard for any external rewards we may gain from seeking our objectives.

Moral hope, then, requires both faith in the value of the ideals we wholeheartedly claim and the use of what Dewey calls the method of intelligence. This method involves not only observation, foresight, and imagination but also respect for the needs of others, honesty regarding our intentions, and sincerity about our commitments. That is, as we engage in intelligent thinking about our goals, we subject them, as well as the beliefs, tastes, and actions that underlie their pursuit, to reflective scrutiny. This sort of reflection begins the continuous process of judging which hopes are best to pursue in a particular situation. It converts hopes that are immediately attractive into hopes that are pronounced good or moral upon critical reflection. Dewey writes, "Intelligence is critical method applied to goods of belief, appreciation and conduct, so as to construct freer and more secure goods. . . . [I]t is the reasonable object of our deepest faith and loyalty, the stay and support of all reasonable hopes" (*LW* 1:325).

Thus, according to Dewey, moral or "reasonable" hopes are those that are supported by the method and habit of intelligently wholehearted living. As I noted at the opening of this chapter, this method is one of the keys to a Deweyan theory of hope. It is the disposition that is most likely to convert disharmony into harmony in ways that satisfy not only the individual's needs but also the needs of his or her social and natural environment. It follows that to hope morally, for Dewey, makes powerful demands upon us. It requires full commitment and risk of who we are and what we possess. It requires faith "in the supremacy of good in spite of all evil" and "in spite of all obstacles" (*MW* 5:371). On the other hand, moral hope offers rich internal rewards. It can yield a sense of belonging, purpose, faith, and unification that allows us to see our "puny" efforts as significant and important in the universe (*LW* 9:15, 19). This sense of belonging and purpose, these feelings of significance, characterize, as I have already pointed out, what it means to live in hope. Thus, for Dewey, striving for moral hope and living in hope are one and the same.

(4) What Is the Object of Dewey's Ultimate Hope?

I believe that most readers of Dewey would agree that the object of his ultimate hope—his most important and inclusive hope—is a society characterized by democratic relationships.[12] According to Dewey, such a society best enables its members to live purposeful and unified lives, ones filled with continuities and interactions, with creative efforts and fulfillments. Put otherwise, Dewey's ultimate hope is for a society that, by helping its members get the most out of their experiences, enables them to live in hope. Dewey tells us much about his ultimate hope in a series of rhetorical questions about why democratic and humane arrangements are preferable to those that are autocratic and harsh. He asks,

> Can we find any reason to promote democratic social arrangements that does not ultimately come down to the belief that democratic social arrangements promote a better quality of human experience, one which is more widely accessible and enjoyed, than do non-democratic and anti-democratic forms of social life? Does not the principle of regard for individual freedom and for decency and kindliness of human relations come back in the end to the conviction that these things are tributary to a higher quality of experience on the part of a greater number than are methods of repression and coercion of force? Is it not the reason for our preference that we believe that mutual consultation and convictions reached through persuasion, make possible a

better quality of experience than can otherwise be provided on any wide scale? (*LW* 13:18)

In short, Dewey's ultimate hope is for a society that enables its citizens to grow. It enables them to develop flexible habits and lead creative lives as they work cooperatively with others to be more intelligently wholehearted about their beliefs, tastes, and choice of ideals.

RESPONSES TO THE CHARGE OF UTOPIANISM

Dewey's ultimate hope for the extension of democracy into all areas of life—economic, social, and educational as well as political—might be viewed by some as so naively romantic and utopian as to promote despair rather than hope. Alternatively put, critics who charge Dewey with utopianism might say that the ideal of extending democracy to all areas of life—and the perpetual social reconstruction that this ideal entails—is such an impossible dream that it is deflating rather than encouraging. It rests on a false notion of what is socially possible and on an overly rosy view of human nature. However, Dewey takes some of the force out of these charges with his analysis of the relation of short-term particular achievements and long-term ultimate goals and his analysis of human nature.

Dewey's Reconciliation of Short-Term Particular Achievements and Long-Term Ultimate Hope Dewey's effort to reconcile short-term particular achievements and long-term ultimate hope is much like his effort to reconstruct our understanding of the role of the future for the present. He argues that the function of ultimate hope is less to provide us with a discrete goal to pursue than it is to help us become more sensitive to present opportunity. In fact, he says, too much focus on reaching an ultimate goal may lead to despair about our efforts to achieve it, and he criticizes those who use such goals as the standard against which to measure progress:

> An office of inspiration and guidance is attributed to the thought of the goals of ultimate completeness or perfection. As matter of fact, the idea sincerely held brings discouragement and despair not inspiration or hopefulness. There is something either ludicrous or tragic in the notion that inspiration to continued progress is had in telling man that no matter what he does or what he achieves, the outcome is negligible in comparison with what he set out to achieve. . . . [T]he fact is that it is not the negative aspect of an outcome, its failure to reach infinity, which renews courage and hope. . . . [What does renew courage and hope is acceptance that] positive attain-

ment, actual enrichment of meaning and powers opens new vistas and sets new tasks, creates new aims and stimulates new efforts. . . . New struggles and failures are inevitable. (*MW* 14:199)

I take Dewey to mean that much contemporary despair about our inability to overcome the gaps between rich and poor, end religious and political strife, and preserve the environment is the result of focusing on how far we are, no matter what we do, from our ultimate hope. Although democratic living and economic justice need to be kept in mind as ultimate ends-in-view, we also need, as Dewey tells us, to be attentive to our particular achievements and what we can learn from them. In other words, having acted in our limited ways, we need to focus on what we have accomplished, however modest, and the new opportunities our accomplishments present rather than the great distance that still separates us from realizing our guiding vision. In addition, Dewey cautions us against being surprised that our very successes leave us with new struggles and failures and even more complex challenges than we faced initially: "New struggles and failures are inevitable. The total scene of action remains as before, only for us more complex, and more subtly unstable. But this very situation is a consequence of expansion, not of failures of power, and when grasped and admitted it is a challenge to intelligence" (*MW* 14:199).

I find Dewey's approach a helpful way to look at my own goals for social reform. I especially agree with his idea that excessive attention to the distance between where I am and my ultimate goal of greater peace and justice can be so discouraging that I miss what I have done and can do. For example, I can become so focused on the small impact that my teaching may have that I overlook the small positive effects of my efforts and the new opportunities they present for further work toward a better, more fulfilling world. Likewise, I can become so focused on completing this book that I forget that the value of writing it is not just about future consequences, ones that I can only vaguely anticipate and over which I have very limited control. Its value also lies in the attention it encourages me to give my present struggles and the immediate satisfaction and engrossment I experience as I overcome particular here-and-now problems. In sum, Dewey argues that an ultimate hope like the extension of democracy is not utopian or deflating when seen as a way of directing present activity rather than as a measure against which to evaluate our distance from a fixed finish line.

Dewey's Analysis of Human Nature　Dewey has often been charged with being naive about human nature.[13] As I read him, however, Dewey has a balanced rather than a naive or overly rosy conception of our basic nature. Just as he sees the world as complex, at times cooperating with us and, at others, defeating us, so, in somewhat similar fashion, Dewey sees human nature as equally complex. Alongside our instincts for domination, ownership, and pugnacity are cooperative, social, and sympathetic instincts. He tells us that in his study of learning outside formal settings, he finds that children imitate adult behavior not because they are natural mimics (as some researchers claim) but because they want to participate in and contribute to adult projects (*MW* 9:39). The child rolls the ball back to the adult not only to join group activity but also to "keep it going" and "take an effective part in the game" (*MW* 9:40). Summing his observation of the cooperative and social characteristics of child behavior, Dewey remarks, "The child is born with a natural desire to give out, to do, and that means to serve" (*EW* 5:64).

In addition, Dewey believes that our impulses, including our more imperialistic as opposed to our benevolent ones, can be satisfied in different ways. For example, in contemporary society, our impulse to compete with others is satisfied for many in the so-called money game, the adventure, drama, risk taking, and labor involved in accumulating personal wealth. To those who argue that because of native human selfishness nothing can be done to ameliorate the prevailing dog-eat-dog economic environment, Dewey answers that the money game is only one way that our needs for competition, drama, and risk can be satisfied. They can also be met in other adventures that demand personal wit, perseverance, struggle, and foresight. For Dewey, these are the adventures of scientific discovery and the adventures, demands, and satisfactions of artistic creativity and work. According to Dewey, what stands in the way of his ultimate hope of extending democracy is not the "old Adam" of human nature, the nature that needs to be transformed miraculously from self-centered to loving one's neighbor. The problem is social custom and tradition, the ways they currently channel our impulses to perpetuate class divisions and the manipulation of the many by the few. In Dewey's analysis, conservatives who say reform is not possible because of human nature rest their case on a false psychology of instincts:

> The conservative who begs scientific support from the psychology of instincts is the victim of an outgrown psychology which derived its notion of instinct from an exaggeration of the fixity and certainty of the operation of instincts among the lower animals. He is a victim of a popular zoology of the bird, bee and beaver, which was largely framed to the greater glory of God. He is ignorant that instincts in animals are less infallible and definite than is supposed,

and also that the human being differs from the lower animals in precisely the fact that his native activities lack the complex ready-made organization of the animals' original abilities. (*MW* 14:77)

In short, Dewey does not deny that we have native needs for domination and combativeness, but he does deny that these needs have "definite" or "ready-made organization." That is, the mode of expression of our instincts, both aggressive and benevolent, is not fixed. Thus, Dewey answers the charge that our aggressive and selfish instincts make his ultimate hope of democratic social reconstruction a pipe dream by arguing that our instincts are both complex and indefinite in expression. The barriers in the way of social reconstruction are not our instincts but the way customs and traditions currently direct the satisfaction of our instincts. Although Dewey does not deny the difficulty of intelligently altering custom and habit, he believes that, at the least, it is worth a try. It is worth trying to alter our patterns of behavior so that human instincts are directed away from war, intolerance, and domination of the many by the few to be satisfied and expressed in more cooperative, equitable, and democratic ways of associated living (*LW* 11:64–65).

DEWEY'S ULTIMATE HOPE AS FOCUSING ON WHAT NATURE GIVES RATHER THAN ON WHAT IT DENIES

In adopting democratic living and its extension to all areas of life as his ultimate hope, Dewey turns his back on more traditional ultimate hopes like eternal happiness or a life free of worry or need. Another way to put this is that by focusing on democracy as his ultimate hope, Dewey celebrates what nature gives us. He recognizes that life is "perilous," a "gamble," and that "in the end the unseen decides what happens in the seen" (*LW* 1:44, 43). He recognizes that new struggles and failures are inevitable (*MW* 14:199) and that, as I have already noted, any attempt to extend our harmonies beyond their natural duration risks withdrawing from life (*LW* 10:23). However, Dewey is equally emphatic in pointing out that although nature does not give us all that we might hope for, namely, a life without worry or doubt, it does give us moments we cherish, moments in which we are most alive, moments made possible by the very challenges and problems that we sometimes wish would go away. Thus, instead of recommending that we adopt as our ultimate hope a life of never-ending bliss or one, as the Stoics or Buddhists might want, free of desire and fear, Dewey urges us to substitute, as more deserving of our most profound hope, a life of challenge, creativity, and cooperative democratic living.[14]

(5) Are We Justified in Hoping for More Than Temporary, This-Worldly Fulfillment?

In discussing Deweyan hope up to now, I have claimed that his focus is on what we can hope for in this world, with its fortunes, misfortunes, and mortality, rather than on a supernatural realm that promises eternal peace or stability. Further, I claim that since Dewey says that nature allows us no more than temporary moments of fulfillment, to live in hope is to value the continued struggle to understand the conditions of such fulfillment so we might make these moments more frequent for ourselves and others. However, there are significant passages in Dewey's work where he seems to go beyond his this-worldly focus and recognize a type of mystical serenity.[15] In these passages, Dewey seems to suggest that it might be reasonable to hope for more than just temporary moments of fulfillment or harmony. He seems to suggest that we can achieve adaptations that allow us to build enduring adjustments and escape the constant movement from disturbance to equilibrium and back to disturbance again that marks organic life. For example, in two 1927 letters to Scudder Klyce, a man with whom Dewey carried on a thirteen-year correspondence, Dewey talks about experiencing a "peace which passes understanding."[16] I take him to mean that in the presence of this peace he achieved a special kind of unification. That is, he leaves behind the distinctions that usually separate self from world and parts of the world from the whole.

Along similar lines, in *A Common Faith*, Dewey says it is possible to achieve adjustments of our deepest being, adjustments that are akin to religious experience. These harmonies, and the resulting peace of mind, are so powerful, Dewey claims, that they endure for those who achieve them even through the darkest times. He writes, "These deep adjustments relate not to this and that want in relation to this and that condition of our surroundings, but pertain to our being in its entirety. Because of their scope, this modification of ourselves is enduring. It lasts through any amount of vicissitude of circumstances, internal and external" (*LW* 9:12). In these adjustments we unify all aspects of ourselves and integrate with "the enveloping whole" in which we live (*MW* 14:181). They introduce us to "a world beyond the world which is nevertheless the deeper reality of the world in which we live in our ordinary experience" (*LW* 10:199).

I find these and similar passages in Dewey's work, at least on the surface, to be in tension with his view that the world is marked as much by disorder and constant peril as by uniformity and good fortune. I say that these remarks are in tension because it seems that to hope for enduring unifications is a will-o'-the-wisp in a world in which, as Dewey claims, as I have already explained, it is dangerous to extend achieved harmonies beyond their naturally limited duration (*LW* 10:23).

Further, and compounding the apparent inconsistencies I note, is Dewey's claim that the experience of enduring harmony and the enveloping whole is noncognitive and difficult to describe. In fact, he says, we cannot even point to it (*MW* 14:181). This vagueness about enduring peace and how we might achieve it seems to conflict with Dewey's claim that all inquiry should provide a trail that others can follow to verify the inquirer's findings (*LW* 12:50). I am left feeling that Dewey has experienced something very important, something that I too want to experience. However, I am also left feeling frustrated, abandoned with no instructions about how to join him on this other shore.

Nevertheless, and despite my doubts and frustrations, I want to follow as best I can the few hints that Dewey does provide about ways to achieve this enduring harmony. I do this in case the tensions I feel are the result not of Dewey's inconsistencies but, rather, of my own inflexibility. It may be that I simply fail to appreciate the radical pluralism and infinite possibilities in the natural world that Dewey is at pains to describe. I begin by setting out a partial road map based on the hints Dewey offers about how we might experience an enduring unification with the world.

DEWEYAN ROAD MAP TO ENDURING ADJUSTMENT AND THE SECURITY OF THE "ENVELOPING WHOLE"

Dewey says, as I have noted, that the enveloping whole in which we find peace is difficult to describe. It is something we sense, a sensation highly charged with emotion that is "ineffable" and "undefinable" (*MW* 14:181). However, Dewey does give some clues about the conditions leading to an experience of this unifying wholeness. In one of his 1927 letters to Scudder Klyce, Dewey responds to Klyce's question about how Dewey achieved a peace beyond understanding. He tells Klyce that it comes from certain experiences he has had but also "from hard work," from his lifelong effort to "resolve certain dualisms."[17] In *A Common Faith*, written seven years after this letter to Klyce, Dewey comments further on conditions leading to enduring peace, saying that religious experiences yielding lasting and harmonious adjustments can come about three ways: philosophic reflection, poetry, and devotion to a cause (*LW* 9:11). In what follows, I discuss these three routes to peace.

Philosophic Reflection   If we take at face value what Dewey says about resolving certain dualisms, then we might understand his philosophic work as a road map to the experience of an enduring harmony and a sense of a reassuring, enveloping whole. I assume that among the dualisms that Dewey spent his life trying to reconcile are the precarious and stable, the perilous and comforting, and the particular and infinite. Thus, although I hear in Dewey that the world is always changing, that all of our steps into the future are full of foreboding and peril, perhaps I overemphasize the precarious aspects of the world. Alongside change and peril, Dewey apparently senses the stable, infinite, and reassuring. It may be that I lack the "negative capability"—the capacity to entertain apparently contradictory positions without choosing one over the other—that Dewey applauds in Keats. It may be that this prevents me from using philosophic reflection to reconcile dualisms in a Deweyan manner and, thus, experience the peace that Dewey finds in our complex world (*LW* 10:39). That is, unlike Dewey, I may lack the ability to hold in balance the particular and infinite, the perilous and reassuring. Instead, I focus primarily on the particular and perilous, and this leads me to neglect the contrary aspects, the infinite and reassuring, that characterize the enveloping whole. This seems to represent a serious incapacity on my part because, as Dewey says, the enveloping whole "belongs" to us, just as much as we "belong" to it (*MW* 14:227).

What might Dewey mean by this mutual belonging? I speculate that, for Dewey, our lives make no sense unless we accept that there is something universal in our particularity. It is as if we are a holograph of the entire universe, the world in a grain of sand, as Blake puts it. We belong to the world insofar as our particular story is part of the world's story. And the world belongs to us insofar as our finite history holds within it the world's history. This may explain why Dewey says that when we experience the enveloping whole, "we live in the universal" and "put off mortality" (*MW* 14:227). In a way that shows the radical nature of Dewey's thinking, the radical possibility of reconciling dualisms—and this point is still difficult for me to accept—each of us has an individualized sense of the whole (*MW* 14:226). Our experiences can be both of the whole and yet unique. That is, the individual and finite, the universal and infinite can be one.

Another way in which Dewey may reconcile the universal and the particular, and explain their mutual belonging, is through his view of change. Rather than speak about "interactions" between individuals and the world, he speaks about "transactions." For Dewey, neither the world nor its parts are complete in and of themselves. In other words, when you and I do something, we change the world, and it changes us. Dewey rejects the term "interactions" because it suggests that we and the world affect each other, but not essentially. It suggests that we are what we are apart from our interactions. By contrast, "transactions" indicates that we and the world affect each other essentially. This is another way of saying that, for Dewey, we cannot tell our story without telling the story of the world and vice versa.[18]

There is also a suggestion on Dewey's part that what humans consider good is also good for the universe and will endure. We are, he says, the world's "manifest destiny" (*LW* 1:315). When we work for ideals, he says, we "carry the universe forward" and can be sure that "our lot is one with whatever is good in existence" (*LW* 1:314). Dewey also tells us that our work is significant for the whole and that we can achieve "a unity with the universe that is to be preserved" (*LW* 1:113–14), a "permanent reshaping of the world" (*MW* 14:19). In effect, Dewey seems to be reassuring us that our efforts, as late products of evolution, are especially significant. He seems to suggest that nature smiles with favor on what humans bring to evolution. That is, we bring a consciousness to animal life that enables us to intentionally control the conditions of fulfillment, conditions that our animal ancestors could only shallowly experience and fulfillments they could experience only by chance (*LW* 10:35).

Dewey's talk of humans and human consciousness as part of the manifest destiny of nature hints of a teleology that, at least at first blush, is in tension with his claim that nature is perilous and human activity always a gamble. Dewey's appearing to have it both ways, claiming that nature is both purposeful and as random as a throw of the dice, is also hard for me to accept. However, it is certainly possible that my thinking is, once again, a sign of my limited negative capability. I may simply have trouble accepting that nature has no favorites but also has favorites.

Poetry   In addition to philosophic reflection, Dewey tells us that poetry can also lead to unifying experiences that promote enduring life adjustments. This is true of art in general, for Dewey, because, when successful, artistic objects have organic unity, a pervasive emotion that infuses all of a work's parts. Just as each of us may be a holograph of the universe, so each part of an artistic work may reflect the whole. According to Dewey, at times the highly emotionally charged sensations associated with aesthetic intuition are so intense that they resemble religious, mystical experiences of communion (*LW* 10:35).

Such highly charged sensations and intuitions of unification can also be brought about by nature. Dewey quotes the British ornithologist and writer William Henry Hudson who had aesthetic experiences in the presence of trees and birds akin to ecstatic religious communion. Dewey also refers to Emerson who said that on crossing a common at twilight he enjoyed "a perfect exhilaration" that made him "glad to the brink of fear" (*LW* 10:35).

Perhaps an even clearer example of unification with nature, of overcoming the dualism of individual and world, is from a 1838 journal entry by Emerson. It is not one that Dewey cites but one that I believe is in the spirit of Dewey's references to Hudson's and Emerson's unifying experiences.

> Every man that goes into the woods seems to be the first man that ever went into a wood. His sensations and his world are new. You really think that nothing can be said about morning and evening, and the fact is morning and evening have not yet begun to be described. When I see them . . . I am cheered with the moist warm, glittering budding and melodious hour that takes down the narrow walls of my soul and extends its pulsation and life to the very horizon. That is Morning; to cease for a bright hour to be a prisoner of this sickly body and to become as large as the world.[19]

What I hear in this journal entry is Emerson's view, one I believe shared by Dewey, that we are not just in the universe, looking at it from a very limited perspective. Rather, at certain times we sense that we are the universe and it is us.

Unlike the path to the enveloping whole through philosophic reflection, art and nature lead us there through immediate experience. Whereas the reason I have trouble following Dewey's philosophic route to enduring peace is my lack of negative capability, I believe my inability to follow his route through poetry and nature stems from my inattention to things noncognitive. I suspect I have a tendency to discount my intuitions and the information my emotions provide since these are, as Dewey acknowledges, so difficult to describe. In a way, Dewey is telling me that I need to attend to and value the intuitions that undergird my discursive, left-brained thinking. As he says, thinking is but a teacup on a sea of emotion.[20] As he also says, consecutive reasoning is less a guide to wisdom than are imagination and sensitivity to the ineffable (*LW* 10:41). It seems clear, then, that if I want to follow the philosophic and poetic road maps Dewey provides for achieving a peace that passes understanding, I need, first, to better comprehend the ways he reconciles the dualisms he finds in our world and, second, to be more sensitive to what my body and my imaginative intuitions tell me about the ineffable background of my focal experience.

Devotion to a Cause   I now consider the third possible route to enduring peace that Dewey mentions in *A Common Faith:* devotion to a cause. In my own experience, I have had more moments of peace as a result of devotion to a cause than as a result of philosophic reflection or poetry. However, my devotion to causes—like being a good caretaker of children or being a good teacher and colleague—has not been unifying enough for me to sense the enveloping whole and the security that such sense provides Dewey. For example, the times when I fail as a teacher, the times when I lack sufficient enthusiasm and skill to win the attention of my students, my devotion to the cause of teaching has wavered. I have wondered whether my efforts are worthwhile. Rather than feeling a sense of peace and security, I have felt anxiety and a sense of despair about life.

More recently, since McCarthy's and my publication of our first book about Dewey in 1998, I have been committed to the cause of trying to better understand Dewey's work, to write about it, and to teach it.[21] This cause has given me more peace than teaching courses that do not have a research connection because, when I can combine teaching and research, there is more unification in my life. I am able to bring together my efforts as instructor, researcher, and writer, as well as enjoy a modest sense of community with other scholars.

In addition, I have felt something mystical in my turn toward Dewey, a feeling that has grown since I first read *Reconstruction in Philosophy* between my first and second years of college. Although I understood very few of the book's details, I responded to Dewey's claim that modern life is without integration for many people. Since my own life as an undergraduate lacked integration, I felt, for the first time, that a philosopher was talking directly to me. When, many years later, I turned to Dewey for help with my teaching, I felt that I was returning home in some way. I was doing what I had to do. That is, I felt—to draw once again from *Human Nature and Conduct* and *A Common Faith*—that something was claiming me and I was claiming it. Whereas teaching seemed like something that I claimed, my work on Dewey involved a mutual claiming, and, thus, it had—and still has—a stronger hold on me. It gives me a greater sense of belonging and purpose than my other causes. When I think about my study of Dewey, I feel connected to him as well as to the long line of Dewey's predecessors who also tried to make sense of life. I feel connected to those people who worked, as I am trying to work, to understand ways to give meaning to life, to understand ways to find strong enough purpose and faith to live in hope despite the many vicissitudes that life inevitably brings.

Although I cherish these feelings of connection and unification with Dewey, I am sad to say that my study of him—including teaching my hope course and, with McCarthy, writing this book—does not give me the enduring peace or sense of the enveloping whole that Dewey speaks about. It does not, to borrow words again from Dewey, help me "put off mortality and live in the universal" (*MW* 14:227). The reason may be, as I have already suggested, that my lack of negative capability does me in. I am so focused on my individual life that I cannot fully appreciate that I am part of a larger universal life.

In conclusion, my construction of a theory of hope for Dewey leaves me with new insights but also new tasks. The Dewey who gives me answers to the first four of my five questions, the Dewey I would like to call my "familiar" Dewey, tells me that the proper object of my ultimate hope should be what the dynamic, ever-changing world gives me: a chance to promote democratic living and to meet the perpetual challenges of life with gratitude and intelligent wholeheartedness. That is, the most I can hope for are moments in which I believe so strongly in the value of what I am doing that I am vitally alive and fully engrossed. These are moments of harmony that are limited in duration but that help make the possibility of such future moments, both for myself and for others, more widely available. By contrast, the Dewey I focus on in my fifth and final question—the Dewey who is, for me, "unfamiliar"—suggests that peace beyond understanding, a deep adjustment that lasts through all vicissitudes, is also a legitimate ultimate hope. This Dewey suggests that I might also aspire to experiences of the enveloping whole that are akin to the religious ecstasy of communion.[22]

Despite the discrepancy I feel between the familiar and the unfamiliar Deweys, I want to live enough in his spirit to keep both Deweyan answers about ultimate hope alive. I want to be both realistic about the limited duration of our fulfillments and, at the same time, accepting of Dewey's invitation to experience the enveloping whole and the feelings of stability and peace that he claims it can yield. I want to be open to his invitation to expand my sensitivities to philosophic reflection, to the poetic, and to the causes to which I am devoted so that I might experience adjustments that are more enduring.

In the next chapter, I further explicate the theory of hope I construct for Dewey by contrasting it to the theory of hope developed by the twentieth-century French philosopher Gabriel Marcel. In doing this comparative work, I try to bring both the familiar and the unfamiliar Dewey into dialogue with Marcel.

TWO

Dewey in Dialogue
with Gabriel Marcel:
Hope with and without God

Steve Fishman

I choose Marcel as the first theorist with whom to compare Dewey because, although Marcel is intentionally unsystematic in his thinking, he is one of the few mainstream twentieth-century philosophers to explicitly discuss hope. The differences I find between Marcel and Dewey are to be expected since Marcel is a theist and Dewey a non-theist. However, what is surprising are the similarities I also find between the two.

Regarding their expected differences, the main one is how they interpret the mysterious dimension of life. Although Dewey is sensitive to it, as I have shown in the previous chapter, as a non-theist he sees all human experience as having a natural origin and a natural end. Thus, the object of Dewey's ultimate hope is democratic living, that is, full engrossment in present experience that leads to individual and social growth. By contrast, Marcel, the theist, views the mystery in life as an intimation of a transcendent realm, and the object of his ultimate hope is salvation in eternal communion with God.

Sharp differences also distinguish Dewey's and Marcel's views of how to overcome hopelessness. For Dewey, as I have said, it requires working for our ultimate hope in intelligent, wholehearted ways. It also requires giving up our desire to prolong the harmonies we achieve into eternity and, instead, accepting the fact that harmonies do not last and some of life's greatest joys come from opportunities to creatively and cooperatively reestablish them. By contrast, for Marcel, overcoming hopelessness requires a transformation of the self: a letting go of one's desiring, acquisitive ego while birthing a selfless, spiritual being.

Whereas these radical differences between Dewey, the non-theist, and Marcel, the theist, are predictable, the noteworthy similarities I find, places where these theorists' footsteps on the terrain of hope overlap, are unexpected. For example, I find that Dewey and Marcel both believe that faith in oneself and in the sources of one's being is important for developing hope. In addition, they both believe that communion—feeling part of a larger whole—is an important condition for maintaining hope. Finally, the overlap I find most interesting is that, for both Dewey and Marcel, this need for communion is satisfied by experiences that are ineffable and indescribable.

I begin this chapter by explicating Marcel's theory of hope, and I do this by presenting Marcel's answers to two questions that get to the heart of his theory: What causes people to become hopeless? And what must people do to regain hope? I then compare Marcel's answers to these questions with answers I construct for Dewey.

Marcel on the Cause of Hopelessness: Lack of Spirituality in a World Focused on Competition and Acquisition

According to Marcel, we become hopeless because the society in which we live neglects the transcendent, spiritual potential of human existence. Our culture's neglect of the spiritual means that death casts a darkness upon our lives that seems unshakable and results in feelings of emptiness. People respond to this darkness not with faith in themselves and others but with distrust and fear, a fear that leads them to become imperialistic and attempt to control everything around them. When I am hopeless, Marcel says, "there is nothing in being to which I can give credit, nothing I can count on, no security" (OM 184). In other words, without a spiritual life, we live like fearful colonial settlers seeking dominion over all we survey.

This imperialistic mentality, for Marcel, has a reductive effect on all aspects of existence: our conceptions of human nature, work, physical objects, and other people. Regarding human nature, the imperialist mentality reduces people's activities to a series of "vital" and "social" functions (OM 173). Our sleep, food, and exercise (vital functions) are evaluated in terms of how well they support the public roles we fill as producers, consumers, and citizens (social functions). We are machines working as cogs in a larger machine, and everything about us is assumed to be predictable. In such a world—one emptied of surprise and choice, of creativity and responsibility—we are left with only "particular hopes" for temporary good fortune and success, bereft of what Marcel calls "absolute hopes" for loving unions that transcend time and space. In short, people become hopeless, according to Marcel, because they no longer believe it is possible to secure what matters most.

As an example of the consequences of this imperialistic worldview, Marcel, in a 1933 lecture, describes the hopeless situation of a railway employee who spends his days punching passengers' tickets in the Metro. This ticket taker is stuck in a cycle of uncreative routine. Further, according to Marcel, when he retires, he becomes worthless and is barely tolerated since he no longer serves a social function. Marcel believes this imperialistic or "functional" worldview, a worldview against which most of us are defenseless, leads to "an increasingly inhuman social order and philosophy" (OM 174).

Although some would disagree with Marcel, arguing that identifying with our social functions helps us gain control over our lives and know our place in society, Marcel contends that we end up without dignity, like parts of a machine that are jettisoned when they no longer work. As he puts it, in an imperialist/functionalist world, in retirement or death we cease to function and thus become "sheer waste to be discarded" (OM 174). In addition, Marcel believes that the imperialistic approach leads people to treat physical objects and other people in functional ways. That is, we reduce things and other people to what they can do for us.

Another way Marcel describes this imperialistic approach is that it is characterized by the desire to "have" rather than "be," to dominate rather than trust and nurture. In this regard, Marcel's analysis foreshadows Erich Fromm's claim that those who seek to "have" things (and people) are in love with death rather than life. Such people, according to Fromm, are "necrophilic" rather than "biophilic" because, in their love of having rather than being, controlling rather than growing, they destroy life.[1]

In a lecture given in 1942, Marcel explicitly connects these imperialistic, functional, and acquisitive tendencies with contemporary societies that claim to be democratic:

> It must . . . be noted that democracy, considered not in its principles but in its actual achievements, has helped in the most baleful manner to encourage *claiming* in all its aspects, the demanding of rights—and indeed to bring a mercenary spirit into all human relationships. I mean by this that the democratic atmosphere tends to exclude more and more the idea of disinterested

service born of fidelity, and a belief in the intrinsic value of such service. Each individual claims from the start to enjoy the same consideration and the same advantages as his neighbor; and, in fact, his self-respect tends to resolve itself into an attitude which is not only defensive but ever claiming rights from others. Thus he considers it beneath his dignity to do anything whatever for nothing. The abstract idea of a certain justice is here oddly connected with the anxiety not to be duped, not to allow another person to take advantage of his simplicity or good nature. But in this perspective how can the spirit of mistrust—mistrust not only of others, but of life itself—not tend to make the human soul less and less a possible dwelling place for hope, or indeed for joy? (*HV* 56–57)

Marcel, in his analysis of modern-day democracies, invokes and extends Ferdinand Tönnies' nineteenth-century criticisms of *gesellschaft* societies (*BH* 233). In such societies, according to Tönnies, all transactions are trades. Every interaction is quid pro quo. In today's society, we see this quid pro quo approach invade even marriage, with frequent prenuptial agreements. Those reflect what Marcel sees as our desire not to be "duped" and to protect our possessions. In other words, even the love between spouses involves constant entries in a ledger to make sure that what each spouse puts into the relationship equals what each takes out. These claims for equality and equal rights are disheartening, for Marcel, because they encourage a lack of trust in and charitable love of others. This is sad for him because trust and charitable love are at the center of his view of hope (DH 282–84). Hope is present when we are available to others without imposing demands about what they must do for us in return. Marcel describes this availability as a gift of oneself, a form of charity that enriches both the receiver and the giver. He writes, "At the heart of charity is presence in the sense of the absolute gift of one's self, a gift which implies no impoverishment to the giver, far from it; and so we are here in a realm where the categories valid in the world of things entirely cease to be applicable" (*BH* 69).

In sum, for Marcel, we who are hopeless suffer from an impoverished, mistaken worldview. Although we are uneasy about seeing ourselves reduced to functions, we give in to this approach and accept its inhuman social order. We accept the idea that our existence is nothing more than our social functions, the result of interactions that are mechanical. Since there is nothing transcendent or spiritual about human existence, death makes a mockery of our ambition for ultimate fulfillment and bliss. Thus, we become aggressively protective of ourselves, imperialistic, unwilling to risk opening to others, unwilling to risk surprise or mystery. However, like drug addicts, the more we try to protect ourselves by using others to our advantage, the more vulnerable, isolated, and hopeless we become. The more we try to preserve the life we believe is so valuable, the more we are unable to leave our fortresses and enter the space where life and hope truly begin.

Marcel's Requirements for Regaining Hope

Having answered my first question for Marcel—What leads people to become hopeless?—I now turn to his answer to my second question: What must people do to regain hope? Marcel names two requirements we must fulfill if we want to sustain our hope for eternal communion with our loved ones, the object, according to Marcel, of our "absolute hope." These are creative fidelity and surrender of desire.

CREATIVE FIDELITY AS A REQUIREMENT
FOR REGAINING HOPE

For Marcel, creative fidelity is unconditional faithfulness to the possibility of goodness and transcendence in another being—a child, spouse, neighbor, or God. The most fundamental of these is creative faith in God. Marcel tells us, "[Absolute] hope consists in asserting that there is at the heart of being, beyond all data, beyond all inventories and all calculations, a mysterious principle in connivance with me, which cannot but will what I will, at least if what I will is really worth willing and is, in fact, willed with my whole being" (OM 184).

Our fidelity to God and others must be creative because it is constantly challenged by unwanted events. As Marcel puts it, our life is full of "trials," the ultimate tests of our fidelity being moments of exile, terminal illness, or imprisonment, moments when we want to say that life is meaningless and all our most fundamental longings will be denied. At such moments, if we are to maintain hope in God and others, we must be creative in the sense that we must freely choose to remain hopeful, and this involves the continual creation of a new self, a new being. That is, to remain hopeful as the result of habit or out of a sense of duty or the fulfillment of a contract does not count for Marcel because we have lost ourselves, given ourselves over to a function or routine. For the fidelity, the hope-in-thou/Thou, to be truly ours, we must freely create it, and it is in these moments, for Marcel, that we truly are. He writes, "A function is, by its very essence, something one has; but in proportion as my function swallows me up, it becomes me, and substitutes itself for what I am. . . . [By contrast,] as soon as there is creation, in whatever degree, we are in the realm of being" (*BH* 150). In other words, for Marcel, as we continually re-create our fidelity, we have intimations of the creative, loving Thou "at the heart of all being" (see also *MAH* 194).

Marcel offers an example of creative fidelity in a mother who continues to hope to see her son again despite the fact that his death has been confirmed by witnesses. She insists that "John will come back." Marcel says that this mother "has within her a loving thought which repudiates or transcends the facts, and it seems as though there were something absurd or even scandalous in disputing her right to hope. . . . What [her] hope gives us is the simple affirmation, 'You are coming back.' And this 'you are coming back' is beyond the reach of objective criticism" (*HV* 65–66; *OM* 184). This woman, by refusing to accept the empirical evidence of her son's death, is being faithful to her longing for unbreakable bonds of devotion and selfless service. Although this may make no sense to people with a functionalist mind-set, the mother, in her creative fidelity to her son, exercises what Marcel sees as her freedom to resist the calculations of the scientific observer. In doing so, she reaffirms her hope in a mysterious force at the heart of being, a force that is in "connivance" with her.

SURRENDER OF DESIRE AS A REQUIREMENT FOR REGAINING HOPE

Marcel requires for hope not only creative fidelity but also the surrender of desire. As I interpret Marcel, our desire to be delivered from life's trials—the ultimate trial being death—does not mean that we can anticipate the details of our deliverance. That is, we must give up the idea that we can specify the nature of our salvation or our eternal communion with our loved ones. Instead, we must let the form of our deliverance and the absolute Thou remain a mystery. The mother in the above example should, therefore, according to Marcel, surrender her desire for a particular sort of reunion with her son, adopting instead a selfless devotion to him. To fail to give up her specific desires indicates a lack of faith in God's goodness. In imposing this requirement on absolute hope, Marcel diverges from theologians like Aquinas and Josef Pieper. Although both Aquinas and Pieper believe, like Marcel, that the realization of absolute hope involves God's grace, neither Aquinas nor Pieper believes that the nature of salvation is, as it is for Marcel, shrouded in mystery and antithetical to desire.[2]

In order to clarify Marcel's view of hope as creative fidelity and surrender of desire, I once again apply his ideas to marriage. To be hopeful about one's marriage is to have faith in the divine presence in one's spouse. For example, it is a husband's availability *(disponibilité)* to his wife, in the sense of his having confidence in her ability to accept and bring to fruition the divine gifts she has received, that is the mark of hope in marriage (*HV* 23). This confidence that a husband has in his wife, according to Marcel, will not seem to her to be imposed from without but, rather, to be working "from within" (*HV* 40). Being present to someone in this way—putting one's hope in another by trusting that they have the ability to make full use of their divine gifts—is to be creatively faithful while surrendering one's own desires. Marcel tells us, "It will be seen that if my love can exercise an action on the beloved, it is only inasmuch as this love is not desire; for in desire I tend to subordinate the beloved to my own ends, to convert the beloved into an object. Thus it is perhaps only absolutely disinterested love that is susceptible of affecting the *thou*" (*MJ* 223). Applying Marcel's notion of disinterested love to our example, the husband who loves and hopes in his wife in this "disinterested" way puts no preconditions on what she will become. I assume that a husband who is available in Marcel's sense will remain steadfast in his faith even if his wife leaves him. He will remain assured that his trust in her establishes an unbreakable bond that will endure in a manner that cannot be foretold. As Marcel puts it, to be absolutely available to another is to love "what God makes of me" (*BH* 69).

Thus, to be faithful in Marcel's sense is transformative. It spiritually heals everyone it touches. This loving, transformative availability is also, for Marcel, an intimation of a transcendent divinity "who is Himself also Love." He explains, "Hope, in this sense, is not only a protestation inspired by love, but a sort of call, too, a desperate appeal to an ally who is Himself also Love. The supernatural element which is the foundation of Hope is as clear here as its transcendent nature, for nature, unilluminated by hope, can only appear to us the scene of a sort of immense and inexorable book-keeping" (*BH* 79).

Whether we agree with Marcel's claim that communion between loved ones is an intimation of an eternal life to come or see it as only his wishful thinking, it is difficult not to respect his efforts to honor the ineffable longing for unending communion—one of the "fixed stars in the heaven of the soul"—that many of us share (*HV* 9). People do sense, in some inarticulate way, the joy of someone's wanting what is best for them while asking nothing in return. We do sense when we are in the presence of someone who has confidence, faith, and high hopes for us. Their presence touches us with a warmth that is somehow healing and lets us feel we are home again.

What I have tried to describe is what I believe many people sense when they are on the receiving end of the charitable love and availability that Marcel describes. In addition, I believe that the need to be on the giving end of Marcel's love is also widespread. It is as if we have a deep longing to get outside ourselves, to merge with something larger, to lose ourselves in some good, trustworthy force where we no longer have to protect our petty borders 24/7. It is as if, like the character Winston Smith in Orwell's *1984*, we know deep in our bones that there is more to life than wasting our time defending our own small territory. Deep down we feel that we are designed to devote ourselves to some cosmic force whose energies are directed toward bringing absolute hope to everyone.

In sum, for Marcel, creative fidelity and surrender of desire rest upon leaving behind our practical, calculating ego and opening to the wonder of being. They rest upon setting aside concern for individual safety, so that, without the limiting straitjacket of self-concern, we can be truly present or available *(disponible)* to others. In this pledge of creative fidelity and selfless openness to others, we deny that the world is bounded by time and space and will dash our hopes for salvation. As Marcel puts it, the pledge of eternal love and fidelity that we make in the face of "verifiable" knowledge to the contrary is a "transcendent" act, one that not only honors our experience of communion but is its first fruit as well (*HV* 67).

Speculating about Marcel's Advice to the Ticket Taker　Having explored Marcel's requirements for hope, I try to apply them by asking what specific advice he might give the railway employee whom he describes as hopeless about achieving lasting fulfillment. To answer this question risks ignoring Marcel's caution that one person cannot tell another how to respond to life's trials, to mysteries that he says are to be lived in contrast to problems that are to be solved in some scientific, generalizable way. Yet I believe Marcel would suggest to the railway employee that he should hope for eternal presence with his loved ones and God, a communion that, after death, will be different from but better than the communion he has shared with them in his earthly life (*HV* 67). Regarding the ticket taker's hopes for his finite existence, I believe Marcel would have as the employee's objective "divine light-heartedness," a life free of the fears and worries that accompany the prevailing cultural focus on egotistic desires (*HV* 61). Although it might be impossible for him to quit his job, when he is shed of ordinary fears and desires, his potential for unconditional love could come to the fore. There would be lightness and youthfulness in his step, no matter his actual age, because of his confidence that "at the heart of being" there is a mysterious principle "in connivance" with him and his absolute hopes.

However, the ticket taker's transforming himself from someone who wants to satisfy his desires through "having" to someone who exhibits creative fidelity and surrender of desire will not be easy. This is because this transformation is a radical one that involves not merely altering the self but giving it up. It is a type of Easter experience in which the having self dies and is reborn as an absolutely available or "being" self. In fact, Marcel admits that very few of us are likely to achieve such change, such "divine light-heartedness." Most people, in his view, are fated to remain in a world of having and desiring, experiencing, at best, only brief moments of absolute hope. Marcel notes, "As far as we can judge, this liberation, this exemption [from the hopelessness of having], must remain the privilege of a very small number of chosen souls. The vast majority of men are, as far as we can see, destined to remain entangled in the inextricable meshes of Having" (*HV* 61).

Although it will not be easy for the ticket taker or anyone else to overcome the prevailing imperialist mind-set, if we are to do so, we need to honor our longing for absolute, enduring loyalty to others. We need to see this longing as an important clue about the spiritual nature of our being. To neglect it, according to Marcel, is to turn our backs on the transcendent and mysterious possibilities of our world. To the contrary, only when we accept such possibilities are we free to reclaim the world as a world that shares our hope for enduring love and communion.[3]

Dewey's and Marcel's Similar Views of the Symptoms of Hopelessness in Contemporary Society

When I compare Dewey's view of the symptoms of hopelessness with the ones I describe for Marcel above, I find numerous similarities in the features of society they focus upon. These include competition for individual gain, a flawed sense of individual independence, and insensitivity to what we owe to others.

DEWEY, LIKE MARCEL, SEES COMPETITION, INDIVIDUALISM, AND GREED AS SIGNS OF HOPELESSNESS

Dewey, in ways that anticipate Marcel's criticisms of contemporary society, tells us that the world has gone "mad" with competition and that we have become too self-centered. In fact, Dewey himself could have written the criticisms of contemporary democracy that Marcel voices in his 1942 lecture. The same sort of self-centered individualism that Marcel finds antithetical to hope is also decried by Dewey (*LW* 5:41–123). Dewey too believes that competition for material goods leads to selfishness, to individuals appropriating for personal profit ideas and technology that are collectively produced. The example Dewey gives is Henry Ford's personal appropriation of the wealth resulting from the collective development and production of the combustion engine. In other words, the form in which democracy presently exists in industrial societies is far from Dewey's ideal, an ideal to which he gives a strong communitarian cast. He makes clear that democracy should not be about grabbing your share of the pie before others grab theirs. Nor should it simply be a series of competitions for public office staged at regular intervals. His ideal of democracy is much more communitarian than that. It is way of life, a "mode of associated living" that features "conjoint communicated experience" (*MW* 9:93). It is an opportunity to join with others in the service of common cause (*LW* 2:235–372).

In a climate that is so removed from his democratic ideal, Dewey believes that a strong step for reform would be a change in the prevailing emphasis in public schools on competition for good grades. He tells us that it behooves educators to promote, above all else, a spirit of social service (*LW* 9:203). Dewey says,

> The acquisition however perfect of skills is not an end in itself. They are things to be put to use as a contribution to a common and shared life. They are intended, indeed, to make an individual more capable of self-support and of self-respecting independence. But unless this end is placed in the context of services rendered to others, services which they need for the fulfillment also of their lives, skills gained will be put to an egoistic and selfish use as means of a trained shrewdness for personal advantage at the cost of others' claims and opportunities for the good life. Too often, indeed, the schools, through reliance upon the spur of competition and the bestowal of special honours and prizes as for those who excel in a competitive race or even battle, only build up and strengthen the disposition that in after-school life employs special talents and superior skill to outwit others and "get on" personally without respect for their welfare. (*LW* 9:201–2, 180)

In this passage, I hear themes that, as I have already indicated, are central to Marcel's concerns about contemporary culture. Both theorists excoriate egocentrism, our imperialistic efforts to dominate or "outwit" others, and our failure to care about the common welfare.

Dewey's and Marcel's similarities increase when we compare the Dewey quotation above, taken from a speech he gave in South Africa in July 1934, with a passage from a lecture Marcel delivered eight years later, in December 1942, in Lyons. Not only do both men decry selfishness and domination of others, but they also both illustrate this feature of contemporary culture with similar examples from school life. Marcel says:

> There is, in particular, every reason to think that the system of perpetual competition to which the individual is subjected in the world today cannot fail to increase and exasperate this consciousness of the *ego*. I have no hesitation in saying that if we want to fight effectively against individualism in its most harmful form, we must find some way of breaking free from the asphyxiating atmosphere of examinations and competition in which our young people are struggling. "I must win, not you! I must get above you!" We can never insist enough upon how the real sense of fellowship which shows itself in such striking contrast among any team worthy of the name, has been rendered weak and anaemic by the competitive system. (*HV* 18)

We know that Marcel personally suffered from school exam competitions.[4] We do not know that Dewey suffered in the same way; he may have only observed this "asphyxiating" competition in his study of U.S. schools. Regardless, it is striking that both men view competition as dangerous because it leads individuals to distance themselves from and dominate others.

Both men also see competition as devaluing the individual. Marcel notes that competition produces "individualism in its most harmful form." This is the case because school exams discount what is unique in each of us. That is, competing with others for the correct answer when there is only a single correct response assumes that an individual's particular skills and particular ways of looking at things are unimportant. Dewey also decries this devaluing of individual differences when, in his South Africa speech, he notes that most school exams are judged by a common standard, and common standards encourage uniformity rather than the pooling of diverse perspectives and skills that he believes is so important to community life (*LW* 9:197).

In short, both Dewey and Marcel see individual competition as a major social problem because it leads to an aggressiveness toward others that is ultimately bankrupt. Despite the protective moats we build around ourselves, our isolation leaves us hopeless because, deep down, we know we can do very little on our own. As Marcel notes, to be exiled or imprisoned—cut off from society with no hope of return—presents individuals with their greatest trial, their greatest temptation to despair. Likewise, Dewey, in an unforgettable phrase, calls solitary confinement "the last term in the prison house of man" (*MW* 13:276).[5]

Dewey's and Marcel's Different Accounts of the Underlying Causes of Hopelessness

Dewey and Marcel share quite similar views of the symptoms of hopelessness in our culture, as I have just shown, both of them focusing on competition, mistrust, and a flawed sense of the individual. However, their accounts of the underlying causes of these phenomena are quite different.

DEWEY'S ACCOUNT OF THE CAUSE OF HOPELESSNESS

Contemporary society's emphasis on individual winning and losing is caused, for Dewey, by a failure to recognize and intelligently utilize changing technology and social conditions. That is, we choose to maintain our dog-eat-dog attitude because we fail to intelligently adapt traditional ways of thinking and behaving to new scientific and technological developments. For Dewey, the fact that we continue to seek dominion over others is the result of our being stuck with certain outmoded ideas about private property and scarcity that perpetuate outmoded habits that keep us from establishing, as our ultimate hope, a truly democratic society. The reason that Dewey calls our embrace of individual competition outmoded is that it ignores the increased ability of technology to sustain a large proportion of the population in a comfortable living style. It also ignores our improved ability to harness the powers of cooperative intelligence, powers best exemplified, for Dewey, by modern science and ones he believes that could be used to ameliorate our social problems. According to Dewey, we still act as if the only way to settle our social problems is to go to war, and we still mistakenly assume that for a few of us to live creative and comfortable lives, a great number of us must live unrewarding ones (*LW* 5:41–123, 11:1–66).

What we hear in Dewey's analysis of the cause of hopelessness is an application once again of his biological model of human life. Living, for Dewey, is marked by rhythms of disturbance and harmony, and to live in hope, in Dewey's sense, is to see these disturbances as opportunities to intelligently, creatively, and democratically achieve new adjustments. As I will show in the next section, Marcel, as a supernaturalist, adopts not a biological model of human life but a theological one. As a result, the principal cause of hopelessness for Marcel is not our failure to intelligently adjust to changing situations but our failure to let spiritual forces in life triumph over material ones.

MARCEL'S ACCOUNT OF THE CAUSE OF HOPELESSNESS

Ironically, the very developments in industrial society that Dewey believes are the basis of hope for perpetual democratic reconstruction—the possibility of sharing the enormous fruits of science and of extending the application of cooperative intelligence to ameliorate social problems—are the developments that Marcel sees as the underlying causes of contemporary hopelessness. As I have shown, for Marcel, science, as a functional approach to things and events, is a form of reductionism. To say that things or persons are best understood as the way they function in society is to miss, according to Marcel, important aspects of human existence. Physical and social scientists dismiss the ineffable features that Marcel finds at the center of our being because these features cannot be explained as instantiations of descriptive laws that apply to large numbers of cases. In their search for the structures of reality, scientists dismiss the concrete, individual encounters that, for Marcel, allow us to give witness to the transcendent, mysterious dimension of human experience.

Scientists' conversion of all human choices into "problems" leads them, according to Marcel, to neglect the unique ways in which each of us experiences the trials of life. For example, to tell people how they should feel when they face terminal illness is to ignore the fact that each person feels the terror and mystery of death in his or her own way. To tell the terminally ill which "stage" in the dying process they are in because of Elisabeth Kubler-Ross's observations of large numbers of dying patients is to deny the terminally ill their freedom to decide how to react to their individual trials.[6] For Marcel, responding to death is one of the mysteries of life because there is no way anyone else can tell us what attitude to take toward it. The meaning of death is up to us. It is up to each of us to decide, as an act of free will, if we will see death as a reason for despair, a reason to fall apart, or as an opportunity for faith, a chance to affirm, "in the teeth" of all scientific evidence, our hope for salvation (*HV* 67).[7] For Marcel, then, individuals' shaping of their own understanding of the significance of life's "trials"—whether these trials afford an intimation of an absolute Thou or an intimation of life's futility—is their initial act of freedom. Modern science, as he views it, with its abstract approach to knowledge and its denial of the uniqueness of our trials and the way we view them, is responsible for the lack of spirituality and, therefore, hope in contemporary life.

In sum, Marcel and Dewey see the cause of hopelessness in modern life as rooted in our notion of the individual as someone caught in a death-clutch struggle with others for scarce material goods. However, their explanations of this development differ because the objects of their ultimate hope and their views of human nature differ. Dewey believes that human origins and ends are natural, whereas Marcel believes that human origins and ends are supernatural or spiritual. Since the ultimate hope for Dewey is to extend the possibility of creative, intelligent, and democratic living to as many people as possible, he wants science—and the technology and methods of cooperative inquiry that it spawns—to be better integrated into our individual and social habits. By contrast, because Marcel's ultimate goal is eternal, loving communion with others and God, he believes that the mind-set of modern science, which dismisses the idea of a transcendent and eternal form of being, needs to be limited in scope rather than extended.

Comparing Dewey's and Marcel's Further Requirements for Regaining Hope: Belonging, Purpose, and Faith in Our Choice of Goals

As I noted at the outset, despite the differences between Dewey's and Marcel's basic orientations toward hope, what makes comparison of these theorists interesting is that Dewey, the naturalist, and Marcel, the supernaturalist, often unexpectedly walk the same ground as they discuss hope. As I have just recounted, although Dewey and Marcel explain the underlying causes of low hope differently, both see individualism, competition, and distrust as symptoms of despair in contemporary society. In the following sections of this chapter, I continue to point out both differences and similarities as I explore Dewey's and Marcel's views of the importance of belonging, purpose, and faith in our choice of goals for resisting modern temptations to despair.

DIFFERENCES IN DEWEY'S AND MARCEL'S VIEWS OF BELONGING AND PURPOSE AS REQUIREMENTS FOR HOPE

For both Dewey and Marcel, a life without belonging and purpose leaves one hopeless. However, for Dewey, their source, as we have seen, is gratitude and piety toward nature. For Marcel, by contrast, their source is gratitude and piety toward God or the absolute Thou.

Dewey on Belonging and Purpose   As I explained in the previous chapter, belonging and purpose are, for Dewey, characteristics of living in hope, and an important source of belonging is recognition of our ancestral connection to nature. Once we recognize this connection to nature, we act piously toward the sources of our being. We work respectfully and carefully to further its most excellent features.

As I also explained in the previous chapter, Dewey's gratitude toward his ancestors resonates with my own experience. However, I stumble when I try to follow his path to gratitude and piety toward all of nature. What I have called the "unfamiliar" Dewey has a reverence for nature that I struggle to achieve. He suggests that this sort of reverence comes to us when we experience the supportive but ineffable background, the "enveloping whole" that is the context of our focal experience (*MW* 14:181). He tells us that if we are open to this dimension of earthly living, then "every act may carry within itself a consoling and supporting consciousness of the whole to which it belongs and which in some sense belongs to it" (*MW* 14:227). In other words, when we sense the type of connection with nature that Dewey refers to, our identity is altered. We and the world become an organic unity. We "belong" to the whole because we, like it, are composed of earth (bone), fire (heat), air (breath), and water (blood). And the whole "belongs" to us because, in its rhythms of one and many, light and dark, regular and mysterious, we see our own rhythms.[8]

In short, gratitude toward others and piety toward nature as the encompassing whole are strong resources, for Dewey, of belonging and purpose. They can help us overcome the isolation we may feel and point out a significant role we might play in the lives of others and nature.

Marcel on Belonging and Purpose   Belonging and purpose are, for Marcel, as they are for Dewey, requirements for hope, but their source for Marcel is quite different from Dewey's. Instead of Dewey's "enveloping whole," which includes nature and other people, Marcel's source is the hidden and loving force at the heart of all being, a mysterious force we cannot name but that favors our existence (OM 174). By truly and freely acknowledging this source of our being, according to Marcel, we bond with it and are no longer "distinct" or "isolated" (*HV* 61). Rather, our acknowledgment of it allows the divine to circulate through us. Without this recognition that our own being is connected to a divine being, we are cut off from our roots and our destination. Without gratitude and piety toward our source, we are victims of hopelessness, left with an existence that is just so many successive events adding up to nothing.

On the other hand, with gratitude and piety for the transcendent, according to Marcel, we find life's purpose, and it excites in us what he sees as the most important human virtue, unconditional love *(caritas)*. Thus, for Marcel, through gratitude and piety we discover that our task in life is to love others unconditionally by helping them bring to fruition their divine gifts. Loving this way, according to Marcel, is not only a requirement of living in hope but also a condition of achieving the ultimate object of our hope, namely, eternal communion with loved ones and the divine.

SIMILARITIES IN DEWEY'S AND MARCEL'S VIEWS OF FAITH IN ONE'S CHOICES AS A REQUIREMENT FOR HOPE

Not unexpectedly, Dewey, the non-theist, has gratitude and piety for nature and other people. Also not unexpectedly, Marcel, the theist, has gratitude and piety for the divine force he finds at the heart of all being. What is unexpected is that both Dewey and Marcel also see faith in one's choice of goals as a requirement of hope.

Dewey on Faith in One's Choice of Goals   As I explained when discussing Deweyan keys to hope in Chapter 1, in addition to belonging and purpose, another important characteristic of living in hope, for Dewey, is having faith in one's choice of goals. This faith is justified, according to Dewey, when we determine our path and activities with intelligence and wholeheartedness. I reproduce once more the passage from Dewey's 1925 Carus Lectures, *Experience and Nature*, that I find so central to a Deweyan theory of hope: "Fidelity to the nature to which we belong, as parts however weak, demands that we cherish our desires and ideals till we have converted them into intelligence, revised them in terms of the ways and means which nature makes possible. When we have used our thought to its utmost and have thrown into the moving unbalanced balance of things our puny strength, we know that though the universe slay us still we may trust, for our lot is one with whatever is good in existence" (*LW* 1:314).

Dewey is not saying that we should trust that others and nature will cooperate with us willy-nilly. Rather, for this trust to be justified some important conditions must be met. Our desires and ideals need to be tempered. They need to pass through the trials of reflection. They need to be sifted by our imagination and forethought to make sure that the cost of reaching our ideals, given what we know of "the ways and means of nature," is worth their promised prize. That is, as we reflect on the wisdom of pursuing our ends-in-view, we must be intelligent about estimating their consequences both for ourselves as well as for the common wealth. Only when our desires and ideals have been tempered or "converted . . . into intelligence" is our hope that nature and others are on our side justified.

In sum, before we can trust nature, we must have faith in our choices. We must have faith in the process of intelligently and wholeheartedly choosing our goals. Yet even when all this is done, Dewey, ever sensitive to the uncertainty and precariousness of human life, does not promise that all of nature and all of society will support us. Rather, as I have pointed out before, he offers something much more modest. He promises only that "whatever is good in existence" is on our side. By this I take him to mean that we may very well be defeated in our efforts to extend justice and equity to all people. But in our failure we can be assured that the good that is in the world, however modest it may be, is with us.

Marcel on Faith in One's Choice of Goals Although the transcendent object of Marcel's ultimate hope is different from the natural one of Dewey, and although Marcel's ultimate hope promises more than Dewey's—eternal life rather than potential social progress—an important aspect of Marcel's view of living in hope, as it is of Dewey's, is faith in one's choice of goals. Marcel expresses the need for confidence in one's choice in a passage I have already quoted, "[Absolute] hope consists in asserting that there is at the heart of being, beyond all data, beyond all inventories and all calculations, a mysterious principle in connivance with me, which cannot but will what I will, at least if what I will is really worth willing and is, in fact, willed with my whole being" (OM 184). It is understandable that readers have focused most of their attention on the first part of this quote in which Marcel describes the nature of hope. Yet the second part is equally important. Marcel says that the principle at the heart of being is only in connivance with me when what I hope for is really worth hoping for and I do so with my whole being. When I read these lines, I think of Dewey who requires that we be wholehearted about our desires and that these "desires and ideas [be] converted . . . into intelligence" (*LW* 1:314).

Thus, despite their different intellectual traditions, Dewey and Marcel share the idea that to have faith in our choice of goals and believe that important elements in the world are on our side we must meet two requirements: we must think carefully and be wholehearted about what we hope for. Although Dewey and Marcel urge us to engage in different sorts of reflection about our goals—Dewey wanting us to be intelligently wholehearted and Marcel urging us to set aside "having" and "desiring" so that we may be spiritually available—they both want us to act and think responsibly about them. This done, faith in our choices and trust that the world will support us are justified.

COMMUNITY AS THE OBJECT OF DEWEY'S AND MARCEL'S ULTIMATE HOPE: DIFFERENCES AND SIMILARITIES

The objects of Dewey's and Marcel's ultimate hopes, as I noted at the opening of this chapter, are very different. Although they both seek community, Dewey's is an earthly democratic association, whereas Marcel's is supernatural. In addition, the fruits they derive from community membership are quite different. For Dewey, to be a member of his ideal community is to share with others the goal of perpetually reconstructing a more equitable and just society and contributing one's unique skills in group efforts to realize this goal. Such community membership is a way of acting on the gratitude we feel toward our ancestors and nature. Thus, membership in a Deweyan democratic community adds not only to our feelings of creativity and personal fulfillment but also to our sense of belonging and purpose.

For Marcel, by contrast, the ideal community adds to belonging and purpose not because it unites us with others in the service of social reform but because it opens us to spiritual being. This spiritual awakening occurs when our communion with others—our openness and presence to them—is the result of a free, creative act that makes no demands on what shall come of the relationship. In other words, for Marcel, in freely choosing to be faithful to and selflessly in communion with others, we open ourselves to what he sees as the creative force at the center of the universe. We trust in the goodness of this force, one that in spiritual communion we allow to work through us.

Having acknowledged these differences in Dewey's and Marcel's approaches to community as the object of ultimate hope, I once again turn to the ground they share. I find that Dewey's focus on social reform helps us overcome the normal limits of time and space in ways that, although not the same as Marcel's transcendent ways, honor needs that are also very important to Marcel.

Dewey's Communal Problem Solving and Marcel's Creative Fidelity In its emphasis on continuous social reform, Dewey's ultimate hope of promoting individual skills to cooperatively and democratically ameliorate collective problems has a distinctively un-Marcellian flavor. I call it "un-Marcellian" because, for Dewey, the central demand of living is problem solving, meeting the organism's and society's continual challenge of adjusting to changes in themselves and their surroundings. This need to solve problems, as Dewey sees it, is one of the reasons that people come together and remain so. By contrast, as I have noted, Marcel is extremely critical of problem solving. It is, in his view, one of the features of contemporary society that keeps people apart. This is because he sees problem solving as a scientific, rule-governed endeavor that ignores the spiritual dimension of life. In doing so, problem solving suppresses our creative process, a process that follows no formulas, allows us to commune with others, and is an intimation of the central mystery and love at the core of all being.[9]

However, when I go beneath the surface of Dewey's and Marcel's different perspectives, there are noteworthy similarities. For example, Dewey's focus on problem solving and communal adjustments to ensure a better future foreshadows Marcel's view that life's trials offer us chances to develop a more authentic or "fuller" self. This is because Dewey does not believe that problem solving for a better future is a good in itself. Rather, as I pointed out when discussing the third key to a Deweyan theory of hope—enriched present experience—he believes that a major value of problem solving is that it provides us with ends-in-view that help us focus better on present experience. That is, as we use our unique skills to achieve cooperatively chosen ends, we become more alive to the present moment and unify our experience. Our self expands as we identify with more of the goings-on in our surroundings. Thus, our need to problem-solve functions, for Dewey, like Marcel's life trials. It affords us opportunities to develop an expanded, more responsive, and unified self. This unification of experience, as I noted in Chapter 1, is, for Dewey, an important characteristic of living in hope.

Thus, Dewey's notion of problem-solving displays at least some of the characteristics of transcendence—the openness and creative presence—that Marcel so values. In creative (rather than routine) problem solving, according to Dewey, we can become so engrossed in our work that we overcome the subject-object distinction. As he puts it, "We say of an interested person both that he has lost himself in some affair and that he has found himself in it" (*MW* 9:133; *LW* 10:199). When so engrossed, we shed a self that has limited interests and give birth to a self that identifies with and has interests in a larger world. That is, in moments of significant problem solving—and Dewey sees art and morality as well as science as creative problem solving—we go beyond our normal limits of space and time. We overcome our normal spacial boundaries by our keen identification with the objects of our inquiry, and we overcome our usual temporal distinctions because our involvement in present activities makes time stand still.

In sum, without discounting the wide gulfs that separate the role and fruits of community in Dewey's and Marcel's objects of ultimate hope, I hear themes about overcoming ego and living beyond time in Dewey that foreshadow Marcel. Like Marcel, Dewey treasures those moments in communal problem solving when our ego, if not left behind or totally transformed as Marcel wishes, at least becomes better integrated with a larger whole. Also like Marcel, Dewey treasures those moments of total engagement when time, if not transcended as Marcel would want, is at least forgotten as past, present, and future are momentarily integrated.

Conclusion

As I have shown, the objects of ultimate hope are, for Dewey and Marcel, radically different. For Dewey—the naturalist—the object of ultimate hope is democratic living, the wholehearted and intelligent pursuit of social reform. By contrast, for Marcel—the supernaturalist—the object of absolute hope is salvation, the development of presence and *caritas* love in pursuit of eternal communion with God. Further, Dewey's hope is ultimate in a different sense from Marcel's. It is unlike Marcel's in that once we achieve some victory in our efforts to extend democracy, we find the victory reveals new problems, and so our efforts must be renewed again and again. Quite the opposite is true of Marcel's goal of communion with God. Eternal bliss is absolute in the sense that once it is achieved, it is a final ending point. Our journey is complete; there is no more traveling to do; we are no longer *homo viator*.

This contrast between Dewey's and Marcel's ultimate hopes shows, once again, Dewey's biological orientation. Contrary to Marcel, although Dewey acknowledges our longing for eternal bliss, for surcease from a life of having and desiring, he denies that this is possible in a world filled with foreboding, a life in which the "dark and twilight abound" (*LW* 1:27–28). It follows that the best that existence offers is the joy we experience when we succeed in answering the challenge of perpetual readjustment. Dewey also tells us that "only a living world can include death" (*LW* 1:47). In other words, to want release from having and desiring rather than the challenge of continuous reconstruction is to want an unchanging world. It is to want a world that is dead and without the wonder, awe, and joy that are available only in a living world. Marcel sharply disagrees with Dewey by saying yes to our longing for transcendence. To do otherwise, Marcel tells us, is to reduce life to the space-time world of modern science. It is to deny the mysterious in life, to ignore those intimations of eternity that we get from selfless love, intimations that cannot be described in function-based science's language of abstraction, distinction, and repetition.

Just as the objects of ultimate hope are radically different for Dewey and Marcel, so are their conceptions of ways to achieve such hope. When I reflect on their different conceptions, two disparate images come to mind. Concerning Dewey, I imagine him urging us to leave the corner of the room in which we sit in order to explore more of our room, to break down our old habits and develop ones that are more sensitive to the richness and wonder of other parts of our room. When I think of Marcel, I imagine him urging us to leave the room altogether, to step through the door that we see only dimly from where we sit in order to gain another world, to step into what Marcel calls "the beyond" (*HV* 9). For Dewey, the means to achieving ultimate hope involves eschewing the routine and familiar for the sake of gaining new and more comprehensive adjustments with our environment. For Marcel, the means to ultimate hope involves throwing off the strictures of conventional, scientific thinking and opening to the absolute Thou that is imminent in our charitable love of others. Dewey's counsel to the hopeless urges a change in emphasis, a shift in focus from unquestioned acceptance of established habits to intelligent reconstruction of them in the interest of more democratic living. By contrast, Marcel, believing in the possibility of transcendence, counsels the hopeless to undertake a radical transformation. He calls for the death of the ego absorbed in self-protection and the birth of a being who identifies with the divine spirit of others, and, ultimately, with the divine spirit of the world.

Alongside the differences I find in Dewey's and Marcel's objects of ultimate hope and the means to attain them, I also discover, as I have shown, noteworthy shared emphases and sensitivities in their views of what it means to live in hope. Both men recognize that competition and isolation are significant contributors to hopelessness. Put positively, they both believe that living in hope means feeling part of something larger than ourselves, something that gives us a sense of belonging and purpose. Most remarkable, the language that both Dewey and Marcel use to describe this feeling of wholeness with the universe echoes the language of mystics. Although Marcel's sense of this mysterious dimension leads him to faith in a transcendent world and Dewey's sense of the mysterious does not, both men emphasize the importance of gratitude and piety toward the sources of our being: for Dewey, nature, including our ancestors and progeny; for Marcel, the absolute Thou.

Both men also take an apparently paradoxical view of the self's role in maintaining hope. They believe that in addition to gratitude and piety toward one's sources, people must have faith in themselves and their choice of goals. People must trust that the objects of their hopes are truly worth hoping for, and both Dewey and Marcel believe this requires that people hope for their goals with their entire being. However, both Dewey and Marcel also claim that in addition to having faith that what we hope for is worthy, we must have faith that we can let go of this very same self to gain a new and better one. That is, both men emphasize that to maintain hope we need to risk letting go of an old, secure self in order to establish a new and fuller one. This means, for Dewey, the continual development of our individual selves in the service of collaboratively determined ends-in-view. For Marcel, it means the transformation of a self-absorbed, egotistical person into a trusting, spiritually available one. In other words, the regaining of hope is not entirely a gift from outside for either Dewey or Marcel. It requires that we act for ourselves. It requires risking a lot to gain a lot.

Finally, both men see death as an opportunity to gain this expanding and fuller self. According to Dewey, we "die" continually as we fall out of step with the surrounding world. These deaths are not to be regretted since they are the condition that brings forward our creative abilities to make new adjustments, to use the gifts our ancestors and nature have bequeathed us in the service of more sensitive, communal living. According to Marcel, our physical deaths provide an opportunity, a chance to see the futility of the possessions we own, the possessions that make us envious of others and turn our relations into quid pro quo trades. The prospect of physical death helps us see that our need to have things masks our real need, our real hope: to selflessly love and form communion with others. Although there are many deaths for Dewey and only one for Marcel, human trials and limits are, for both men, chances to lose a despairing self and gain a more hopeful one.

THREE

Dewey in Dialogue with Paulo Freire: Hope, Education, and Democracy

Steve Fishman

> Democracy is . . . faith in the capacity of human beings for intelligent judgment and actions if proper conditions [freedom of communication, inquiry, and consultation] are furnished.
>
> —John Dewey, *Human Nature and Conduct* (*LW* 14:227)

> Hope is rooted in men's incompletion, from which they move out in constant search, a search which can be carried out only in communion with others. Hopelessness is a form of silence, of denying the world and fleeing from it. . . . As long as I fight, I am moved by hope.
>
> —Paulo Freire, *Pedagogy of the Oppressed* (*PO* 91–92)

In this chapter I pick up a number of threads that I have developed in previous chapters. By comparing Dewey and Freire, I bring Dewey into conversation with another philosopher who, like Marcel, is strongly influenced by the Christian and existential traditions. However, unlike Marcel, Freire's ultimate hope parallels Dewey's. Freire's focus is this-worldly, social reform, rather than otherworldly, individual transcendence. Thus, in the present chapter, we will hear in Freire themes of *caritas* love, being and having, and I-thou relations that ricochet fruitfully off my previous discussion of Dewey and Marcel. We will also hear in Freire themes of communication, critical reflection, action, and democracy that help me further develop the theory of hope I construct for Dewey. This is because Dewey and Freire, although coming from significantly different cultural traditions and employing significantly different language, both view being active in the world as people's primary need. As a result, they share the belief that social action—intelligently wholehearted, critical action—is essential to living in hope. And the direction of this social action is, for both, perpetual democratic reform. This means that Dewey's and Freire's theories of hope hit the ground, that is, get played out in practice, in ways that Marcel's does not.

One of the common arenas in which Dewey and Freire put their theories into action is the field of education. Thus, in this chapter I explore hope in the context of the classroom. That is, I study Dewey and Freire to see how they might be a source of inspiration for reform-minded teachers like me, educators living in a world that is, in my view, as I have said, short on collective hope for social reform.[1] Put differently, I turn to Dewey and Freire in order to better understand their visions of democracy and their confidence that educators can promote a more democratic future. I need to believe that there is something I can do in my classroom to resist what appear to be overwhelming barriers to social reform and hopeful living. Given that Dewey and Freire remained convinced that schools could serve the interests of reform despite the terrible injustices they witnessed in their own lifetimes, I believe it worthwhile to look to them for guidance in our own period of crisis.

My Dewey-Freire dialogue yields three discoveries about the way their theories of hope hit the ground in education for democracy. First, I discover that although both men recognize that curriculum and instruction are not easily modified since they reflect the interests of the ruling class, both remain hopeful that individual teachers can take steps—however modest—to alter educational practice. I also discover that Dewey, in his discussions of pedagogical reform, sometimes, especially in his early work, fails to emphasize the political dimension of education. By contrast, Freire never misses a chance to make clear that education is always about either promoting social reform or reinforcing the status quo.

Second, I find that although both Dewey and Freire rest much of their hope for a more just future on reforms in education, they rely on different human potentials and, thus, favor diverse means of achieving social reform. Dewey, writing in the context of Anglo-American liberalism and class mobility, emphasizes human intelligence and people's ability to adjust their established practices to changing conditions (*LW* 13:59). This leads Dewey to argue for the gradual amelioration of social ills. By contrast, Freire, writing in an environment marked by neocolonialism and intractable class differences, emphasizes what he calls *"conscientizacao"* (CWL 4), that is, people's ability to join with others in renaming and transforming themselves and the world. This leads Freire to argue for social revolution as the way to address our social ills. Although I realize that fixed characterizations of Dewey's and Freire's positions are dangerous since both men wrote voluminously over long periods of time, I believe my characterizations are true to the overall thrust of their work.

Finally, I discover that Dewey's and Freire's visions of democracy complement one another. Both see democracy not so much as a particular constitutional arrangement but, rather, as a way of life. It is a way of living that celebrates certain virtues, like respectful dialogue with others, critical reflection, and cooperative action. In doing so, both men believe that democracy promotes a life of hope. For Dewey, this is because democracy encourages the formation of collaborative associations, ones that help people overcome individual competition and find belonging, purpose, and unity in their activities. For Freire, sounding like a social reform–minded, leftist version of Marcel, democracy promotes hopeful living because it encourages dialogue, the I-thou relationships that help people transcend self-centeredness and experience the *caritas* love and liberation that, for Freire, characterize living in hope. I find the fact that Dewey and Freire present complementary visions of democracy particularly interesting given that they write in very different political contexts and employ quite different theoretical lenses. Dewey, writing in a "first world" context, aligns himself with the Anglo-American liberal tradition and favors, for the most part, biological, evolutionary terms such as "adjustment," "environment," and "reconstruction," whereas Freire, writing in a "third world" context, aligns himself with the humanist, Marxist, and anticolonialist traditions and favors Christian-existentialist terms like "love," "humanization," "salvation," and "rebirth."

In what follows, I explore the three discoveries I have just described and conclude by explaining how this Dewey-Freire dialogue bolsters my hopefulness about what I and other reform-minded teachers can do in our classrooms.

Pedagogical Reform and Social Reform:
Dewey's and Freire's Contrasting Emphases

Despite Dewey's and Freire's recognition of the conservative and institutional constraints on teachers, both believe that schools are an important means to their ultimate hope for continuous social reform. However, although both men believe that our chance for a better future rests largely on education, they differ in the emphasis they give this social reform dimension of schooling. It is front and center in Freire's best-known works, whereas it is possible to overlook this dimension in Dewey's. That is, Dewey, by contrast with Freire, discusses pedagogical change without always emphasizing its important role for social reconstruction.

DEWEY FOREGROUNDS PEDAGOGICAL REFORM

Dewey's occasional failure to present pedagogical reform as central to his hopes for social reconstruction can be seen, for example, in his final book-length discussion of education, *Experience and Education*, published in 1938. In this volume he seems to neglect the politics of education altogether as he discusses the danger of certain misinterpretations of "progressive" teaching. Likewise, Dewey's most famous discussion of education, *Democracy and Education*, published in 1916, can leave readers with the same mistaken impression. Instead of beginning with explicit attention to the politics of schooling, Dewey opens *Democracy and Education* by discussing the importance of education for community survival. In his opening chapters, he tells us that education is the means by which a community's knowledge and customs are "transmitted" to the young and that the challenge of formal schooling is to capture the "vitality" that accompanies informal education, the sort that children experienced in pre-industrial societies.

When Dewey does eventually discuss the social function of democratic education in chapter 7 of *Democracy and Education*, he does so in very general terms. He points out that schools in a democratic society need to educate students to be open to one another, engage in free communication, and avoid erecting class barriers. However, he does not use this discussion of democracy's social function as an opportunity to analyze the political realities of U.S. public schools or the ways they are used to perpetuate the status quo. It is not until chapter 19, when the reader is 250 pages into the book, that Dewey finally speaks specifically about his political concerns: his worries about U.S. class divisions—the separation of labor and leisure classes, vocational students and liberal arts students, those who are educated to serve and those who are educated to lead. The possibility of reading Dewey as neglectful of the ways schools reproduce the inequities of the larger society partially accounts for the harsh criticisms occasionally directed at him from the political Left. One critic has gone so far as to call Dewey the "high priest" of bourgeois values in America and the "head salesman" of its theology.[2]

A reader has to examine articles written by Dewey in the 1920s and 1930s to find clear connections between his fight for pedagogical change and his hope for social reconstruction. In a 1934 address to the American Association of Teachers Colleges, he exhorts instructors to help students develop the "intelligent skepticism" they need to be responsible participants in the reform of U.S. social and economic structures (*LW* 9:160). In a 1922 piece Dewey asks teachers to help students get below the "froth and foam" of government and media pronouncements to learn what is really going on (*MW* 13:329, 332). This 1922 piece ends with a passage that dramatically shows the intimate connection between Dewey's struggles for educational reform and his ultimate hope for a more democratic, humane society:

> [When schools] cultivate the habit of suspended judgment, of skepticism, of desire for evidence, of appeal to observation rather than sentiment, discussion rather than bias, inquiry rather than conventional idealizations . . . [then] schools will be the dangerous outposts of a humane civilization. But they will also begin to be supremely interesting places. For it will then have come about that education and politics are one and the same thing because politics will have to be in fact what it now pretends to be, the intelligent management of social affairs. (*MW* 13:334)

In a 1934 pamphlet published by the League for Industrial Democracy, Dewey again connects pedagogical and social reform when he urges teachers to help themselves and their students overcome their "economic illiteracy" (*LW* 9:183). A year later, he tells school administrators they are either with social reformers or against them. They must choose between seeing the social function of schools as perpetuating existing social conditions or as taking part in their transformation (*LW* 11:347). In addition, in his later works, Dewey gives an increasingly political flavor to his discussions of the method of intelligence (*LW* 13:59), or what he calls "good habits of thinking" (*MW* 9:163). Dewey comes to see this method, as I have said, as crucial to his ultimate hope for social reform.

FREIRE FOREGROUNDS SOCIAL REFORM

Whereas understanding Dewey's views concerning the relationship of education and social reform requires a reader's close attention, Freire's views concerning teaching as a political activity is the major chord on almost every page of his work. In a 1985 interview with Donaldo Macedo, Freire reflected on the centrality of politics for his work, saying that "the educational proposals that I have been making for years basically derive from two rather obvious, nonsimplistic ideas." The first is that at every level of schooling—formal and informal—education is political. The second is that one's pedagogy should be consistent with one's political hopes, and, for liberating teachers, this means helping students become "Subjects" or active, critical, and creative learners.[3]

Dewey's and Freire's Diverse Means of Achieving Their Hopes for Social Reform

In this section, I explore Dewey's method of intelligence and Freire's theory of "conscientization," these men's quite different plans for achieving social change. As I will show, Dewey's "first world" context and the U.S. liberal tradition lead him to believe that negotiation and step-by-step social adjustment can yield gradual amelioration of class differences and extension of democracy to all areas of life. By contrast, Freire's "third world" context and Brazil's neo-colonial tradition lead him to believe that only dramatic individual and social transformation can reduce class differences and result in true democracy.

Before going into more detail about the method of intelligence and con-scientization, I once more acknowledge the danger, given the complexity of these theorists' work, of characterizing Dewey as a gradualist and Freire as a revolutionary. In fact, there are times when Dewey sounds more radical than gradualist. For example, in one of his most famous books, *Liberalism and Social Action* (*LW* 11:1–65), he explicitly calls for liberalism to become radical and give up piecemeal reforms (see also *LW* 9:76–80). Conversely, Freire sometimes sounds more gradualist than revolutionary. For example, in *Pedagogy of the Oppressed* and elsewhere, Freire indicates that people who want to transform the social structure must, at times, be content with what they can achieve through patient negotiation with the dominant class (*PO* 101, 217–18).[4] However, despite these complexities, I believe my characterization of Dewey as pinning his hopes on gradual reform and Freire as pinning his hopes on revolutionary transformation captures the overall spirit of their work.

"THE METHOD OF INTELLIGENCE" AS DEWEY'S MEANS OF ACHIEVING HIS HOPES FOR SOCIAL REFORM

Dewey's hopes for a more just future are pinned to widespread adoption of the method of intelligence (*LW* 5:276; see also *MW* 12:273–76). As the Dewey quotation I use for the first epigraph to this chapter indicates, this method is, for him, central to his ultimate hope: the extension of democracy. In fact, at one point he labels it "the method of democracy" (*LW* 11:56). What Dewey means is that acting intelligently enables us to engage in the collaborative inquiry that characterizes democracy, the sort of inquiry that helps us have faith in our choice of goals and live in hope of a better future.

Dewey's reliance on the method of intelligence reflects—not surprisingly—his evolutionary, biological approach to the human situation. As I explained when comparing Dewey and Marcel, the challenge for people, according to Dewey, is not to make revolutionary changes but to gradually "readapt" their environments to achieve what they consider to be desirable ends (*LW* 9:11–13; 10:19–20). For each individual, this means altering habits that are no longer appropriate for changed conditions. Collectively, the challenge is similar, according to Dewey. Communities must modify established beliefs and inherited social institutions that prove unsuitable for meeting new cultural demands and exploiting new cultural opportunities (*LW* 11:48–50, 58–61).

It follows that, for Dewey, if schools are to further his ultimate hope for democratic social reconstruction, they must do more than provide pupils with technical and professional skills so that students can earn a living. Schools must also help students develop the ability to think critically about the social and political context in which they will be using their professional skills. Dewey gives the example of students studying math and bookkeeping who should also understand the social and political implications of the ends for which their potential employers will use their accounting skills (*EW* 5:73–74). More generally, educators need to help students practice the method of intelligence so that they can engage in collaborative efforts to modify established practices, beliefs, and institutions in order both to meet present-day challenges and to recognize new opportunities for social reform.

Although Dewey refers to "the method of intelligence" throughout his work, he never provides an elaborate account of it. However, what he says about "reflective thinking" and "intelligent thinking" offers a good idea of what he has in mind. It is a process involving three stages. In the first, we analyze a "perplexing" situation, one in which our plans are blocked, in order to generate possible solutions. By engaging in analysis at this point rather than blindly striking out in a new direction or sticking stubbornly to our original plan of action, we begin to act intelligently rather than capriciously or in accordance with fixed habit. In the second phase, we use our possible or "hypothetical" solutions to reexamine our perplexing situation and refine our possible solutions. In a final stage, we test the hypothesis that seems most likely to resolve our dilemma. If it fails, the advantage of the method of intelligence is that our "failure" yields new and valuable information about our situation. We then experiment with other possible solutions (*LW* 8:113–24; *MW* 9:163). The following statement provides one of Dewey's most succinct accounts of intelligent thinking: "[Intelligent thinking entails] observation of the detailed makeup of the situation; analysis into its diverse factors; clarification of what is obscure; discounting of the more insistent and vivid traits; tracing the consequences of the various modes of action that suggest themselves; regarding the decision reached as hypothetical and tentative until the anticipated or supposed consequences which led to its adoption have been squared with actual consequences. This inquiry is intelligence" (*MW* 12:164).

What I have said so far may make it appear that the method of intelligence is based exclusively on cognitive skills. However, as readers might suspect from my discussion in Chapter 1 of intelligent wholeheartedness as one of the keys to Dewey's theory of hope, this is not so. The method of intelligence, according to Dewey, also requires moral traits of character like "wholeheartedness," "courage," and "responsibility" (*MW* 9:173–79; *LW* 8:303). In addition, Dewey makes clear that the need for such traits is especially pronounced when we apply the method of intelligence to our social problems. He says that for the method to be used effectively in the service of reform, people must master the skills of communication, negotiation, and consultation (*LW* 13:187). They also need traits like open-mindedness, toleration of uncertainty, and the ability to experiment with "unaccustomed lines of behavior" (*LW* 13:165–67).

"CONSCIENTIZATION" AS FREIRE'S MEANS TO HIS HOPES FOR SOCIAL REFORM

Whereas Dewey looks to the method of intelligence to promote gradual reconstruction of oneself and one's environment, Freire looks to the use of conscientization to promote revolutionary change. More specifically, for Freire, liberatory teachers must help students develop *conscientizacao*, that is, help them go beyond naive awareness of the world, or mere opinion *(doxa)*, to active investigation of the world, or critical knowledge *(logos)*. Freire's *conscientizacao*, like Dewey's method of intelligence, involves a probing of reality, a deconstructing, in Freire's case, of the "myths" that the oppressor class has foisted on the oppressed to keep them in submission. Although Dewey's method of intelligence takes on political overtones in the 1920s and '30s, it still remains a general method of responding to any and all troubling situations. By contrast, Freire's *conscientizacao* is always a method directed toward fulfilling his hopes for political and cultural liberation. Freire tells us, "Conscientization implies . . . that when I realize that I am oppressed, I also know I can liberate myself if I transform the concrete situation where I find myself oppressed. . . . [It] implies a critical insertion into a process, it implies a historical commitment to make changes" (CWL 5).

Conscientization's connection to political liberation means that, when taken seriously, it involves dramatic personal transformation. Whereas Dewey's method of intelligence gradually refines individual and communal views and behaviors in a trial-and-error process, Freire's method of conscientization requires a complete break with one's former life and rebirth in total commitment to the liberation of the oppressed. In this regard, Dewey's position on intelligence and Freire's on conscientization reflect their overall philosophic approaches, with Dewey emphasizing continuities and Freire emphasizing striking contrasts.[5] Freire, describing conscientization more fully, explains, "Conscientization is a painful birth. There is no palliative for it. . . . Conscientization . . . involves an excruciating moment, a tremendously upsetting one in anyone who begins to conscientize himself, the moment when he starts to be reborn. Because conscientization demands an Easter. That is, it demands that we die to be born again" (CWL 10; see also PO 50).

Although Freire's description of conscientization, and its resulting "rebirth," echoes Saint Paul's language in 1 Corinthians when Paul claims that we die in our physical life to be reborn as spiritual beings, this is not what Freire has in mind. Freire sees the reborn person as someone dedicated to transforming this earthly world, not as someone reborn into a changeless, immaterial world. In addition, the transformation that Freire speaks of is more than just an individual's commitment to work for liberation. Freire's rebirth also involves an individual's solidarity with the oppressed. In other words, if individuals who are successful at naming the world and changing it are not working to help the voiceless and impotent do the same, they are not, according to Freire, truly reborn. Thus, Freire's talk of an Easter experience is not just a rhetorical flourish. He sincerely believes that salvation lies in action for this-worldly liberation, in fighting against exploitation and resisting resignation (PHEART 105).

Thus, Freire views the core of hope as the freedom to make the world more humane, not, as Marcel does, to establish eternal communion with others in a spiritual, transcendent existence. Put differently, although Freire's Christianity contrasts with Marcel's, Freire also takes his Christianity seriously. He says that his God pushes him "toward world transformation" so as to restore the humanity of both the exploited and the exploiters (PHEART 103–4). He says one can walk with Christ only if one challenges race, sex, and class discrimination (PHEART 105). In what I see as a bold move, Freire manages, by finding salvation and true "being" in struggle for this-worldly liberation, to blend his Christianity and his Marxism (ELC 129). He gives religious value to the Marxist communion of all people as free people in a perpetually changing earthly world, and he substitutes this sort of communion for Marcel's more traditional Christian vision of people as spiritually connected in a mysterious and unchanging divine world.

Given the Marxian perspective from which Freire writes, and given his belief that the obstacle to personal and social reform is the elite class's determination to hold on to its supremacy, it is not surprising that revolution, for him, seems the only reasonable way for men and women to regain their freedom and become creative, historic beings (see *ECC*). I quote the Freire passage that serves as the second epigraph of this chapter: "Hope is rooted in men's incompletion, from which they move out in constant search, a search which can be carried out only in communion with others. Hopelessness is a form of silence, of denying the world and fleeing from it. . . . As long as I fight, I am moved by hope" (*PO* 91–92).

Freire's belief that revolution is the only way to restore hope and achieve social justice was forged by his experiences in Brazil. Initially, in the 1950s and early 1960s, he thought Brazilians could peacefully create a democracy that would give voice to the silenced masses through voluntary reform from within. In this era, he saw Brazil as a society in the process of "opening" and developing its own cultural identity. However, after the 1964 military coup and Freire's own subsequent exile, he became radicalized (see *ECC*).⁶

Thus, as I read Freire's post-1964 work, his hopes for social reform rely on conscientization leading, as I have said, to individual and communal death and rebirth in the service of revolutionary social transformation. In a 1970 work, Freire writes, "For the First World to hear the Word [of God], it must previously undergo an Easter. It must die as First World and be reborn as Third World" (LYTS 12). And again, "A church like that [which wants to stay politically neutral] refuses to live the Easter experience it is always talking about" (ERC 17; see also CWL 10; ELC 122–23, 127; and *PO* 132–33).

For Freire, then, the struggle for individual freedom and voice parallels state and class struggles at the national and international levels. Just as members of the oppressed class are silenced by members of the oppressor class, so dependent nations and churches are silenced by metropolitan nations and churches. Just as individuals must wrest control of their own destinies from their masters, so dependent nations and churches must wrest "the point of decision" from metropolitan cultures (*ECC* 130).

In sum, Freire takes a revolutionary approach to social reform and believes the best path is conscientization and our ability to die and be reborn in solidarity with the poor. By contrast, Dewey takes a gradual approach to his ultimate hope of social reform and relies on our ability to employ the method of intelligence and engage in cooperative negotiations to adjust outmoded beliefs and practices. Of course, many factors lie behind these men's different approaches to social change. I have already mentioned the different political traditions and social contexts in which they wrote. Another factor is their own experiences with revolution. Whereas the revolutions that Freire witnessed—in Guinea-Bissau, Cuba, Nicaragua, and China—allowed him to be more optimistic about the possibility of dialogic revolutionary leadership, Dewey's experiences with revolution were markedly different. The ones Dewey witnessed—in Russia, Germany, and Italy—led to the tyrannies of Stalin, Hitler, and Mussolini. These events hardly soothed Dewey's worries about working for wholesale rather than gradual change or his fear that violent means lead to violent ends.

Dewey's and Freire's Ultimate Hope: Democratic Living

Despite Dewey's and Freire's different analyses of the appropriate paths to achieve individual and collective reform, they share, as I have said, a similar ultimate hope: the continual extension and fuller realization of democracy. Further, both see democracy as a way of living in hope. That is, for Dewey and Freire, democracy is not just about individual rights, about ensuring people as wide a berth as possible so they can go their own ways. It is not just "anarchy plus a constable," as Thomas Carlyle derisively described laissez-faire capitalism in the 1860s.[7] This "don't tread on me" approach is anathema for both Dewey and Freire because it forces people into egoistic competition that ends up in feelings of isolation, loneliness, and, thus, hopelessness about leading a meaningful life. To the contrary, for both men, democracy depends upon collaborative fraternity—as much as equality and liberty—to maintain perpetual social reconstruction.

DEWEY'S EMPHASIS ON COLLABORATIVE LIVING

The U.S. Constitution, the Bill of Rights, and federal and state laws ensuring regular election of public officials are, for Dewey, important features of American democracy. However, the success of a democracy's ability to promote hopeful living, as he sees it, depends upon the vitality of its infrastructure. This means, for Dewey, that democracy should help its citizens develop a social spirit by extending their individual interests beyond themselves and their immediate families to include concern for wider community issues. In fact, Dewey goes so far as to say that to be so insensitive to one's relations to others as to believe that one can really stand and act alone is an "unnamed form of insanity" (*MW* 9:49). He also tells us that "what one is as a person is what one is as associated with others, in a free give and take of intercourse" (*MW* 9:129). Thus, the keys to social reform and hopeful living, for Dewey, parallel the keys to educational reform and hopeful learning: development of individual skills—including a spirit of social service, faith in intelligent wholeheartedness, and enriched present experience—in the service of collaboratively agreed-upon group needs.

Alternatively put, Dewey believes that when a democracy is working well, what makes its citizens hopeful is also what makes groups hopeful. This is based on Dewey's view that individuals flourish best (are most alive and engaged in their activities) when they are members of mutually considerate, cooperative associations, and these associations flourish best (see themselves as parts of a larger unified whole) when they are in open interaction with other cooperative groups (*LW* 2:235–372). These transactions among individuals and groups not only enrich individuals' personal experiences but also help break down class divisions, divisions that lead to alienating competition and, in the end, to feelings of despair about the possibility of meaningful living. Dewey's idea that living in hope depends upon the vitality of interacting, cooperative groups is reflected in his most widely quoted definition of democracy: "A democracy is more than a form of government; it is primarily a mode of associated living, of conjoint communicated experience. The extension in space of the number of individuals who participate in an interest so that each has to refer his own action to that of others, and to consider the action of others to give point and direction to his own, is equivalent to the breaking down of those barriers of class, race, and national territory which kept men from perceiving the full import of their activity" (*MW* 9:87).

In sum, for Dewey, feelings of isolation and doubts that one's individual actions are meaningful are overcome—replaced by hope—in democracy. This is because in democracy we are, ideally, valued members of a cooperative group whose goals we share, a group that encourages individuals to act intelligently and wholeheartedly in the service of the common wealth.

DEWEY'S CRITIQUE OF CAPITALISM AS ANTITHETICAL TO HOPE

Dewey criticizes various aspects of U.S. democracy, as I explained in Chapter 2, with his most trenchant criticism aimed at laissez-faire capitalism and competition for personal gain. In particular, Dewey worries about Americans' equation of laissez-faire competition with democratic freedom. This equation of unfettered moneymaking with democratic freedom is, as Dewey sees it, one of the roots of hopelessness in our society. In Dewey's view, the drive for personal wealth—to the exclusion of other activities that promote artistic endeavors, science, and companionship—impoverishes everyone. Its negative impact on the life chances of the poor is obvious, but Dewey views this competitive, materialistic ethos as limiting the quality of life of the wealthy as well (*LW* 3:223; see also *MW* 9:84, 317–18; and *LW* 11:61).

Further, competition for wealth, according to Dewey, leads to manipulation of the media, and manipulation of the news impedes informed public debate and, thus, our ability to understand public issues or develop what Dewey calls "social intelligence" (*LW* 13:47; *MW* 5:497–98). Such competition also, according to Dewey, alienates workers and citizens from one another. In turn, this alienation inhibits the formation of cooperative associations, associations that, as we have seen, are the backbone of Deweyan democracy and hopeful living.

Dewey attributes the demoralizing competition for "private pecuniary profit" to eighteenth-century liberalism gone awry (*LW* 5:84; *MW* 9:351):

> As the new [industrial class] won power [in the nineteenth century], their doctrines hardened into the dogma of the freedom of the industrial entrepreneur from any organized control. . . . The idea of hands off, which was practically sound under [those] circumstances, was stiffened into the dogma of *laissez-faire* "individualism." . . . Consequently, that which began as a movement in the direction of greater liberty for expression of the energies of man . . . has almost resulted in identifying the power and liberty of the individual with ability to achieve economic success—or, to put it in a nutshell, with ability to make money. (*LW* 11:366)

As the above quotation indicates, Dewey finds that whereas capitalism was once a midwife for democracy and hopeful living, this is no longer so. Worse yet, capitalism has become a hindrance to democracy's extension and development, to its goal of giving every individual "new opportunities and powers" (*LW* 11:366). No matter how great the success of capitalism in expanding productivity and broadening our horizons, in its twentieth-century form, according to Dewey, it works against the central values of Anglo-American liberalism: individual liberty, development of individuals' unique talents, and freedom of communication and inquiry (*LW* 11:1–66). In other words, the ethos of capitalism, according to Dewey, has so narrowed people's interests to competition for personal gain that they live in protected fortresses, leery of one another and fearful of being taken advantage of by their neighbors.

This means that the feelings of belonging and faith in the value of the contributions we make to the group—feelings that are, for Dewey, at the core of democracy and hopeful living—are sorely diminished. As Dewey tells us, people do not live by wages alone. Instead, what people need is an outlet for what is humane in them, and this means being able to satisfy their inclination to work creatively and wholeheartedly with others (*MW* 12:9).

In sum, Dewey is very much the Jeffersonian democrat in his idea that the backbone of hopeful living is membership in face-to-face, voluntary cooperative associations. Dewey wants the state to promote conditions that foster such collaborative organizations, whether they be focused on professional, religious, political, or other issues of mutual concern (*LW* 2:235–372). Dewey also wants citizens to extend their interests beyond personal concerns to national issues. He believes this can happen when citizens have access to information that goes beneath the "froth and foam" of mass-media messages and when local groups openly communicate, interact, and learn from one another.

FREIRE'S EMPHASIS ON DIALOGUE AS ESSENTIAL FOR DEMOCRATIC AND HOPEFUL LIVING

Freire, like Dewey, believes democracy is the key to humans' hopefulness. However, whereas Dewey views collaborative community as the core of democracy, Freire's emphasis is on dialogue. More specifically, the key to democratic governance for Freire is dialogue between revolutionary leaders and "the people." Such interaction is important because it is in dialogue that respect for one another is established. In dialogue we treat one another as intrinsically valuable beings rather than as objects or things to be manipulated for selfish, individual purposes. For Freire, there is something religious about dialogue because, echoing themes we hear in Marcel, Freire tells us that dialogue depends upon *caritas* love, on replacing I-it with I-thou relations, and on leaving the world of having to enter the world of being, a realm where we satisfy our ontological need and regain true hope (*PO* 58–60, 167–68; *PHEART* 44–45).

Although we hear the religious language of Marcel in Freire's account of dialogue, there is a distinctive Marxist and pragmatist sound to the way Freire fills out his view of dialogue. For Freire, the dehumanizing world of having is not, as it is for Marcel, primarily about people's acquisition of things. It is, according to Freire, primarily about people's "having" each other, about one social class dominating and oppressing another. To step out of the world of having and into the world of being is not, for Freire, as it is for Marcel, to participate in the mystery of spiritual communion. It is to participate in collaborative humanization of this earthly world. In other words, although both

Freire and Marcel believe that true hope depends upon leaving the realm of having for the realm of being, their understanding of what it means "to be" is different. For Freire, we participate in true being and ultimate hope when we enter into the perpetual struggle for democratic liberation, whereas, for Marcel, we participate in true being and ultimate hope in eternal communion with God. Alternatively put, for Freire, unlike Marcel, the object of *caritas* love and dialogue is not something mysterious or transcendent. The object is changing this earthly world. This is why Freire tells us that authentic dialogue requires "true" words, that is, words that affect our actions in the world. Otherwise, for Freire, dialogue is not genuine but mere "verbalism," just so many "false" words (*PO* 87–88).

This is to say that Freire, like Dewey and others in the pragmatist tradition, believes that words, when used authentically, are like beliefs.[8] They are plans for action, and it is only in action that we test our words by seeing how well they work. Further, Freire, although he does not use Deweyan terms like "adjustment," "accommodation," and "adaptation," is clearly not talking about dialogue that leads to acts of accommodation, that is, mere subsistence or resigned routine. For Freire, dialogue functions properly only when it transforms and humanizes the world, when it serves the cause of liberation.

But how is dialogue—specifically, the leader-people dialogue that Freire sees as central to democratic governance—to be carried out? "The people" are vast in number, and leaders are few. Although Freire offers no particulars in response, his own life offers clues about the sort of caring and listening he has in mind when he speaks of dialogue as an existential requirement of hope and democracy.

Arguably, no encounter had more impact on Freire's professional life than a worker's response to a public lecture Freire gave in Brazil in the 1950s about the immorality of corporal punishment for children (*PHOPE*). This worker's comments, and the manner in which Freire heard them, show the potential power of leader-people dialogue. Freire was speaking at a social center in one of the poorest sections of Recife and had just completed his talk when a middle-aged man rose to ask, "Dr. Paulo Freire, sir—do you know where people live? Have you ever been in any of our houses, sir?" After describing his own small and minimally equipped dwelling, he tells Freire that although he has never been to Freire's house, he can describe it. The urban worker then paints a picture of a luxurious home with a big yard, bedrooms for the children, a kitchen with appliances, a study for the doctor professor, and even a room for the family maid. Freire, looking back, had to admit, "There was nothing to add or subtract. That was my house." The laborer did not have to elaborate to the audience the point of his remarks to Freire. It was obvious: before experts feel comfortable about their proposed solutions to social problems, they had better engage in dialogue with the people they are advising; that is, "advising" had better be a two-way street with listening, talking, caring, and trusting on both sides. (*PO* 35, 42–46; RES 306–7). Put another way, the dialogic moment is, for Freire, an example of the dawning of "I-thou" cooperation that he believes should mark all communication. In such communication, for Freire, people acknowledge their mutual dependence and the fact that neither would be human without the other (*PO* 167).

Just as Dewey's approach to democratic governance and educational reform parallels his approach to hopeful living, so it is with Freire. Whereas Dewey's focus in both politics and pedagogy is on helping individuals contribute intelligently and wholeheartedly to a meaningful whole, Freire's focus in both democratic governance and school reform is on overcoming the imperialistic relations between leaders (teachers) and followers (students) that are antithetical to the trust and mutuality of hope. As other commentators have pointed out, Freire's decision to call his most widely read book *Pedagogy of the Oppressed* rather than *Pedagogy for the Oppressed* is significant.[9] That is, for Freire, learning is something teachers do *with* students; it is not something they do *for* or *to* students (*PO* 93; LNAT).[10] Similarly, political revolution is something leaders undertake *with* the people, not something undertaken *for* or imposed *upon* the people. Imposing revolution on the people without genuine dialogue with them indicates that the putative leaders have not truly died to their previous class identities and been reborn in thorough solidarity with the oppressed. It indicates that the leaders do not truly trust the people, and this means that neither can live in hope with one another.[11]

FREIRE'S CRITIQUE OF CAPITALISM AS NEOCOLONIAL EXPLOITATION

Freire's critique of capitalism parallels Dewey's in many ways. Like Dewey, Freire decries the focus in capitalism on pecuniary gain, a system, he says, in which "money is the measure of all things, and profit the primary goal" (*PO* 59). The result of this ethos is that instead of economic development being a chance to enhance the life opportunities and hopes of everyone, it makes conditions hopeless for the great majority. In addition, Freire, voicing Dewey-like criticisms of the equation of laissez-faire competition with democratic freedom, suggests that the capitalist world has, in effect, turned ethics upside down. It has made the freedom of commerce (for a few) more important than the freedom to be human (for the many) (*PF* 116).

Finally, Freire, once more like Dewey, argues that capitalism hurts not just the powerless but the powerful as well. For Freire, capitalism robs both the rich and the poor of hope. The elite have nothing to hope for because they fear change. That is, they fear any developments that might alter their position of power (*TWT* 14; *EDL* 20). The poor are also robbed of hope, but for different reasons. As the result of the myths perpetrated by the elite, they believe their poverty is part of the natural order of things, and, thus, they feel impotent to affect their future. As one young peasant told Freire, "I have no tomorrow that is any different from today that is any different from yesterday" (*PHEART* 42). This fatalistic stance toward the world is reinforced, according to Freire, by the message of the "traditional" Church: the more people suffer, the more they are purified (*ERC* 20). In sum, current capitalist relations between rich and poor rob both classes of the chance to realize their true humanity. The elite become so focused on their possessions and maintaining their power over others that they only "have" and no longer "are." The poor become so accustomed to internalizing the oppressors' attitudes toward them that they have no confidence in themselves and live a submerged, passive, and hopeless existence (*PO* 59–61, 97–101).

Although Freire's criticisms of capitalism parallel Dewey's in many ways, Freire's contrasting theoretical lenses and language give the tone of his criticisms a strikingly different color. More specifically, for Freire, unlike Dewey, capitalism has not just gone astray from its original alliance with liberalism and the promotion of individual liberty. Rather, Freire views capitalism as the bedfellow of colonial exploitation. Present-day capitalists do not have to use bayonets and soldiers to keep the poor in line as the early European settlers did. Instead, they use dehumanizing factory work, banking methods of education, and media messages to ensure the docility of the poor.[12] They also use a variety of palliative measures and "charities" to keep the poor falsely hopeful that some day they may join the elite and earn "the right" to oversee the poor. Although capitalism as colonial-like exploitation may be thought by some to exist only in the third world, Freire assures us that the third world is not a matter of geography. It is a mind-set. The third world is very much in the first world, he says, although many of the poor who live in the first world refuse to recognize their status (*PO* 57; *PHOPE* 55–56).

Freire's critique of capitalism through anticolonial, Marxist lenses is also reflected in his language. He calls the routines of industrial factory work "brutalizing," suggesting that modern laborers are no more than slaves. How-ever, instead of being slaves to a visible owner, they are slaves—via factories and their machines—to invisible, distant owners.[13] The language of Freire's discussion of unemployment also reflects his view that capitalist exploita-tion of workers is like colonial exploitation. He tells us that, for laborers, unemployment is a sentence to "a kind of living death" (*PF* 117). In other words, capitalists, like their colonial forebears, see modern workers as less than human, as animal-like creatures to be exploited and discarded without a backward glance. Chiding those who claim that with the collapse of the Berlin Wall capitalism "stepped forward in its excellence once and for all," Freire reminds us of the terrible cost extracted by capitalism on human life. He reminds us that thirty million children die every year from causes that could be prevented for the cost of what American cigarette manufacturers spend annually on advertising. He reminds us that eight million Brazilian children do not have the opportunity to attend school and that 52 percent of the people in Recife live in slums. In these slums, "little boys and girls, women and men, [vie] with starving pups, tragically, like animals, for the garbage of the great trash heaps outlying the cities" (*PHOPE* 94–95).

In sum, although Freire's critique of capitalism points to many of the same shortcomings as Dewey's, his analysis of their etiology is quite different. Freire views capitalism and contemporary hopelessness as rooted in a regime of exploitation that has its source in European colonialism. This source helps explain, for Freire, how the elite can see workers as less than human, how they can justify the great chasms that separate their lifestyles and opportunities from the lifestyles and opportunities of laborers and the unemployed. It also explains, for Freire, how capitalism's focus on having and dominating leaves us competitive with others, blotting out the virtues of love and trust that are essential to living in hope.

By contrast, Dewey sees the hopelessness of contemporary life as resulting from the ruling class's misidentification of classic liberalism with laissez-faire individualism, their continued but inappropriate emphasis on "rugged indi-vidualism," independence, and self-reliance as our most important virtues (*LW* 5:41–123). That is, unlike Freire, Dewey believes that the capitalist class is even more credulous than the people they appear to be "duping" (*MW* 13:333). He believes it would be "a great mistake" to view the emphasis in schools on personal advancement rather than social service as a deliberate effort by the capitalist class to maintain its power (*LW* 9:178). Instead, Dewey insists that the problem Americans face today is not a malevolent elite that needs to be overthrown. No, according to Dewey, our dilemma goes much deeper than the conscious intention of those in power. Our problem is the widespread failure to use our intelligence, to recognize that the habits and beliefs that helped us successfully meet the challenges of late-eighteenth- and nineteenth-century America are no longer appropriate for present-day conditions.

Conclusion

I conclude by describing the implications of my Dewey-Freire dialogue for my own hopefulness as a teacher.

TAKING HOPE FROM THE IDEA THAT
EDUCATION IS POLITICAL

Both Dewey and Freire argue that what we do in the classroom is political. This may appear frightening at first, but I find it uplifting to realize that we, as teachers, are either supporting the status quo or challenging it. In other words, every day that we teach, we have opportunities to work for reform, social reconstruction, and more hopeful living. Certainly, neither Dewey nor Freire wants teachers to see their classrooms as bully pulpits; this would hardly promote use of the method of intelligence or conscientization. However, my study of Dewey's and Freire's work suggests two ways in which, regardless of teachers' subject matter or curriculum, we can take better advantage of the politics of our teaching, using it more consciously to achieve democratic ends.

First, we can pay better attention to our listening. Dewey argues that teaching should not be a matter of "'telling' and being told" (*MW* 9:38), and Freire argues that much of present instruction suffers from "narration" sickness, whereas, to the contrary, teachers, like liberatory leaders, must be good listeners (*PO* 71, 76). Given the importance that both men place on communication and dialogue for reform (and, similarly, the importance Marcel places on "presence" and "availability"), we should work toward making conversation a two-way street in our classes. How do I expect to do this? My intended initial steps toward this goal are modest. At the least, I want to be more aware of my body language as students speak. For example, I can make sure that I turn toward students who are speaking, make better eye contact, and try to take in what they are saying instead of interrupting too quickly with a defensive or prerehearsed response. At the least, I want to be more aware that the tone and manner in which I conduct myself in my classroom—what Dewey calls "collateral" instruction (*LW* 13:29)—are political. In fact, according to Dewey and Freire, our collateral messages are just as politically important—maybe even more important—than the content of what we teach.[14]

Second, I want to be more politically self-conscious by attending more carefully to the sorts of examples or data that I present to students for classroom analysis and discussion. Regardless of our subject matter—whether philosophy, English, math, or biology—we can use examples that bring to center stage current economic and political realities as we help students practice their particular discipline-based skills.[15] For instance, in my own college philosophy classes, as I plan my curricula and assignments, I intend to keep in mind that the United States has a strong democratic tradition and that I need to watch for opportunities to present this tradition and its relationship to capitalism for problem-posing analysis with my students. I also intend to keep in mind that the wealthiest 20 percent of the world's population uses 86 percent of the world's resources. By contrast, the world's poorest 20 percent uses 1.6 percent. And the United States, which has 6 percent of the world's population and appropriates 25 percent of its resources, allows 20 percent of its children to live in poverty.[16] With these ideas and figures at hand, I want to watch for opportunities to use Dewey's indirect teaching and Freire's problem posing to ask myself and my students how this inequitable situation has come about, how, historically, it has been "justified," and what might be done about it.

Of course, neither Dewey nor Freire wants just talk. They both insist that learning and conversation should be connected to doing. Both would insist that any classroom discussion is meaningless unless it leads to changes in practice. In this regard, I believe it is reasonable to expect that if we can help ourselves and our pupils become more aware that most U.S. lifestyles are too costly to be extended to the rest—or even a majority—of the world's population, this new self-consciousness might lead us to action, even if, at first, this action is only minimal. I have in mind, for example, "belt tightening" by myself and my middle- and upper-class students, purchasing less and simplifying our lives where we can. I also have in mind getting involved in local community affairs or just treating more sensitively those I encounter who are victims of oppression of whatever sort—economic, political, or cultural.[17]

In short, I am heartened by this study's reminder that, for both Dewey and Freire, we have no choice about whether we, as teachers, are engaged in politics. The very nature of our profession means that we are in the thick of it, and I value Dewey's and Freire's reminders that we need to be self-conscious about this important dimension of our work. Borrowing Dewey's language, we need to be intelligent about the politics of our teaching and not just allow this dimension of it to be shaped by caprice, drift, or fixed routine.

TAKING HOPE FROM STUDENTS' POTENTIAL

In addition to being buoyed by Dewey's and Freire's insistence that teaching is a political activity, my optimism that I can be an agent of reform is bolstered by Dewey's and Freire's positive views of our students' potential. As we meet with our pupils, Dewey, in effect, urges us to see them as capable of intelligent, wholehearted, collaborative, and critical behavior. If we can help our students and ourselves avoid the sort of competition that both Dewey and Marcel decry, and if we can help them get beneath the "froth and foam" of media and government messages, we can engage in the sort of shared inquiry and intelligent readjustment of our practices that Dewey sees as necessary for democratic, cooperative, and hopeful living.

Freire's faith in human nature also strengthens my resolve. He believes that a problem-posing approach with our students, a chance to dialogue and name the world in common inquiry, can make both our students and ourselves more critical and humane. It can transform us from passive fatalists about the future to hopeful and active agents in solidarity with the oppressed. In fact, for Freire, hopefulness that we can affect the future is "an ontological need" (*PHOPE* 8). That is, in Freire's view, to give up hope that we as teachers—or people in any walk of life—can effect reform is to become passive or less than human. Although at times it is easy to fall into despair, Freire, like Dewey, is adamant that this is not our natural condition or who we really are. Instead, we should see despair as a sign that we have fallen out of dialogue with others or have succumbed to the ethos of "having" rather than "being" that marks much of our contemporary world (*PO* 59–60, 77; *PF* 116–17). In other words, we should see despair as a signal—by the deepest part of our being—that we need to reconsider our present behavior and be open to others in order to generate honest, genuine dialogue and new action.

TAKING HOPE FROM THE DEMOCRATIC REFORM TRADITION

A third optimistic residue I take from my comparison of Dewey and Freire is that we are not alone. Dewey traces his political origins to eighteenth- and nineteenth-century Anglo-American liberalism. Freire's social critique is rooted in nineteenth-century humanist Marxism, whereas his belief in human freedom and the transformative power of love and trust is as old as first-century Christianity.

Dewey's and Freire's visions of democracy not only have a rich past; they have also been taken up and extended by a number of contemporary scholars. In particular, this is true of Dewey's and Freire's insistence that ways be found for allowing all citizens a fuller role in governance and public policy. I have in mind the work of Benjamin Barber who, like Dewey and Freire, wants broad-based citizen power over public decisions, what Barber calls "strong" as opposed to "thin" democracy.[18] I also have in mind the work of liberation theologians who, like Dewey and Freire, want us to focus our ultimate hopes on this-worldly reform rather than passively waiting for justice to come in a supernatural, transcendent world.[19]

As I have shown, these reform traditions, as exemplified by Dewey and Freire, have similar political and social goals but also diverge in many ways. However, rather than seeing these differences as inconsistencies or contradictions that we need to reconcile, I suggest that we stretch our capacity for the "negative capability" that Dewey values, our capacity, as I explained earlier, to hold apparently contradictory positions without yielding to the desire to resolve them or let one triumph over the other (LW 10:39). We should see these differences or apparent inconsistencies as strengths. That is, I am not only uplifted by these reform traditions; I also am uplifted by their tensions (and the tensions they create within us). For example, I value Freire's urgent tone and the force of his Manichaean, either-or language. I want his outrage at injustice to percolate within me, to keep waking me from my all too familiar first world slumbers. However, I also value Dewey's more considered and conciliatory tone, his incremental and experimental—let's be careful not to throw out the baby with the bathwater—approach to social reform. I want his incremental, experimental approach to remind me that although I need to keep an eye on long-range goals, I also need to take advantage of even the most limited reform opportunities that my situation presents. Likewise, I recognize the strong antidote to despair of Freire's exhortations to overcome our "necrophilic" having tendencies and totally refashion ourselves in solidarity with the poor. However, I also value Dewey's advice that change is always with us and that we can use it to challenge settled habits and open ourselves up to new ways of believing and doing.

In sum, I find that one of the values of my Dewey-Freire dialogue is that it helps me overcome the natural tendency—one that both Dewey and Freire resist—to look for absolutes, to settle on some final truth about the classroom or ourselves. In terms of my teaching, my new appreciation of the value for inquiry of suspending closure means that I can profit from Dewey's and Freire's contrasting means to their similar ultimate hope of democratic educational and social reform. I can try to keep in tension their various suggestions. I can experiment in my classroom with ways to promote both the method of intelligence and conscientization, both collaborative community and humane dialogue. I can do this not only for the sake of my students but also for my own sake, a teacher striving to find ways to live in hope in dark times.

FOUR

Dewey in Dialogue with Positive Psychology and C. R. Snyder: The Morality and Politics of Hope

Steve Fishman

> The notion that every object that happens to satisfy has an equal claim with every other to be a value is like supposing that every object of perception has the same cognitive force as every other. There is no knowledge without perception, but objects perceived are *known* only when they are determined as consequences of connective operations. There is no value except where there is satisfaction but there have to be certain conditions fulfilled to transform a satisfaction into a value.
>
> —John Dewey, *The Quest for Certainty* (*LW* 4:214)

In my comparison of Dewey to Marcel and Freire in the previous two chapters, I hold Dewey's ideas up to those of fellow philosophers, men who, despite their diverse locations within the philosophic tradition, share with Dewey an understanding of that tradition's history, methods, and issues. For example, although Dewey is a naturalist and Marcel a supernaturalist, and although Dewey rejects Marxism and Freire embraces it, both Marcel and Freire share Dewey's concern about the morality of our ultimate hopes. Dewey's focus on the morality and politics of ultimate hope, rather than on the tools and strategies for achieving particular hopes, comes into strong relief as, in this chapter, I put Dewey in the company of researchers from a very different tradition, contemporary clinical psychology.

Specifically, I further explore a Deweyan theory of hope by comparing it to the most fully developed approach to hope in contemporary psychology, that of C. R. Snyder. I do this by engaging Dewey in a dialogue not only with Snyder but also with the contemporary movement within psychology known as "positive psychology," a movement whose emphasis on building positive qualities like contentment, happiness, and hope is shared by Snyder. I begin this dialogue by offering a Deweyan response to programmatic statements by leaders in the positive psychology movement. I then describe Snyder's theory of hope and critically consider it from a Deweyan perspective.

A Deweyan Response to Positive Psychology's Programmatic Statements

I believe that, in general, Dewey would be enthusiastic about positive psychology's interdisciplinary potential. In particular, he would be encouraged by recent programmatic statements that indicate positive psychology is interested in becoming more self-conscious about the political and moral potential of its research. I have in mind Martin E. P. Seligman and Mihaly Csikszentmihalyi's recent characterization of positive psychology as "a science of positive subjective experience, positive individual traits, and positive institutions." Seligman and Csikszentmihalyi's third defining characteristic of the terrain of positive psychology, "positive institutions," would especially please Dewey.[1]

I say it would please Dewey because he believes that social science has the potential to assist in ameliorating social problems. He argues against the long-standing view that the concerns of science and morality are disparate, that answers to *is* questions (science) and answers to *ought* questions (morality) belong in separate realms (*MW* 3:6). To the contrary, Dewey claims that only with the help of science can people properly evaluate their moral ideals. Only with the help of science can people intelligently gauge the full consequences of their actions and the desirability of available alternatives. He writes, "Science must have something to say about *what* we do, and not merely about *how* we may do it most easily and economically" (*MW* 6:78–79). As Dewey points out in the epigraph I chose for this chapter, only when we place our perceptions in the larger context of their causes and consequences do we *know* them. Likewise, only when certain conditions are fulfilled do satisfactions become values. For Dewey, these conditions include evaluating the relative merits of different satisfactions by placing them in the larger context of their consequences for ourselves, for others, and for our environment.[2]

Thus, Dewey urges us to bring together answers to the *is* questions of science (what are the consequences of our satisfactions?) and the *ought* questions of morality (which of our satisfactions should we value?). Just as Dewey urges us to use the method of intelligence to ensure that our hopes are moral, so he urges us to use it as we decide upon the sort of persons we want to become, the individual habits and social institutions we want to nurture and develop. Although he was roundly criticized as naive for believing that people whose views are in serious conflict can peacefully settle their differences,[3] Dewey held firmly to his claim that applying the method of intelligence to moral conflicts was worth a try (*LW* 9:108). It is, in Dewey's view, a method whose potential for bringing about a just society is far greater than the means we currently use: violence and war or, on the other hand, "continuation of drift with improvisations to meet emergencies" (*LW* 11:61).

What stands out for me in recent programmatic statements by positive psychologists like Seligman and Csikszentmihalyi is that they appear to be moving their research in the direction that Dewey strongly advocates. They seem to recognize that psychology is not politically and morally neutral when they propose that positive psychology be a science of positive institutions—and by "positive institutions" I take them to mean institutions that are morally worthy. The opening paragraphs of Seligman and Csikszentmihalyi's article, the lead piece in an issue of *American Psychologist* devoted exclusively to positive psychology, support my reading, my sense that positive psychology wants to move beyond the disciplinary boundaries that presently separate science from morality and politics. They write,

> Entering a new millennium, Americans face a historical choice. Left alone on the pinnacle of economic and political leadership, the United States can continue to increase its material wealth while ignoring the human needs of its people and those of the rest of the planet. Such a course is likely to lead to increasing selfishness, to alienation between the more and less fortunate, and eventually to chaos and despair.
>
> At this juncture, the social and behavioral sciences can play an enormously important role. They can articulate a vision of the good life that is empirically sound while being understandable and attractive.[4]

Explicit in this opening statement is Seligman and Csikszentmihalyi's negative evaluation of current U.S. priorities. They suggest that these are immoral because they overemphasize competition for material wealth, an overemphasis that neglects other human needs, perhaps for companionship, creativity, and community. They suggest that our current social and political orientation is also immoral because it leads us to ignore not only our own needs for more than just material wealth but also the needs of people materially less fortunate. Recognition by Seligman and Csikszentmihalyi that positive psychology should "articulate a vision of the good life" and, by implication, the individual habits and social conditions that nurture it would be especially gratifying to Dewey. He would also be gratified by Shelly L. Gable and Jonathan Haidt's wish that "positive psychologists will become more daring in their theory and their interventions and will try, in the coming years, to actually improve the functioning of schools, workplaces, and even governments."[5]

I say that Dewey would be gratified by such declarations by positive psychologists because he believed that no profession or job is morally and politically neutral. Whatever our daily tasks, if we do not see them as reforming the status quo—for example, reducing what Seligman and Csikszentmihalyi see as Americans' current selfishness and the "alienation between the more and less fortunate" that follows in its wake—then we are, if only unwittingly, helping to perpetuate the injustices of the status quo. As a result, Dewey would urge positive psychology to go against the grain that says science is politically neutral, that what scientists choose to study and what they do with the results of their research are amoral and apolitical. He would urge positive psychologists to take seriously Seligman and Csikszentmihalyi's declaration that "the social and behavioral sciences can play an enormously important role" as the United States faces the choice of what sort of country it wants to become in the new millennium.

Stepping outside the disciplinary practices of one's field is not easy, however, and this can been seen even in Seligman and Csikszentmihalyi's programmatic article. Although they write that they want to articulate a vision of the good life, they quickly add that they intend it to be "empirically sound."[6] Their qualification may be in the Deweyan tradition of using the information that science provides to better evaluate our moral choices, predict their potential outcomes, and modify them in light of new experience. However, invoking the idea of "empirical soundness" could also be a way of suggesting that a vision of the good life can result from simply administering sophisticated questionnaires to broad population samples over appropriate periods of time. In other words, it might suggest that social scientists themselves—their attitudes, values, and social locations—are nonfactors in their own work. If this is the case, then Dewey would be disappointed. He would see it as an unwillingness to bridge the gaps between disciplines that he believes is necessary if we are to intelligently ameliorate our social ills. Nevertheless—and despite the fact that positive psychologists themselves recognize that the field has not yet done much studying of "positive institutions and communities"[7]—I believe Dewey would see this intention of positive psychology as a bold step, one that he would fully support.

In sum, I see positive psychology moving in a Deweyan direction as it seeks to study moral values and ways to modify them in light of what it identifies as our social and global dilemmas. Likewise, I see Dewey's effort to show that science and morality are best joined rather than kept in separate compartments as evidence that he may legitimately be seen as a precursor—a part of the theoretical foundation—of the emerging field of positive psychology.

I now turn to the theory of hope of C. R. Snyder, a major figure in hope research who has aligned himself with the positive psychology movement. In my presentation of the main elements of Snyder's theory, I intersperse Deweyan comments as I engage Snyder and Dewey in dialogue about hope.

C. R. Snyder's Theory of Hope and Dewey's Responses

In *The Psychology of Hope*, C. R. Snyder tells us that hope consists of willpower, "waypower," and clear goals. More specifically, willpower is "mental energy" that helps us reach our objectives (*PH* 6). It is the strength of our determination and commitment to get from one place, point A, to another place, point B. Persons with high willpower say things to themselves like "I can," "I'm ready to do this," and "I've got what it takes" (*PH* 6; see also PPFH 13; and HT 251). People who say these sentences to themselves are high in what Snyder calls "willful thinking" (*PH* 7). Regarding the second component of hope, waypower, people with high levels of this ability are good at what Snyder calls "planful thinking" (*PH* 9). He finds that waypower is a "mental capacity" to find ways to reach our goals, and those who are strong in this capacity are able to find multiple pathways to their objectives.

HOPE AND GOAL SETTING

Snyder reports that the three components of hope—willpower, waypower, and clear goals—are equally important and that all three components interact to mutually promote one another. Regarding goal setting, Snyder, in his study of more than ten thousand people, observes that those who are very specific about their goals are higher in willpower and waypower than those whose goals are vague or poorly defined (*PH* 7–8; HT 250; HIM 108). That is, he discovers that specific goals stimulate greater motivation; they energize us and increase our willpower (*PH* 219). Similarly, specific goals enhance our waypower, prompting us to use the mental capacity we have for finding multiple avenues to our objectives (*PH* 255).[8]

Dewey would certainly agree with Snyder about the need for specific goals. As I said in my account of Dewey's idea of disciplined hope in Chapter 1, he believes that unless we make concrete plans to reach our goals, they remain simply pie-in-the-sky wishes, objectives to which we merely give lip service (*MW* 12:139–55). He is insistent that real conditions and the objectives we hope to achieve need to be integrated. However, Dewey seeks to maintain a healthy balance between developing specific, concrete goals and remaining flexible about them, remaining sensitive to the uncertainties of the future and the vast, dimly lit context in which we live and act.

Given Dewey's position about maintaining this balance, I believe he would caution Snyder and other positive psychologists about putting too much focus on fashioning concrete goals and keeping our eyes on the prize. As Dewey points out, we usually do not fully understand our problem until we find the solution (*LW* 8:201). We often need to get going and investigating without fully knowing just what our problem is and how we are going to solve it. That is to say, we do not want to become so wedded to the concrete, specific goal we have set before us that we fail to attend to the clues and vital evidence from experience as we move forward. Too much attention to the specific form we have given our objective may hinder the balance between doing and undergoing, continuity and interaction, commitment and flexibility that Dewey advocates (*LW* 13:17–30, 10:50–53). Such a balance between articulated goals and attention to changing conditions, for Dewey, allows us to maintain purpose while, at the same time, remaining open to learning by expanding our interests and revising our beliefs in light of new experience.

Snyder himself is aware of the need to maintain a tension between setting concrete goals and remaining flexible. He reports that high-hope people are good at what he calls the "Getting-there/Being-there balance" (*PH* 229–31; *HIM* 111). Whereas Snyder does not make this tension a major focus of his theory of hope, it is central for Dewey's. According to Dewey, the importance of concrete goals can be easily misunderstood. It can lead to what Erich Fromm calls the "idolatry" of the future.[9] Reaching our intended goal, for Dewey, is not as important as it often seems because, if and when we do reach it, our experience usually turns out to be not what we expected and so we always have to generate new goals. For Dewey, as I indicated earlier, the real function of goals is to help us be more attentive to the present, to help us figure out what to do in the here and now. That is, given the limits of our intelligence, the best its dim spotlight on the future can do is provide an objective that helps us decide how to act and what to focus on today. Dewey writes,

> The "end" is the figured pattern at the centre of the field through which runs the axis of conduct. About this central figuration extends infinitely a supporting ground in a vague whole, undefined and undiscriminated. At most intelligence but throws a spotlight on that little part of the whole which marks out the axis of movement. Even if the light is flickering and the illuminated portion stands forth only dimly from the shadowy background, it suffices if we are shown the way to move. (*MW* 14:180)

Thus, for Dewey, when goals function properly, they are not so much about future accomplishments since the future is largely unknown. Rather, when goals function properly, it is because they do something important for us in the present.

HOPE AND OWNERSHIP OF GOALS

Snyder finds that high-hope people not only generate specific goals that energize their willpower and waypower. They also generate specific goals that are truly theirs, not ones that others have chosen for them (*PH* 213–14; *HT* 253). In addition, he reports that high-hope people experience a sudden sense of excitement and purpose when they hit upon a goal that they really value. He writes, "Vague goals . . . do not provide the mental spark to get us moving. . . . Once people clarify their goals, they often are filled with active and empowering thoughts" (*PH* 7).

When Snyder observes that the truly "owned" goals of high-hope people energize them, he touches on another theme that, as we have seen, is central in Dewey's work. Like Snyder, Dewey advises against pretending to care about what we are doing when we really do not. Owning our goals is especially important for Dewey because otherwise we cannot give ourselves wholeheartedly to them. To the contrary, for Dewey, when we are wholehearted as well as intelligent about our work, we can have faith in the worthiness of our efforts, one of the qualities, as we have also seen, that, for Dewey, is a key to living in hope (*MW* 9:180–85; *LW* 9:12–15). In these Deweyan ideas about wholeheartedness and its role in hopeful living, Snyder and positive psychologists can find theoretical support for their observations about high-hope people and the importance of goal ownership. They can also find in Dewey grounds for asking members of their high-hope target group additional questions, ones that might reveal something about the roles that gratitude and piety toward nature and the human community play in these's people's high levels of hope.

For Snyder, then, having specific goals that we truly own, along with will-power and waypower, is important for hope. He also reports that self-con-fidence is crucial. He finds that people who have high hope also have confidence that they can muster the determination to see their projects through and figure out ways to surmount any obstacles that may arise as they pursue their objectives. Someone who has high willpower, waypower, and specific goals might still not have high hope if they have no confidence that they can marshal their abilities in a particular situation (*PH* 12). Thus, Snyder observes that people's estimation of their success in achieving their objectives is even more important than their past history of reaching their goals. He writes, "If you were placing a bet on [how well a person will perform], you probably would win far more often if you wagered on the person's level of hope rather than previous record of achievement" (*PH* 23–24).

In addition to high-hope people's self-confidence about meeting their objec-tives, Snyder says that his studies show that these people display numerous other desirable traits as well (*PH* 58–64). For example, they do not find the world frightening because they believe they are in control of their lives. They see the cup as half full rather than dwelling on the half that is empty. Their self-confidence is modest rather than showy. They have friends they can call upon for help, but they do not "use" others. Instead, their relationships are based on mutual consideration (*PH* 60–61; HT 261). High-hope people also generate goals in many areas of life rather than putting all their eggs in one basket (*PH* 214–15; HT 253). They enjoy competition as a chance to extend their skills, are chosen for leadership positions, and do not worry about death because they see it as simply a part of life (*PH* 64).

MOVING FROM LOW HOPE TO HIGH HOPE

One of the main strengths of Snyder's theory is that, as he puts it, "hope is a learned way of thinking" (*PH* 22; HT 249). Although he says that parents influence their children's levels of adult hope and that "the human basis of hope is usually set in the first two to three years of life" (HIM 109), Snyder finds that low-hope people can become high-hope people (*PH* 211–12). How can they bring about this change?

Making Goals More Specific and More Numerous　Given what I have already said, it is not surprising that one of Snyder's first pieces of advice to low-hope individuals is that they become more specific about their goals. For example, Snyder suggests that those who are overly shy should try to talk to at least one stranger every week or two and then increase this activity to longer conversations in subsequent weeks (*PH* 251). Snyder also suggests that when striking up a conversation with a stranger, one should ask questions and try to learn about the other person. However, he cautions against "cross examining" one's conversation partner (*PH* 252). Further, he tells a shy young man that it is often helpful to confess to another that one is shy, and this sometimes allows others to commiserate and help figure out how to overcome shyness (see HT 251, 261).

Besides urging low-hope people to make their goals specific, Snyder also advises that they develop multiple goals. He counsels that they examine various areas of their lives—work, recreation, health, family, and romantic relations—and write down specific goals they have in each of these areas and prioritize them. This way, if they fail to achieve a goal in one area, instead of getting bogged down by that failure, they can turn immediately to other goals on their list. The possession of multiple goals in various areas of life is what Snyder says he has observed in high-hope people he has studied. That is, rather than spending a lot of time ruminating about their failures, high-hope people protect themselves against overattention to failure by quickly moving on to other objectives (*PH* 59, 214–20; HIM 110).

Snyder's recommendation that low-hope people try to emulate high-hope people in having multiple goals makes good sense. This is helpful not only for dealing with failure; it also helps people who reach their goals generate new ones and thus avoid what might be called "post-goal-fulfillment blues." However, Snyder's advice could be seen as running counter to Dewey's emphasis on unity as a mark of living in hope. That is, Dewey worries about jumping from one goal to another for fear that an individual may fail to find unification or integration in a life that is episodic, filled with stops and starts that keep its different experiences in separate compartments. Dewey's concern reflects his view of the importance of temporal integration as well as the integration of success and failure in helping us enrich present experience and find connections among all parts of our lives.

Although at the close of this chapter I identify two general research recommendations that Dewey might offer positive psychologists, before concluding this current section I present a specific research suggestion that Dewey might make to Snyder about the latter's advice to low-hope individuals regarding goals. Snyder's emphasis on having multiple goals in multiple areas of our lives might lead Dewey to recommend study of the different degrees of integration of people's multiple goals and the effects of this differential integration on individuals' levels of hope. In other words, Dewey might be concerned that people could very well succeed in achieving goals in different areas of their lives and still come away feeling that their lives do not add up to much. The fragmented quality of their living might leave them feeling that they are making no overall progress toward the sort of unifying, ultimate goal that Dewey suggests is central to living in hope (*LW* 9:3–58).

My own experience with undergraduates leads me to be sympathetic with Dewey's concerns. Over the years, numerous students have spoken to me of their frustration that their courses—especially those they must take to satisfy distribution requirements—seem to have nothing to do with one another. These students indicate a need to try to find connections among the different disciplines represented by their courses, and they express disappointment that they cannot give their schoolwork a unified direction so that their efforts in different areas can support and enrich one another. That is, my students seem to feel firsthand what Dewey describes as the importance for hope of choosing goals that enrich present experience, ones that allow our various activities and relationships to come together into a unifying whole.

Increasing Willpower   Not only does Snyder suggest ways to clarify and multiply our goals, but he also makes the comforting claim that we can increase our willpower or the mental energy we have for reaching our goals. He suggests we do this by bolstering our self-confidence. He suggests that if we repeat mantras like "I can," "I'm ready to do this," and "I've got what it takes," we can become more self-conscious at the moments our willpower energy is depleted and take steps to increase it (*PH* 6). He also suggests that we say to ourselves, "Anyone would make similar mistakes on something this hard" and "The task I am undertaking is difficult, but it is a challenge that is worthwhile, one that will expand my skills" (*PH* 248, 225). In other words, he observes that people can successfully use mantras to increase their willpower and take a more positive attitude toward the challenges they face, seeing their difficulties as opportunities rather than hardships or signs of their own inadequacies (see HT 255).

Once again, I believe that Snyder and positive psychology can find theoretical underpinnings in Dewey's writing for their recommendation that low-hope people see roadblocks to their goals as opportunities to expand their individual skills. As I indicated in Chapter 1, Dewey recognizes that in a world as uncertain as ours it is natural to want assurances that we can reach our goals. However, he advises us not to fret over the fact that such assurances cannot be given. Instead, he advises us to focus on what the world *does* give us: chances to collaboratively employ our creative abilities to ameliorate our individual and social ills. In sum, I believe that Dewey's metaphysics and worldview provide additional theoretical support for Snyder's recommendation that low-hope people can avoid letting their failures get them down if they focus on the very real opportunities for goal achievement and growth that their environment provides.

Increasing Waypower   Snyder also offers a variety of remedies for low way-power. Perhaps the most important is to think of different ways to reach our goals. He also recommends that people visualize taking their first steps toward their goals while also anticipating what might go wrong. This is help-ful because if something does go awry, we are in a better position not to be surprised and to have available to us ways around the obstacles we encounter. In addition, Snyder says that we should not hurry this process of planning for alternative routes and ways around roadblocks (*PH* 244–47).

Dewey would certainly agree with Snyder that persistence and discipline about planning are essential to hopeful living. In *Democracy and Education*, he says that we need as much discipline in making our plans to achieve our goals as we need in actually accomplishing them (*MW* 9:134–37). In addi-tion, one could understand Snyder's suggestions about increasing waypower as a concrete development of Dewey's theory about the need to combine impulse and thought. Dewey tells us that when we are stuck or thwarted, our impulse is to quickly get going again. However, according to Dewey, what people need to do is stop and think about ways around current impediments to their objectives. They need to generate new "ends-in-view," or subgoals, that allow them to realign their habits, get their habits working in harmony again, and resume their pursuits (*MW* 14:117–26). In other words, according to Dewey, impulse and thought need to be combined if we are to be disci-plined in our planning (*MW* 14:178). Otherwise, we are likely to strike out blindly or choose routes to our goals that are not well thought out and prone to fail, leading us to surrender our objectives. In sum, Dewey's view of the relationship among thought, impulse, and habit may provide an additional theoretical underpinning to Snyder's observations about the importance of being patient not only as people set their goals but also as they devise ways to achieve them (*PH* 216, 226–29, 243).

Differences in the Role of Despair in Snyder's and Dewey's Theories of Hope

Snyder devotes minimum attention to despair. Instead, as I have just related, although he says that high-hope people are prepared for defeats and describe their defeats in positive terms (*PH* 226; HIM 111–12), his strongest advice for low-hope people is to quickly get past their failures and focus on achieving alternative objectives. Snyder takes this approach because he observes that the high-hope people he has studied waste little time ruminating about their failures or worrying about the brevity and apparent insignificance of their own existence (*PH* 59, 64). Snyder writes, "Higher-hope persons do not dwell on failures . . . because they are mentally invested and focused on accomplishing their goals. Accordingly, hope is a way of thinking that moves us toward good outcomes and thereby protects us from bad outcomes" (*PH* 18).

By contrast, Dewey assumes that there is an intimate connection between hope and despair. For Dewey, we begin to hope, and to employ thinking to reach our goals, only when our habits are interrupted and things go wrong (*LW* 8:123). Thus, for Dewey, hope always arises in the context of anxiety and potential despair. Hope is born when we have lost our footing and are struggling to regain our direction.[10]

PARTICULAR HOPES VERSUS ULTIMATE HOPE

Dewey's assumption of an intimate connection between hope and despair is the result of his focus on ultimate hope rather than particular hopes, or, put differently, social, altruistic hopes rather than individual, self-centered ones. Given the real-life barriers to achieving the sort of ongoing democratic reform that Dewey advocates, it is not surprising, as I remarked earlier, that those who share Dewey's sort of ultimate hope are tempted by despair. As I have said, Dewey's few explicit remarks about hope seem to be directed at those who are disillusioned about the possibility of ever achieving thoroughgoing social reform. It is as if people must, in order to test their commitment to their absolute hopes, successfully work through their despair about the unlikelihood of ever fulfilling them. For example, Dewey tries to assure us that although we may not see the fruits of our efforts at social reform, if we have chosen our ultimate hopes intelligently and wholeheartedly, we can have faith that there are good forces in the universe that are on our side and will carry them on. He also tries to assure us that although we do not want to be naive, our youthful idealism and sense of power should not be totally abandoned because of adult sensitivity to human limitations. According to Dewey, our ideals and youthful visions are products of nature and deserve to be nurtured: "[Our] juvenile assumption of power and achievement is not a dream to be wholly forgotten. It implies a unity with the universe that is to be preserved. The belief, and the effort of thought and struggle which it inspires are also the doing of the universe, and they in some way, however slight, carry the universe forward" (*LW* 1:313–14).

In short, Dewey suggests that we need to understand and work through despair if we are to plant a life of hope on solid ground. He suggests that only when we come to grips with the fact that our lives are short and may end without dramatic issue, "wither[ing] away like the grass of the fields," can we fully appreciate the importance for living in hope of qualities like gratitude, intelligent wholeheartedness, and enriched present experience (*MW* 14:19).

Whereas Dewey sees hope as arising from coming to terms with life's trials and the barriers in the way of achieving our ultimate hopes, Snyder, as I have indicated, observes that hope, in the main, results from focusing on particular, individual goals and avoiding ruminating about the limits of the human situation. Thus, in comparison with Dewey, Snyder might be seen as finding a less painful road to hope. Snyder discovers that people can increase their hopefulness without the anguish of having to fully explore those aspects of life—its uncertainties, inequities, and absurdities—that may drive some thoughtful people to despair. To the contrary, Dewey's approach implies that this sort of anguish avoidance may not be possible. His recognition of life's hazards suggests that those who are short on hope may need to do significant revising of their worldview. In the face of life's tragedies, they may need to find ways to nurture feelings of belonging, purpose, faith, and unification if they are to maintain and not surrender their ultimate hopes.

Alternatively put, Dewey assumes that the Enlightenment perspective—the view that if we are smart enough about our goals and ingenious enough about ways to reach them, then we will get what we want—is flawed. Although Dewey underlines the fact that at times nature cooperates with us and allows us to reach our objectives, he is equally realistic about the fact that nature often defeats our best-laid plans. That is, for Dewey, failure is an ever present possibility in any human endeavor, and, thus, ultimate hope, if it is to be maintained, must be husbanded in the context of a post-Enlightenment perspective that recognizes that life is never fully controllable, is filled with mystery and chance. Thus, ultimate hope, as distinguished from ordinary hopes, is that to which we are committed despite the likelihood that we will never achieve it, no matter how intelligently wholehearted we are in shaping and pursuing it. Our commitment to it is based on a strong disposition toward altruism, a willingness to work for a good that we would like others to experience even if we are unable to. It is also based on the sort of strong faith that Dewey calls for, a faith that if we act intelligently and wholeheartedly, others will continue our work after we are gone. In sum, for Dewey, unlike Snyder, one of the keys to living in hope is accepting that our joy comes from knowing that although we may never see the full fruits of our labor, our "lot is one with whatever is good in existence" and that, in a modest way, our struggles to achieve our ultimate hopes "carry the universe forward" (*LW* 1:313–14).[11]

Differences in the Roles of Morality and Politics in Snyder's and Dewey's Theories of Hope

Besides the intimate connection that Dewey sees between hope and despair, Dewey's work raises a moral and political question that Snyder acknowledges but leaves unexplored. This question is, what is moral hope? Snyder acknowledges this question in his forecasts about hope research. He predicts that as researchers come to understand the great variety of people's goals, they will be "forced to grapple with value-related issues." He adds, "In this regard, it would be fascinating to conduct content analyses of the goals that occupy the thinking of high-and-low hope people" (PPFH 22). In addition, in a recent coauthored article, he writes that the question "What lies ahead for positive psychology?" sparks excitement in both him and his coauthor. This is because "the positive psychology perspective presents opportunities to address philosophical issues (e.g., What is the good life?) and practical questions (e.g., How do positive emotions affect us over time?)" (FPP 751).

Snyder also raises the question of what moral hope is in the moving and dramatic final paragraphs of *The Psychology of Hope*. In these final paragraphs, Snyder echoes Dewey's deep gratitude and piety toward nature and other people (*MW* 4:176). Snyder writes,

> Whenever there is a personal goal, a "me" goal, I would ask you also to think of the implications of this goal for the rest of us as a "we" goal. In the extent to which the me and we goals relate positively on each other, much like images in a reflecting pool, then our goals are in synchrony.
> . . . Each of [us] stands in a long evolutionary line. Looking back, we honor the memories of our ancestors. Looking forward, we have an unknown and yet undeniable impact on our descendants. Individually and collectively, we are time travelers who, for better or worse, are making a difference in what happens next. The link between what was and what might be rests in our thoughts today. If our minds are filled with willpower and waypower for goals profiting only ourselves and not others, we advance the forces of unhappiness, divisiveness, fear, aggression, and destruction. If our minds are filled

with hope for shared goals, however, our legacy will be a positive one. The changes necessary for this latter scenario are not easy, but they are doable. It is our choice, and the decision will be made in the most powerful polling booth of all—the human mind. My vote, for what it is worth, is that we can get there from here. (*PH* 297–98; see also HIM 114–15)

Despite Snyder's taking this stand for "we" rather than just "me" goals, he issues a qualification. Snyder also tells us that "hope theory is meant to be neutral in its treatment of the value of the goals selected by people. Therefore, because a person has high hope, there is no theoretical premise that prosocial, positive goals are being pursued" (HT 267; see also PPFH 21–22). Snyder's finding that individuals with antisocial goals may also be high-hope people does not seem surprising. However, the illustrative example Snyder offers—"a [high-hope] gang leader who wants to secure his turf and turn a handsome profit on the sale of illicit drugs" (*PH* 267)—does not, at least on the surface, appear to be fully consonant with the traits that Snyder correlates with high-hope individuals. These traits include better overall psychological adjustment (HT 261), better care of their health (*PH* 63), give-and-take reciprocal relations (*PH* 60), and consideration of the desires of other people (HIM 112, 114). Regardless, by not distinguishing high-hope individuals whose goals are prosocial or considerate of others from high-hope individuals whose goals are egotistic or self-centered, Dewey would say that Snyder misses a valuable opportunity to learn about the conditions and habits that enable people to think carefully about the consequences of their activities. That is, Snyder misses a chance to help us find effective ways to develop and work for "shared goals," misses, as he himself puts it, a chance to help us "get there from here."

In short, whereas the morality and politics of hope are central issues for Dewey, Snyder, despite his own and other programmatic statements by leaders in positive psychology, still, understandably, finds it difficult to bring these issues into the arena of his professional concerns.

ACCOUNTING FOR THE DIVERSE ROLES OF MORALITY AND POLITICS IN SNYDER'S AND DEWEY'S THEORIES OF HOPE: DIFFERENT ACADEMIC DISCIPLINES

When I wonder why Snyder does not focus on the relative merits of different goals and their political implications, I believe one of the reasons is the power of his discipline's traditional methods and practices. Social and behavioral scientists generally adopt the posture of neutral observers, researchers who organize their observations according to various theories and then report their findings and their studies' implications for further research. Thus, from a traditional social scientist's perspective, judging the moral merits of the objects of people's hopes would involve invoking the researcher's own personal values and, therefore, betraying his or her obligations as a scientific observer. Snyder takes this stance explicitly in the multiauthored "Authors' Response" in the issue of *Psychological Inquiry* devoted entirely to his work on hope. He and his coauthors write:

> In our estimation, the theoretical slope gets especially slippery when we come to the question of who is to decide what is a virtuous goal? Should we truly make hope our own, as belonging exclusively to Western society in general and America in particular? What is a virtue to those in the West may not be a virtue to someone born and raised in another culture.
>
> Just as someone from a different culture may not share our values, a young person [like the gang leader used as an illustration by Snyder] may pursue goals that are unacceptable to mainstream citizens. The gang member, however, probably is pursuing goals that are congruent with his own personal value system. (SOR 322)

Although Dewey, like Snyder and his co-investigators, observes that values vary from culture to culture and person to person, he strongly disagrees with the position of moral relativism that Snyder and his coauthors adopt. As Dewey says in the epigraph of this chapter, noticing what people find satisfying is only the first step in deciding which satisfactions are truly worth valuing. In parallel ways, he would argue that observing various cultures and individuals is the initial step, and only the initial step, in working for social reform. According to Dewey, we need to begin with such observations if we are to fashion ideals that are rooted in reality and not just castles in the air. However, a crucial second step is to decide upon the most desirable traits of the groups and individuals we observe so that we can use these desirable traits to criticize existing groups and individuals, including ourselves, so that they and we can improve. Dewey tells us:

> In seeking this measure [of the relative value of different forms of group life], we have to avoid two extremes. We cannot set up out of our heads, something we regard as an ideal society. We must base our conception upon societies which naturally exist, in order to have any assurance that our ideal is a practicable one. But . . . the ideal cannot simply repeat the traits which are actually found. The problem is to extract the desirable traits of forms of community life which actually exist, and employ them to criticize undesirable features and suggest improvement. (*MW* 9:88–89)

When Dewey moves to the second step—extracting the desirable traits of group life—he comes up with the two criteria that, as I indicated in Chapter 3, distinguish different levels of democratic living: how open the members of the group are to each other's different needs and interests and how open the group is to the needs and interests of other groups. When Dewey applies these criteria, he is able to distinguish criminal groups from civic-minded ones:

> In any social group whatever, even in a gang of thieves, we find some interest held in common, and we find a certain amount of interaction and cooperative intercourse with other groups. From these two traits we derive our standard. How numerous and varied are the interests which are consciously shared? How full and free is the interplay with other forms of association? If we apply these considerations to, say, a criminal band, we find that the ties which consciously hold the members together are few in number, reducible almost to a common interest in plunder; and that they are of such a nature as to isolate the group from other groups with respect to give and take of the values of life. (*MW* 9:89; see also *LW* 13:19)

In short, for Dewey, it does not follow that because different cultures and people deserve equal respect, all cultures and everyone's *values* deserve equal respect. Quite the contrary, Dewey claims that those groups and people whose ethical judgments display sensitivity to the emotional and intellectual dispositions of their members and members of different groups are superior to those that are constructed casually and without sympathetic consideration of others (*MW* 9:8). By contrast, Snyder implies that there is no satisfactory way of rank-ordering the goals of different groups and individuals. Attempting to do so risks going down the "slippery" slope that he and his coauthors want to avoid and moving beyond the established methods and practices of the social sciences.

ACCOUNTING FOR THE DIVERSE ROLES OF MORALITY AND POLITICS IN SNYDER'S AND DEWEY'S THEORIES OF HOPE: DIFFERENT VIEWS OF THE INDIVIDUAL

A second reason that Snyder chooses not to evaluate the relative desirability of various goals may be the picture of the individual that emerges in *The Psychology of Hope* as someone generally working alone to maximize his or her own interests. Although Snyder certainly recognizes that we are influenced by others and, at times, need to negotiate with others or seek help to solve our problems (*PH* 213, 253), the broad moral and social consequences of the way people choose their goals does not receive much attention. At the opening of *The Psychology of Hope*, Snyder reports that when he observes people, they are always pursuing goals. The pursuit of various objectives is, in Snyder's view, human beings' basic occupation. Snyder then claims that high-hope people are those who are successful in reaching their goals. As a result, the research that Snyder reports attends primarily to the characteristics and skills that enable high-hope people to be so successful in reaching their objectives. Although Snyder does not fully develop the picture of the individual with whom he begins his study, the main image that emerges for me is of individuals focusing on their own interests as they decide upon their goals and only occasionally seeking advice or attending to the interests of others.[12]

With this portrait in mind of individuals making decisions with primary regard for their own needs, it is understandable that Snyder's Adult Trait Hope Scale questionnaire does not ask individuals if they are concerned about the effects of their goal choices on the overall human community or the natural environment (*PH* 26; *PPFH* 25; *HT* 274). That is, Snyder's concentration on people trying to get from point A to point B leads him, understandably, to focus on the skills that enable individuals to do so while generally neglecting individuals' consideration of the fallout upon those beyond their immediate view. As a result, Snyder's approach and his Adult Trait Hope Scale do not lend themselves to exploration of the morality or political implications of the goals people choose.[13]

Although Dewey, like Snyder, believes that humans are goal directed (*LW* 8:141), the picture of the individual with which Dewey begins is more social. Dewey's individual is also moving from point A to point B, but point B is, for Dewey, primarily group membership, not solitary achievement. Whereas the mental picture I have of Snyder's individuals is of people moving on a path from one point to another with their eyes on their targets, I imagine Dewey's individuals somewhat differently. I see them acting in a social setting with other people and with the goal of participating in others' ongoing activities. To repeat one of Dewey's most striking observations, "Solitary confinement is the last term in the prison house of man" (*MW* 13:276). In other words, for Dewey, isolation from others is people's worst punishment since they are social through and through, and, thus, their goals are social through and through. As partial evidence for this view, Dewey claims that we learn our mother tongue because we want to become part of the group, and to become part of the group we learn its language so we can contribute to its activities and earn group membership (*MW* 9:21).

In sum, despite the very Deweyan, communitarian sound of the closing paragraphs of Snyder's *Psychology of Hope* and his coauthored article "Hope: An

Individual Motive for Social Commerce," Snyder generally presents a picture of the individual as choosing goals regardless of their long-term moral and political consequences for others. He implies that individuals need to be careful that they are not too much influenced by those around them, that they need to act independently if they are to identify goals that will really motivate them.

Although Dewey wants people to be wholehearted about, or fully own, their objectives, his view of the individual as dominantly social leads him to a different approach to goal setting than the one adopted by Snyder in *The Psychology of Hope*. In choosing goals, Dewey claims, as I have said, that not only must we be wholehearted, but we must also be intelligent. We must fashion our goals and actions according to what we view as good for society at large, what others expect of us, and what we believe will best preserve the natural environment (*LW* 5:279–89). In other words, for Dewey, if our choices are to be moral, we have to consider the interests of people in our own country, people in other nations, and the physical environment that supports us (*MW* 9:104).

Research Suggestions That Dewey Might Offer Snyder and Positive Psychologists

I believe Dewey would offer two general research suggestions to Snyder and positive psychologists: study ultimate democratic hope in relation to despair, and study hope with the objective of promoting social reform. These two suggestions are closely related. Adopting the first recommendation would, for Dewey, be one way of achieving the second. I turn now to Dewey's first recommendation.

CONSIDER STUDYING ULTIMATE, DEMOCRATIC HOPE IN RELATION TO DESPAIR

I speculate that Dewey would want positive psychologists to explore ultimate democratic hope in relation to despair. I believe he would urge this sort of exploration because human betterment depends upon understanding the conditions that nurture prosocial hopes, habits, and dispositions. Although Snyder discusses a variety of objects, relations, and accomplishments that people pursue (*PH* 5), he provides few examples of people who experience low hope because of frustrations about reaching prosocial ultimate hopes. Instead, most of Snyder's detailed explorations of people who have low hope deal with problems that, although serious, are more particular and manageable. He discusses problems like the difficulties graduate students have finishing their dissertations (*PH* 10–11), the challenges people experience juggling their responsibilities as single parents (*PH* 39–40), and a family's uncertainties about how to let a child know that the family pet has to be put down (*PH* 245). I believe Dewey would say that Snyder's research would be enriched by including in his study examples of other sorts of experience of low hope, like the kind people experience when their hopes are focused on overcoming social injustice and creating a more humane world.[14]

To summarize, without denying the importance and representative nature of the high- and low-hope people that Snyder observes, I believe Dewey would urge Snyder to expand his research. He would ask Snyder and positive psychologists to study and offer more help to people whose low hope is a consequence of their commitment to prosocial, democratic goals, commitments that may require strategies to deal with unusual sensitivity to the precarious and tragic dimensions of life.

CONSIDER STUDYING HOPE IN WAYS THAT PROMOTE SOCIAL REFORM THROUGH HOPE

Although Snyder is personally sensitive to the ethical implications of hope, his disciplinary tradition, as I have already suggested, encourages him to avoid evaluating the relative merits of people's goals. It also encourages him to present his work as morally and politically neutral. However, I believe Dewey would claim it is not neutral at all. He would claim it has important moral and political consequences. From Dewey's perspective, Snyder, despite his own intentions, may be read as saying that it does not matter whether your goal is a new car or a vow of solidarity with the poor. From Dewey's perspective, Snyder may, thus, unwittingly and indirectly, be supporting the greed and drive for personal pecuniary profit that Dewey claims reduce the quality of life in U.S. and world society.

Put differently, I believe that what Dewey said to educators in 1935 he would say to positive psychologists and all other professionals today: You're either with us, or you're against us (*LW* 11:347). You are either for reform, or you are for the status quo. He would recommend that Snyder and other positive psychologists attend more to the morality and politics of hope—for example, by studying the conditions that nurture prosocial hopes, dispositions, and habits—in order to better forward democratic, social reform and minimize the risk of working, however unintentionally, to preserve the status quo. In this regard, Dewey would view Sympson and Snyder's forty-eight-item Domain Specific Hope Scale as a potentially important early stage in studying how to develop and pass on the habits of prosocial, democratic hope (DIV).[15]

He would be similarly enthusiastic about positive psychology's interest in studying how to transfer optimism from individual to collective concerns.[16]

In sum, Dewey would say that it is possible to interpret Snyder as finding that for high-hope people the only apparent considerations surrounding their goal setting are determining what they want and how best to achieve their objectives. Because of the moral and political questions that Snyder's study neglects, his findings may be taken to imply that we, as Americans, do not have to consider what price others, both in this country and around the world, must pay for the goals we choose. Thus, from Dewey's point of view, Snyder, without intending to do so, may reinforce the dominant pattern in the United States of walling ourselves off from the impact that our relatively lavish and wasteful lifestyles have upon the standard of living and health of the rest of the world. Inadvertently, and however slightly, his work may help keep at bay, for those of us who are among the world's relatively rich, the consequences of the false idea that the earth can sustain our way of living without exacting a tragic toll on both the environment and the world's poor.

Dewey's Challenge: Reconciling Particular and Ultimate Hopes in Order to Live in Hope

In conclusion, Dewey would certainly recognize that it is not easy for most of us to see the moral and political implications of what we do. It is not easy to find ways to work for social reform while carrying out our professional practices and working to realize our particular hopes. That is, Snyder and positive psychologists are hardly alone in struggling to reconcile the demands of their daily activities with their ultimate hopes for moral and political reconstruction. When we give first rank to ultimate hope and the responsibilities it implies—as Dewey would have us do—our daily cargo becomes profoundly heavier. We then cannot escape the fact that, our best intentions notwithstanding, every time we teach a class, take on a new client, or engage in research without explicitly working to understand and change the present social system, we perpetuate it. In effect, we condone the status quo and unwittingly act as conservative rather than reforming agents. Given the prevailing view that politics is only for politicians and ethics only for ethicists, I believe that Dewey would ask all of us to recognize and embrace Snyder's and positive psychology's challenge as our own.

FIVE

Conclusion to Part I: Highlights of a Deweyan Theory of Hope

Steve Fishman

I conclude Part I of this book by briefly summarizing what I see as the highlights of a Deweyan theory of hope. At the outset of my effort to construct such a theory for Dewey, I said that what stands out for me is his recognition that misfortunes dog all living creatures, his recognition that "every day brings us one day nearer death" (*LW* 14:98). In this regard, Dewey's approach contrasts sharply with the findings of C. R. Snyder who observes that high-hope people avoid ruminating about their failures and see goal achievement as the best antidote to despair. However, I agree with Dewey, contra Snyder, that failure and hope are intimately connected. I also agree with Dewey that goal achievement is not itself a sufficient condition of high hope. That is, I believe it is possible to be highly successful and still feel empty if one does not have faith in the worthiness of one's goals.

At the outset I also said that what stands out for me is Dewey's effort to maintain a life of hope without appealing to God and a future heavenly existence to give meaning or purpose to life. In this regard, Dewey's naturalistic approach to hope dramatically contrasts with Marcel's supernatural approach. Although I am sympathetic to Marcel's insistence that without faith in an eternal and loving communion with others human existence makes no sense, I find Dewey's naturalism more reflective of my own experience. As much as I want to share Marcel's faith that my life has transcendent meaning, I suspect that it does not.

But, then, why go on? If the sun is going to blow up someday, and if I, along with all humanity, will vanish to be forgotten forever, why continue? Why should I bother with my "puny" and "flickering" actions (*LW* 1:314, *MW* 14:227)? It is Dewey's attempt to answer these questions that I find most attractive about his orientation to hope, and I find his most powerful answer is gratitude and piety toward nature and the human community. This is why, as I explained in Chapter 1, I chose gratitude as the first key to a Deweyan theory of hope. Dewey's calling attention to what we owe past generations and our responsibility to future ones reflects his cognizance of our markedly social nature and our ontological need for action. Like Freire, and unlike Snyder, Dewey sees us as thoroughly social and historical creatures, and so, for Dewey, gratitude to the long human chain in which we are links helps answer the human thirst for belonging as well as for purposeful action.[1]

I chose intelligent wholeheartedness as the second key to Deweyan hope because once we decide to go on, it is so difficult to know the right path to take. It is difficult to know the best way to throw our "puny" efforts into the "moving unbalanced balance of things," into the constant rhythm of disturbance and equilibrium. The way to choose a path and move forward, Dewey says, is to trust ourselves. More specifically, he says that if we embrace our causes wholeheartedly, and if we do our utmost to "intelligize" our practices, then we can have faith that our goals are worthy. We can have faith that we are using our puny efforts in the best possible way.

I highlighted enriched present experience as the third key to Deweyan hope because hope traditionally is seen as prospective, as future oriented. However, Dewey's sensitivity to the hazards of life and to its perpetual rhythm of disturbance and quest for new harmony leads him to suggest that a life of hope is marked by a sense of the importance of the present moment. Since no harmony endures indefinitely, there is no resting point in life, and every moment is potentially as valuable as any other. This is why, for Dewey, to subordinate the present to the past or future is to exchange what is relatively under our control to what is incapable of control (*MW* 14:183). This is why, for Dewey, in a life of hope, every moment is mined for meaning. The here and now is listened to closely for reverberations of the past and preludes of the future. In each and every moment, we sense our connection and unity with the larger world in which we live and find the source of our being.

Dewey's sensitivity to life's perils and rhythms, his awareness that all fulfillments are of limited duration, is also reflected in his choice of democracy as his ultimate hope. Not only is democracy, for Dewey, a way of life that promotes the development of open, cooperative inquiry and service for the common good. It is also a dynamic goal, not a static one. It is not the sort of final state of eternal peace at the core of more traditional ultimate hopes like Marcel's. Quite the contrary, Dewey, like Freire, envisions democracy as never-ending reconstruction. It is, for Dewey—as the Constitution was for Jefferson—an ongoing experiment that so values new experience that it provides for constant revision.[2]

The "Familiar" and the "Unfamiliar" Dewey

In Chapter 1, I also talked about a "familiar" and an "unfamiliar" Dewey. I presented the familiar Dewey as content with the opportunities and risks of intelligently, wholeheartedly, and creatively meeting our challenges, challenges that never end. I presented the unfamiliar Dewey as suggesting that it is reasonable to hope for more, for an equilibrium that lasts through "any amount of vicissitudes of circumstances, internal and external" (*LW* 9:12). As I indicated then, what I call the familiar Dewey rings truer to my own experience than the unfamiliar one. The familiar Dewey never tires of reminding me that the world is hazardous, the future filled with foreboding, and that famine and failure are as likely to be "just around the corner" as abundance, festival, and song (*LW* 1:43). He never lets me forget that the wonderful opportunities for new growth presented by disparities between me and my environment are also, if the disparity is too wide, the onset of death (*LW* 10:29–30). In other words, the line between triumph and disaster is a thin one. Since I do not feel especially at home in or trusting of the world, I am more comfortable in the company of the familiar Dewey. He too seems to be wary of the world. He too seems to expect nothing more from nature than the never-ending rhythm of disturbance and struggle for new harmony. In fact, he tells us that to try to escape this rhythm would mean leaving a living world and entering a finished and unchanging—a "dead"—world (*LW* 1:47). In sum, the familiar Dewey tells us that we must do our best to hand on, in better shape than we received it, what we find most valuable in our culture, and we must do this without any guarantee that we will succeed.

By contrast, the unfamiliar Dewey is more trusting or sure of the world than the familiar one. He seems to promise more than just the opportunity to grow as we seek creative and cooperative ways to meet our inevitable disturbances. He seems to have confidence that the world is on our side, that good acts will somehow be preserved, that enduring peace of mind is possible. I want to be open to the invitations that the unfamiliar Dewey offers me to expand my view of the universe. However, in Chapter 1, I also described the troubles I encounter when I try to follow Dewey's path toward the enduring harmony that he describes to his correspondent Scudder Klyce as a "peace which passes all understanding."[3]

Hope, Climbing Mountains, and Creativity

Although study of Deweyan hope has not yet brought me the peace and understanding that Dewey found and describes to Klyce, it has given me other residues. It has made clearer to me the importance of gratitude, intelligent wholeheartedness, and enriched present experience. It has made clearer to me the ways in which these qualities can help me live in hope by promoting a sense of belonging, purpose, faith, and unity.

These Deweyan insights about living in hope are captured for me in Max Otto's story, the one I related in the Preface, about Dewey's advice, at age ninety, to a young physician: life is about climbing mountains to see the other mountains to climb. For me, this image captures Dewey's belief that the exhilarating and joyous experience of creatively meeting our inevitable disturbances takes some of the sting from death. That is, I take these creative experiences as one of the reasons that Dewey could say "yes" to life in the face of all the disappointments he knew, including the loss of his young sons, Morris and Gordon. I believe these creative moments are the reason Dewey wrote continually and with passion his entire life and why he called the idea of art, that is, all intentional and reflective problem solving, "the greatest intellectual achievement in the history of humanity" (*LW* 10:31).

I claim that creative moments can, for Dewey, take some of the sting from mortality for several reasons. First, as I interpret his advice to the young physician, scaling mountains puts us very much in the present. Climbing requires full attention and, as a result, takes focus away from future death. Second, creative moments can reduce the sting of death because, in both retrospect and prospect, they are enjoyable. That is, creativity's exhilaration and the prospect of more such experiences can be strong motivators for soldiering on despite the shadows of mortality. Finally, if the problems we creatively address are chosen intelligently and wholeheartedly, mountain climbing can lessen the sting of mortality by unifying us with others. That is, scaling mountains to find new ones to climb connects us with other climbers as well as with those whose labors provide the rope, harness, and pulleys on which the very possibility of our adventure depends.

Dewey's image of scaling mountains is especially valuable to me because of my own struggle to make peace with mortality. The idea that "every day brings us one day nearer death," as Dewey puts it, hit home for me long ago on an otherwise quiet Yom Kippur afternoon in the fall of the year I entered first grade. My family was returning to our East Bronx apartment from synagogue when I overheard my father talking about the cemetery plot where he would be buried when he died. My mother tried to stop him. She said, "Shush, Danny, the *kinder*, the *kinder* is turning white." But it was too late. On that late fall afternoon death came home to me and has remained a strong presence within me ever since. Dewey's image of climbing, his satisfaction and faith in the worth of creativity, helps me deal with mortality. It helps me understand my own need to write, my own feeling of being lost when I have no mountain to climb, and my chilling fear at the thought of finding no new mountain when I finally approach the pinnacle of the one I am on. In short, Dewey's image helps me reconstruct and better understand the ways I have been using my own version of scaling mountains to take some of the sting from death and increase my chances of living in hope.

I would be less than candid if I ended this summary without acknowledging that I hold these Deweyan insights about hope tenuously. I suspect that I may surrender them in future moments when my failures, limitations, and new trials pull me forcefully in the direction of low hope. However, I also suspect that the familiar Dewey will remind me that to expect these insights to guarantee full protection from despair is to risk overlooking the creative opportunities to recover hope that only a living world—only a world that continues to threaten me—can give.

PART II

The Practice of Hope

SIX

Teaching a Course on Hope

Lucille McCarthy

[The teacher] has to know how to give information when curiosity has created an appetite that seeks to be fed, and how to abstain from giving information when, because of lack of a questioning attitude, it would be a burden and would dull the sharp edge of the inquiring spirit.

— John Dewey, *How We Think* (*LW* 8:144).

In Part II of this book, I report my findings about Steve Fishman's Philosophy and Practice of Hope course, an undergraduate class he taught at the University of North Carolina at Charlotte (UNCC) in the spring of 2005.[1] My primary focus will be on the ideas about hope that students were most able to use in their own lives. However, before reporting in the next chapter on the ideas students took from the course, in this chapter I provide some details about the class: the students who enrolled, Fishman's pedagogical approach, the course materials and assignments, and the general atmosphere in the classroom. I do this so that readers can understand the context in which student learning occurred. I also do this so that readers who might want to offer such a course can determine which aspects of Fishman's class might be appropriate in their own settings and which features they would need to modify to fit their particular teaching styles and student population. I start with a description of the students who took Fishman's course on hope.

The Students: Who They Were and Why They Enrolled in Steve Fishman's Hope Course

In January 2005, ten students enrolled in Steve Fishman's upper-division philosophy course, The Philosophy and Practice of Hope, at the University of North Carolina at Charlotte, a regional branch of the state university that enrolls some twenty thousand undergraduate and graduate students. Of Fishman's ten undergraduates, nine were philosophy majors, some with double majors. Nine were juniors or seniors, and six of the ten were women. All were Euro-American except Shoua Lao, a nineteen-year-old sophomore Hmong pupil, and three of the ten were returning students, older than typical-age undergraduates. Thirty-six-year-old senior Beth Blalock had dropped out of college seventeen years earlier when her mother got sick and had returned two years prior to taking Fishman's hope class; junior Carolyn Kamionka, age forty-two, had also resumed her education two years earlier after staying home to raise her family; and senior Christopher Vernarsky, age twenty-eight, had quit college in Wisconsin when he was twenty-two because he was "wasting his parents' money." Chris said he had no idea at that time what he was interested in, but, in 2004, he decided to study philosophy and registered at UNCC. One unusual feature of the class makeup was that it included a mother-son combination: Carolyn Kamionka was joined in the course by her twenty-three-year-old son, Bob Glahn.

All of Fishman's ten students were full-time at the university, and, in addition, eight of them worked outside school, some spending as much as thirty to forty hours a week at their jobs. Of the ten who began the course, eight finished. Because I was able to stay in contact with the two who dropped out midway through the semester—both for "financial reasons"—I will include all ten students in my report.

During my first interview with each student in February, I asked why they had signed up for the class. Their answers fell, generally, into one of two categories. They said they enrolled either because they wanted to take a course with Fishman or because they saw the word "hope" in the course title and knew they "needed more hope," as one student put it. Leaving out the one non-philosophy major, Faith Dennison, a twenty-three-year-old senior political science major who said she took the course simply because it fit her schedule and looked like an easy A, students were about equally divided between these two categories. Of the four who enrolled in the course because Fishman was teaching it, three students—Rebecca Hinson, Stan

Lefcoski, and Carolyn Kamionka, all philosophy majors—said they had taken courses with him before and enjoyed them. The fourth person, Christopher Vernarsky, said that he had not previously taken a course from Fishman, but a friend said he was good, and this motivated Chris to enroll.

That five students fell into the second category—taking the course because they needed more hope—surprised me. I went into this project thinking that undergraduates would be quite hopeful, if not about the world situation then at least about their personal prospects for the future. I thought these young people would say that they were in college because they expected, upon graduation, to get the job, house, car, family, and life they wanted. Of course, I know many undergraduates have experienced troubles in their lives, but I was not expecting such a high proportion of the class to tell me that they had recently been or were now in despair. I describe these five students at some length because, as people who were suffering, they approached the class differently from the others. They seemed to come saying, "Maybe I can help myself here."[2]

The first such student was nineteen-year-old sophomore philosophy major Shoua Lao. She told me that although she felt underprepared for the class—it was only her third philosophy course—she knew she "had to take it" because she "didn't have enough hope." In the past six months her grandfather had died, her young uncle had been crushed to death by a tree, and her boyfriend had committed suicide. "I was hopeless," she told me, "and I wanted to hear what others say about hope. I needed something to uplift my spirits. Even though I was worried about keeping up with the class, I took it anyway."

Like Shoua Lao, Lindsey Weston, a twenty-one-year-old senior with a double major in philosophy and psychology, told me in mid-February that she needed to understand hope. "I have a love-hate relation with hope," Lindsey said. "Sometimes hope is good; sometimes it's not. I want to figure out when I should hope and when I shouldn't, when it's emotionally effi-cient and when it's not. I suspect this course won't help me figure it out, but maybe it will get me to think more." Lindsey explained that she had been in Kuwait the previous summer with the Air National Guard, the only woman in her group, and she had been the victim of ugly rumors, with her friends not only failing to defend her but actually fanning the flames of the stories. Lindsey said this had caused her to lose her faith in humanity. She no lon-ger trusted people and tended to see only the bad in them, which she hated, she said, and she wanted to get back to her pre-Kuwait openness and trust in others. She concluded, "I'm hoping this course will make me look at my life differently. But that won't be easy because I can't accept truths that are handed to me by others. I have to make sense of things myself."

Charles Dautun, a twenty-year-old junior philosophy major, enrolled in the course because he had taken Deductive Logic with Fishman his freshman year and "loved" it and had, since then, taken several more philosophy classes. In addition, like Shoua and Lindsey, Charles said he "needed hope." In the previous year, he too had experienced devastating losses. His best friend, a young man Charles's age with whom he worked at the local YMCA, had died of bone cancer, and just before Christmas, three weeks before the course began, his girlfriend's brother had been killed in Iraq. The week before Charles and I spoke, his girlfriend had gotten back the ten-page letter she had written her brother on the day he died. Charles fought back tears as he told me, "You don't know what you're gonna do until you're in this situation. . . . My sense now is that I've already hit rock bottom. I can't get no lower. I can only have hope to get better."

The fourth student who said in mid-February that she enrolled in the course because of its subject matter was Beth Blalock, the thirty-six-year-old returning senior philosophy student. Beth told me she was taking the course "to learn about hope." She had had several "traumas" in her life, she said, including a mentally ill mother, a good friend's suicide several years earlier, and a recent divorce. In addition, she told me, she had lost her religion. "If hope isn't in religion, where does it lie?" she asked. "Does it really exist? . . . What I really want to find out is how do you go on when the bottom falls out?"

Finally, Bob Glahn, a twenty-three-year-old senior philosophy major, said that in the month before the semester began he had found himself so depressed that, on some mornings, he "couldn't get out of bed." Among other problems, he told me, he was suffering because the girl he loved had rejected him. Then, as he was deciding what courses to take, he went to the bookstore and saw the books for Fishman's course. He bought one of them, Thich Nhat Hanh's *Touching Peace: Practicing the Art of Mindful Living*, and read it. According to Bob, it helped him so much he signed up for the course. When it turned out that *Touching Peace* was on Fishman's optional list and the class would not discuss it, Bob said he was very disappointed. However, he stuck it out and, at semester's end, told me he was grateful he had done so.

I return to these students in the next chapter when I report on the ideas about hope that they drew upon and most frequently referred to across the semester. In the sections that immediately follow, I describe Fishman's goals in his Hope course for himself and his students, and I outline his assignments and students' reactions to them.

The Teacher's First Goal for Himself and His Students: Co-inquiry

I find that Steve, like most teachers, functions in a variety of ways in the classroom, but the role that he says he strives to adopt—and the one that students most frequently commented on—is that of co-inquirer: a teacher studying a topic who invites his students to join him. This encourages pupils to be somewhat more active in class, to become co-investigators who occasionally play instructor to the teacher and their classmates. In this arrangement, Fishman downplays one sort of authority for another. Rather than gaining authority based exclusively upon knowledge he has already acquired and which he presents to his students, his authority is also based on his ability to lead an investigation, his ability, in this situation, to lead students in an exploration of the nature of hope and its importance for their lives.[3]

As Fishman planned the course, he constructed the syllabus so students could be co-travelers on the journey he himself was taking.[4] He thus assigned readings from Dewey, Marcel, Freire, and Snyder, the theorists who had most influenced his thinking, as well as selections from the twentieth-century German theologian Josef Pieper and contemporary American psychologists Randolph Nesse and Richard Lazarus. Of course, Fishman knew that his students could not follow his exact footsteps since he had spent three years reading in the area before deciding which books of Dewey to include and how to contextualize Dewey with other commentators on hope. Nevertheless, Steve was certain that hearing his students' reactions to the material would be helpful to him, and he also suspected that his students would profit from the fact that he was actively trying to make sense of these same texts himself.

That Fishman wanted to be a co-inquirer with his students is evident from his frequent comments to this effect in class. He told students from the start that he was studying and writing about hope and assured them he had no definite answers about it. He was, he said, "struggling to understand" and "trying to pull threads together." In any case, he told them, it would do them no good even if he did have answers and gave them to them. Echoing the spirit of the Dewey quote I use as the epigraph to this chapter, Steve told the class, "To truly learn something you need to be able to work with others to construct answers to problems you really own." He then made students smile when he told them about one of his undergraduate teachers at Columbia University, Sidney Morgenbesser, who once, when Steve asked Morgenbesser a question, responded, "Fishman, it took me years to figure this out. You think I'm just going to tell you?!"

Steve's genuine desire to engage students in inquiry with him was further evident in his reactions in class. When he felt he understood something in new ways—that he or his students had made new connections or found new "harmonies," to use a Deweyan word—Steve became excited. He waved his arms, punched the air, and spoke animatedly in response to the pupil whose comment had provoked the insight. In my interviews with students, they smiled when they spoke of these occasions and referred to them as Fishman's "aha" moments. In fact, in late February, Shoua Lao told me that she believed she would get an A on her first essay if she could "teach Dr. Fishman something. . . . I've noticed that he gets most excited when he hears something that he hasn't heard before, especially when it's coming from one of us. . . . He also likes it when we see things for the first time."

The Teacher's Second Goal for Students: Bringing the Academic and Personal Together in "Constructed Knowing"

If Fishman's first goal for himself and his students was to become co-investigators of hope, his second was what all teachers want for their students, namely, learning. However, the learning Steve values most is of a special sort, what Mary Belenky and her colleagues call "constructed knowing." In this sort of learning, people use their own lives to connect to and make sense of new material and use new material to shed fresh light on their personal experiences. According to Belenky and her associates, constructed knowers "work to weave together subjective and objective strategies for knowing, to connect personal knowledge with knowledge learned from others." By contrast, the most common form of learning in school involves what Belenky and her colleagues term "received knowing," that is, knowing that devalues personal experience and, instead, involves "receiving and reproducing knowledge from all-knowing external authorities." Belenky and her associates also distinguish "constructed knowing" from "separate knowing." The latter, like received knowing, is extremely common in academia and requires knowers to distance themselves from a belief in order to "doubt" it. That is, separate knowing involves "taking an impersonal and skeptical stance and applying methods that promise objectivity."[5]

THE TEACHER'S HISTORY: LITTLE CONSTRUCTED KNOWING

It is no accident that Fishman works to make space for constructed knowing given his history as a student and a writer. As an undergraduate, Steve himself was, he says, a victim of too much received and separate knowing. He recalls that, in one philosophy class after another, he was trained to learn and then destroy people's arguments, and he was never encouraged to develop his own. Neither was he ever invited by his teachers to ask about the connection between philosophic concepts and his own life. In fact, Steve became so alienated from his studies that, much to his parents' dismay, he refused to participate in his undergraduate commencement ceremony at Columbia. Although he was unable to articulate exactly what had gone wrong, he recalls explaining to his mother that it would be fraudulent to participate since he felt he had accomplished so little. In the end, as Steve tells it, he stuck it out at Columbia and was, eventually, able to complete his Ph.D. But he still felt downhearted. When he left New York City for Charlotte, North Carolina, in 1967 to teach at UNCC, he says that although he was pleased to be joining the philosophic tradition, which he greatly respected, he still felt "empty-handed." That is, he knew quite a lot about philosophy, but he had no idea how to use it to help him live his life. It was not until years later, when he got involved in his university's Writing Across the Curriculum program and began studying learning and writing in his own classroom, that Steve was able to use philosophy—in particular, the work of Dewey—to better understand and reconstruct his own life successes and failures.

Referring to Dewey's essay "Construction and Criticism," Steve told me, "When I first read that piece, I thought Dewey was talking about me. He tells of meeting people who say they were disappointed in—even damaged by—their college education because they were taught only how to criticize others' views but never how to use those criticisms to construct their own positions" (LW 5:134). Steve concluded, "I don't want what happened to me to happen to my students."[6]

THE STUDENTS' HISTORY: LITTLE CONSTRUCTED KNOWING

Fishman's determination to have pupils engage in constructed knowing turned out to be unusual in the experience of eight of his ten students.[7] Although some welcomed constructed knowing and some struggled with it, only one said she did not like it. This was Faith Dennison, the twenty-year-old senior political science major who took the class because it fit her schedule. Faith said Fishman's essays were the first "opinion papers" she had ever been asked to write. In all her previous college courses, she "learned the facts, gave them back to the teacher, got [her] A, and got out." She regretted enrolling, she told me, when she learned that this course would require a different sort of thinking and more work than she had expected.

When I spoke with the other nine students, all philosophy majors, they told me that, unlike Faith, they appreciated Fishman's efforts to apply philosophy to "real life," but they echoed Faith's comments regarding the rarity of this teaching approach. In their philosophy classes, they said, they had seldom been asked to relate academic learning to their personal experiences. Only two said they had previous experience with constructed knowing. Shoua Lao told me that in her Introduction to Philosophy course the previous semester her instructor occasionally welcomed students talking about their lives. Similarly, Beth Blalock said that her Narrative Philosophy instructor, like Fishman, wanted students to use philosophy to explore their personal stories.

Just as most of the philosophy majors in Fishman's class reported that constructed knowing was unfamiliar to them, they also agreed—unanimously—that Fishman's effort to make a place for it altered the tone of class discussion. Fishman sits with his students in a circle and appears, they said, "to really want to know what we think." In fact, Fishman's constructed-knowing stance seemed so unusual to Bob Glahn that he asked me in late February if it were really genuine. "Is Dr. Fishman really interested in understanding what this material means to us? Or is he just making us think that?" Carolyn Kamionka, the forty-two-year-old returning student and Bob's mother, commented in a separate interview about the respectful listening she felt from Fishman and, thus, from her classmates. Carolyn explained that this was a group of veteran philosophy majors with whom she had taken numerous courses, and they often engaged in win-loss, separate-knowing debate. "In other classes, we argue," she told me, "and we sometimes leave not liking each other very much. But we seldom convince each other; we just harden our positions." By contrast, "in the Hope class," Carolyn said, "it's not a debate or argument. The point of this class is to see things differently, and we listen to one another. . . . I often leave class full of thoughts, feeling I have so much left I want to say. Bob and Lindsey and I continue talking as we walk to the parking lot. That's rare."

Senior philosophy major Rebecca Hinson, in an April interview, also contrasted the atmosphere in the Hope class with the disputational climate in the other philosophy class in which she was enrolled that semester. Rebecca commented, "It's not so easy to speak up in my other philosophy class, because I know I'll be attacked by one or more classmates every time. . . . However, in [the Hope] class, because we put so much of ourselves into it, we don't get into those objective conflicts. Instead, we're trying to come to an understanding about something, and we learn by hearing different ways of responding to it." Bob Glahn, at semester's end, returned once again to what he saw as Fishman's unusual teaching style, summing it up with a term he had learned from Gabriel Marcel: "Dr. Fishman doesn't feel it's his automatic duty to argue with us or find holes in what we say. The best way to describe him is that he is 'present' to us."

THE WRITING ASSIGNMENTS: PRACTICING DIFFERENT WAYS OF KNOWING AND SETTING THE CONDITIONS FOR STUDENTS TO BECOME CO-INQUIRERS

Making connections between theory and real-life problems, between school and nonschool concerns, is, then, in Fishman's view, an important part of learning and growth. He thus designs his writing assignments not only to bolster students' skills in critical, separate knowing. He also wants them to engage in constructed knowing, relating ideas from the reading to their own experiences. In addition, Fishman's writing assignments helped students prepare for and practice co-inquiry with him and their peers. These two goals, making space for a variety of ways of knowing and setting the conditions for collaborative teacher-student investigations, lie behind all three types of writing that Fishman assigned: informal in-class writing, homework papers, and end-of-unit essays.

Informal, In-class Writing   Fishman often begins class with a ten-minute free-write that he completes alongside his students.[8] This start-of-class informal writing is Fishman's way of helping pupils gather their thoughts and articulate their own stances before class discussion begins. This is because he not only wants his students to have something to say in class; he also wants them to have a stake in class inquiry. That is, he tries to ensure that their ideas and questions, not just his, shape class discussion. To get at students' concerns, he asks them in their freewrites to respond to a variety of kinds of questions. For example, to promote critical knowing, he may ask them to reflect on a particular quote he selects from the reading or compare this quote with an earlier class text. To promote constructed knowing, he may ask students to describe what stands out for them from the reading and what it means to them. With this same end in view, he may ask them if the assigned reading resonates with their own experiences, and, if so, how it helps explain their own moments of hope or despair.

When I questioned students about how Fishman's informal writing assignments worked for them, the answers I got suggest that these assignments not only helped students practice various ways of knowing; they also helped them move at least part of the way into a co-inquirer role. For example, sophomore Shoua Lao, the least–academically prepared student in the class, said she appreciated them because "it's hard for me to express myself in class, so I would rather do it in writing. Through the freewrites that Dr. Fishman gives us, it's easier for me to release my thoughts. And then, in class, when we discuss them, I sometimes feel I can speak up." At the other end of the spectrum, Rebecca Hinson, probably the class's most academically skilled student, approved of the freewrites for a different reason. For Rebecca, who was, unlike Shoua, comfortable participating in class discussion, these freewrites served to make her contributions more effective. She said, "It's really easy when you start a discussion to jump into it and lose your train of thought and forget what you were going to say. The freewrites help me be more coherent in class." Rebecca added that she was most excited when Dr. Fishman or one of her classmates took something she reported from her freewrite and put it at the center of class discussion.

Eleven Homework Assignments   Nearly every Tuesday of this Tuesday-Thursday class, students were required to bring in typed homework responses to Fishman's questions about the assigned reading for that day. For these homework assignments, Fishman had the same two goals as he had for the in-class writing. I offer as an example the homework assignment that students brought with them to the February 15 class discussion of chapter 1 of Dewey's *Common Faith*, the discussion I describe at some length later in this chapter.

Homework Assignment 6—Chapter 1 of A Common Faith, February 15

Although Dewey denies the existence of a transcendent God in *A Common Faith*, he affirms that certain experiences are dominantly religious.

1. How does Dewey characterize the nature and function of experiences that are dominantly religious?
2. Dewey's view of religious experience leads him to reconstruct the concepts of moral faith, religious faith, and the "unseen power controlling our destiny" (*LW* 9:4, 17). As best you can, please describe Dewey's reconstructions of the concepts of moral faith, religious faith, and the unseen power having control over our destiny.

3. In what ways are these Deweyan reconstructions important for developing a theory of hope for him?
4. In what ways do Dewey's ideas of religion resonate with your own experiences of religion?

In this assignment, students are being asked, in questions 1 and 2, to do separate, critical readings of the text. That is, they must interpret and present material from the text that Dewey himself does not describe clearly. They are also being asked to do constructed knowing, to bring Dewey's ideas together with their own experiences in question 4. In addition, in question 3, Fishman invites students to join him in the class's shared inquiry into a Deweyan theory of hope.

When I interviewed students about the value for them of the homework, they disagreed about it, with some indicating, in effect, that it failed to achieve either of Fishman's objectives and others suggesting that it succeeded, at least in some respects. For example, Christopher Vernarsky complained that for him, the homework was just "busywork." Similarly, Faith Dennison was unhappy with the homework because it took too much time, requiring her to read the selection over and over. "Twenty pages of Dewey!" Faith exclaimed. "When I saw that on the syllabus before the semester started, I thought this course would be easy. But twenty pages of philosophy is not the same as twenty pages in a poly sci text!" Faith admitted, however, that the homework's requiring her to reread the text and try to put her ideas on paper was helpful. "At least I have some idea about the readings and, therefore, am not as silent in class as I might be. But I'm still frustrated," she said. "I'm used to facts and numbers, right and wrong, rather than these endless ethereal discussions of ideas."

By contrast, several students spoke more positively about the homework. For example, Beth Blalock, the thirty-six-year-old senior philosophy major, found that the homework assignments helped her figure out what she cared about in the readings. She told me, "When it came time to write the first essay, I had already done a lot of investigation in my homework papers, so I could go back to the places where I talked about the parts of Dewey I loved. I made index cards of the quotes I wanted to use, and these helped me pull my essay together."

Three Essays   Like the in-class and homework writing, the essays Fishman assigned required critical and constructed knowing and asked students to report on their progress as active investigators into the nature of hope. That is, Steve asked students in their essays to report on what they learned from the assigned literature, how this contributed to their emerging theory of hope, and how this emerging theory affected their lives. The three essays that students were required to write came at the ends of major units: at the close of five and one-half weeks spent reading Dewey, after three weeks discussing Pieper and Marcel, and at the end of two weeks reading Freire and Snyder. For all of the essays, students spent the class period prior to the due date in small groups responding to one another's drafts. Fishman read and graded the essays, and, for essays 1 and 2, he audiotaped his comments, recording a cassette for each student that lasted between eight and twelve minutes. On the third and final essay, Steve wrote his comments on each student's paper.[9]

These essays presented a challenge to nearly all of Fishman's students who, as I have said, were inexperienced with constructed knowing. Although by the time the first essay was due on February 24 students had been given opportunities to practice this sort of thinking, speaking, and writing in their homework and class work, six of the ten told me they were still uncomfortable, for a variety of reasons, when it came to writing this essay. Generally speaking, they had trouble balancing the two sides of constructed knowing. That is, either they struggled to understand and articulate what they had read from Dewey, or they were unable—or unwilling—to find the relevance of Deweyan theory to their own lives.

Among those students who struggled with the personal side of constructed knowing was Stan Lefcoski. This twenty-one-year-old junior philosophy major brought no personal issues at all into essays 1 and 2. This may be because Lefcoski was a philosophy student who clearly enjoyed "separate knowing," a young man who saw himself as skilled at the sort of win-loss debate that students told me characterized many of their other classes, and he was unwilling to give it up. Stan explained, "You've got to be sharp when you enter a philosophy class. You've got to be ready to argue." And, he said, he enjoyed recounting to his non-philosopher friends the arguments advanced by the philosophers whom he had studied. Stan's unwillingness or inability to engage in constructed knowing characterized his homework and in-class writing as well. Across most of the semester, he seemed to avoid Fishman's questions, using them instead as an opportunity to speak only generally about the assigned reading. He adopted a kind of universal, omniscient voice that he evidently thought characterized philosophic writing and argumentation. In addition, Stan could not profit from the peer-response days because he either was absent or came to the group sessions without a draft. However, in Stan's third essay, and without help from peers, he finally took Fishman's invitation seriously to say something about how the course had affected him and what he might take from it. Ironically, what Stan said was that the course, along with other life events, had called into question for him the value of the sort of philosophic, separate knowing discourse around which he had so shaped his identity.

Like Stan Lefcoski, Beth Blalock struggled with the personal side of constructed knowing, but unlike Stan, she participated in and profited from small-group response to her draft of essay 1. Beth, a student whose academic record was, she said, a "disaster," came to the response group with some nervousness. However, she told me, "when I read my draft aloud to the group, they heard things that needed adjusting, like I had too many quotes from Dewey and not enough connections to my own life." Beth also explained that her experience in the small group gave her the same sense of cooperative community that she felt in the classroom. "People in my group," Beth said, "actually stopped and listened and helped me get my point across. They reminded me, like Dr. Fishman does in class, to tell why I like these passages and what they meant to me." With this support from her group, Beth did manage to write a paper that Fishman, knowing her difficulties as a student, considered a remarkable effort to use her own concerns to organize some very complicated sections of Dewey's texts.

In the group that struggled with the other side of constructed knowing—the academic side—was Shoua Lao who had had little experience with reading and writing about philosophic texts. So, in all three of Shoua's essays, she presented personal narratives that were never convincingly related to the readings. Her peers, as they read her first-draft accounts of her life experiences, pointed to places they thought she might insert ideas and quotes from the readings. She tried to do this before handing her final drafts to Fishman, but her essays remained first and foremost personal narratives and suffered from what Fishman deemed an inadequate understanding of the philosophic literature.

Like Shoua Lao, twenty-year-old philosophy major Charles Dautun struggled with the academic side of constructed knowing. His draft of the first essay recounted a life experience he wanted to explore: the death of his best friend a year earlier. Charles's challenge was to theorize his personal narrative with Deweyan insights. After class on the day he handed his finished essay to Fishman, he told me in an interview, "Trying to bring Dewey in was the hardest thing. . . . There was so much material, and every time I tried to bring in something, I felt like I couldn't use that without adding something else. But I did it, and I think it's a paper I'll want to keep and reread down the road." Ultimately, as I show in the next chapter, Charles managed to connect philosophic theory to his personal life in ways that brought both alive.

Like Beth Blalock, Charles Dautun spoke in glowing terms about his experience in his draft-response group. He commented that he had never seen a group of students working so hard to help each other. "Usually we just read each others' papers and pretty much ignore them, maybe write a couple of remarks on them. I guess it's the way Dr. Fishman brings his class together, like we all feel part of the class, and this is the way we all work together. We all try to learn from each other. We're not just trying to get through."

Some students struggled with constructed knowing for reasons other than their inability to master the texts or find ways the texts were personally meaningful. For example, some had difficulty with constructed knowing because they did not believe Fishman was really serious about his request for it. For this and other reasons, they could not surrender their belief that academic papers are about giving back to the teacher what the teacher already knows. One student who found herself in this position was Lindsey Weston, the twenty-one-year-old Air National Guard reservist who hoped Fishman's course might restore some of her faith in humanity. Lindsey found herself in a contradictory position because she was sensitive to Fishman's call for constructed knowing but, at the same time, fearful of surrendering her normal received-knower stance. On the one hand, she told me that she was a person who had to construct her own solutions to problems and insisted that Fishman's role as a teacher was not to "hand out answers" but to lead her to her own. In line with her desire to do constructed knowing, Lindsey chose in her first paper to explore her Kuwait experience, trying to examine it through Deweyan lenses. Yet Lindsey was also a person who cared desperately about grades since she was headed for graduate school, likely in her other major, psychology. Thus, on draft-response day, Lindsey seemed far less concerned with what she wanted to say or with feedback from peers than she was with getting to Fishman after class to ask him what he *really* wanted, what, in effect, she needed to do to get an A.

Fishman told me later that he found the conversation with Lindsey—and Faith Dennison, who joined Lindsey—very difficult. "I can't tell Lindsey and Faith what Dewey means to them and their lives." Indeed, as a teacher who values constructed knowing and active inquiry, he can only try to set conditions that lead students, with help from their peers and teacher, to generate their own answers. This was frustrating for both Lindsey and Faith, but Lindsey, as I show in the next chapter, was able by her third essay to apply hope theory to her life in fruitful ways.

These students' essay writing experiences show the challenges for teachers who want to adopt a co-inquirer stance and make space for constructed knowing. First, they have to help students like Lindsey Weston, pupils who are attracted by constructed knowing but conditioned to be received knowers, trust that they are serious about wanting students to explore new material by talking about what it means to them. Second, they need to help students like Stan Lefcoski, pupils who view personal experience as irrelevant to learning new material, see constructed knowing as a potentially fruitful way to master new material. That is, even if students disvalue reconstructing and getting insight into their own experiences, constructed knowing can be presented as a useful tool for making philosophic texts more interesting and memorable. Finally, teachers have to help students like Shoua Lao, pupils who have trouble reading the texts, see that struggling to master the reading is worthwhile. If such pupils are patient, they can use their own life concerns to help them make their way into new literature.

CLASS DISCUSSION: PRACTICING DIFFERENT WAYS OF KNOWING AND TEACHER-STUDENT CO-INQUIRY

In this section, I show Steve Fishman, in one class session, trying to orchestrate various ways of knowing while engaging in co-inquiry with his students. To do this, Steve takes what I call an "indirect" teaching approach.[10] That is, instead of going directly into Dewey's text and lecturing about it, Steve tries to set the conditions for students to use their personal experiences to get into new academic material. This indirect approach often works effectively to involve students with new literature. However, as I will show, it also has its dangers.

Central among these is that when Fishman invites students to lead with their personal experiences, he cannot know in advance where the discussion will go. He poses a question about students' own lives that he intends will result in meaningful interaction with the assigned text, but it does not always work this way. For example, in the class I am about to describe, Steve worries, as students recount their personal experiences, that they are leading the group further away from, not closer to, Dewey's text. At times like these, Steve must make split-second decisions about whether to intervene, and, if so, how best to do it. On the other hand, using students' personal concerns to initiate discussion can lead to heightened interest. Because students set the table, so to speak, they are in a position to be genuine co-investigators; they cannot easily adopt the familiar role of passive received knower that, as I have shown, is sometimes hard to surrender. Indirect teaching of this sort is not easy, as Dewey himself points out, since it is never routine and the instructor must not only know the subject matter but also be sensitive to student psychology and group dynamics. Yet, Fishman says, for him, it is worthwhile when the class achieves the sort of ricochet he wants among the personal, the text, and the group.[11]

Problems Using Students' Personal Experiences to Master New Material: Too Much Personal Experience and Not Enough New Material In order to illustrate the challenges associated with Fishman's teaching approach, I roll the tape of the February class discussion of chapter 1 of *A Common Faith*. When students arrived in class that day, the eleventh meeting of the semester, they brought with them typed answers to the four homework questions I listed on pp. 114–15. Fishman began class by giving students a five-minute history of *A Common Faith*—the debate among Douglas Macintosh, Henry Wieman, and Max Otto that led Dewey to write the book in 1934,[12] and then Steve put them in pairs. He asked students to exchange their homework papers and become, in effect, co-inquirers. After reading each other's homework, he wanted students to write two things on their partner's paper. "First, tell your partner what you learned about *A Common Faith* from reading their home-work, and, second, ask them a question about Dewey's work that remains puzzling to you." To complete this assignment, students moved across the circle to join their assigned classmate, and the two worked together, first silently, reading and writing, and then chatting with one another. In asking students to read and comment on each other's work, Fishman is giving them an opportunity to see that it is not only the teacher who has answers and insights. Their peers—and they themselves—do as well.

After about fifteen minutes of working in pairs, students complied with Fishman's request to come back into a circle. He started discussion with a constructed knowing question that he intended would lead the group to important issues in or questions about Dewey's text. Fishman called first on Christopher Vernarsky who was sitting two seats to his left.

"Well, Chris, what did you think of this chapter?" Steve asked.

Chris glanced down at his copy of *A Common Faith* and then looked back up at Fishman. "I love this book. I read it last semester in Dr. Eldridge's class, and I've gone through it once or twice since then. When I first read it, I felt like Dewey was saying something that I had believed for a long time. I was raised Catholic, and although I have lapsed, I still believe in God, but I don't like the Church's organizational structure. . . . When I read this book, I couldn't believe someone wrote it seventy years ago and I didn't know about it."

Fishman listened and nodded, and, at the point Chris said he had read the book several times, responded, "Really!" When Chris finished, Steve prodded him to say more with another constructed knowing question: "Can you tell us why you like the book so much?"

"Because Dewey agrees with me about how limiting organized religion can be. And he says you can have religious experiences that change your life that have absolutely nothing to do with the Church. He wants us to turn our focus from the supernatural to the natural. . . . Finding out that there was respectable support for my position kind of gave me hope for the future. The comfort of company made me feel more secure somehow." Chris then read the passage from chapter 1 in which Dewey says that the adjective "religious" is not necessarily connected with an institution or system of beliefs. Rather, "it denotes attitudes that may be taken toward every object and every proposed end or ideal" (*LW* 9:8).

When Steve and I reviewed the videotape of this class, he recalled that, at this point in the discussion, he was not sure what to do next. He was tempted to pursue an avenue that Chris had opened, going directly into Dewey's text to clarify what Dewey means by "religious experience." However, Steve sensed that it was too soon for that, that pushing students too early back to the assigned reading might make them feel that their own experiences with religion were irrelevant. So he decided that rather than asking students to be separate and received knowers at this point in class discussion, he would, instead, keep going indirectly at the text by asking another personal-experience question. That is, he would assume students had a rough-and-ready idea of what Dewey means by "religious experience" and see if they could use their own lives to work their way into the text rather than the other way around.

"Chris, let me ask you this," Steve said. "Have you ever had a religious experience? I don't want to be too personal, but I wonder if you have ever had the sort of religious experience Dewey talks about."

Steve remembers that the minute he posed this question he felt relieved and energized. Although he had no idea what students would say, he was genuinely interested in finding out. Furthermore, he believed his question would help students feel that they were crucial to this inquiry. They would, thus, he believed, become more involved in the discussion than if, too early, he had made Dewey's text the sole focus of attention. Steve turned out to be correct: his question started a conversation that engaged the class for the next twenty minutes.

Before answering Fishman's question, Chris stopped to think. He seemed to need a moment to consider how the Deweyan ideas he had just praised actually played out in his own life. "Yes," Chris said, "I've had what might be called a religious experience. But it's not a specific moment, like Tuesday morning at ten o'clock. It's more like the process of having a religious outlook. It's not like you get it today. You've got to keep working on it."

When Chris finished, three students indicated they wanted to speak. In what followed, all three, like Chris, described their falling away from organized religion and their appreciation of Dewey's notion that, despite rejecting the Church, they could still have religious experiences. Although they all mentioned an aspect of the text they found personally relevant, they focused more on their reasons for leaving the Church than on Dewey's notion of religious experience and whether they had ever had such an experience.

The first student to speak after Chris was Carolyn Kamionka who described her own rejection of established religion. Noting an idea from chapter 1 of *A Common Faith*, she remarked that Dewey says that non-Church-related religious experiences happen more frequently than we appreciate. Carolyn told of being raised Catholic in an oppressive situation in which she had been punished by her parents and teachers for questioning Church dogma. She finally left the Church, she said, when she had children. "I knew I had to break the cycle. I said, 'I can't teach this to my kids.' I wanted them to be able to think for themselves. . . . Like Chris says, you have to focus on the natural. . . . And you don't have to go into a Catholic church and see a statue. Religious experiences can be anywhere."

Fishman nodded appreciatively, pleased that Carolyn had noted something she remembered from the text, but her comments did not achieve the balance of personal experience and exploration of Dewey that he wanted. Steve felt that her criticism of the Church did not really drive her into the heart of chapter 1, that is, into Dewey's efforts to redefine religious experience in a broader, more inclusive way than does organized religion. However, Steve decided not to interrupt the line of discussion at this time. Instead, he called on the next student whose hand was raised, Faith Dennison, to see how she would answer his question and whether she would take the class further into Dewey's work.

Faith Dennison, although a practicing Catholic, offered support for Carolyn's assessment of the dogmatic nature of the Church, describing the "ruler-on-the-knuckles" Catholic schooling she herself had endured. "Although my family still goes to church, we jokingly refer to ourselves as Catholic Lite," she said. Faith then described a movie she had seen recently, *Stigmata*, that had opened her eyes to the notion that "Jesus is in nature." "Ever since I saw that movie," she said, "I now look at small moments as being religious." Faith then described such a "small moment," picking up on one aspect of

Dewey's religious experience—that it provides a sense of security and peace. "I was having a horrible day last week," she explained, "but, then, as I was driving home from work, a great song came on the radio. I rolled down the windows, let the air blow through my hair, and I felt like I was flying. I felt calm, at peace, like I sometimes do when I'm sitting outside and see the sun break free from the clouds. . . . I try to build on these small moments so I can be, as Dewey says, a religious person rather than just a person of religion."

Although Fishman, once again, was gratified by this student's picking up on Dewey's idea that a renewed sense of peace is one consequence of religious experience, he feared that Faith might be trivializing Dewey's notion of religious experience or that she might not have read Dewey carefully. However, he did not want to point this out to her. It might seem too much like an attack, one that would discourage her and her classmates' efforts to work their way into Dewey's reconstruction of religious experience. So Steve thanked Faith for her comments and turned to Bob Glahn, the third student waiting to comment.

Bob contributed another condemnation of institutional religion but did not, as Steve wished, take the class to a careful consideration of what Dewey means by "religious experience." In fact, Bob brought a new idea to the discussion, espousing the radical—and un-Deweyan—position that traditional communities have no redeeming features at all. Taking off from Dewey's critique of established religion as being too authoritarian, Bob explained how his own individuality had been so suppressed by church groups—both Catholic and Protestant—that he concluded that, for people like himself who are concerned with individual creativity (Bob is minoring in theater), such groups are just downright dangerous. Bob concluded that people who attend church on Sundays are not really religious. They are just going through the motions, acting, according to Bob, like "sheep." "Why should I follow a shepherd and join the flock? When is it ever good to be a sheep? I personally feel that religion destroys the concept of religious experience!" After apologizing to the group for his "personal diatribe," Bob went even further, claiming that prayers that are recited by memory across generations are "meaningless, just empty words. They lose any significance because they aren't created by the people who mouth them. Prayers should come with a warning: Do not repeat." He then told the class that a religious experience for him is what Thich Nhat Hanh describes as being able to live in the present moment.

As Chris, Carolyn, Faith, and Bob critiqued institutional religion and described their own alternative religious experiences, another pupil, Beth Blalock, had been listening carefully. But Beth looked puzzled. She raised her hand, and, in a moment of critical knowing that she later told me was very important for her, she posed a question that she "was afraid to ask." She recalled, "All these people were talking about their religious experiences, and I wondered if these were really what Dewey had in mind. Is it enough just to have a great moment driving your car, or seeing the clouds part and the sun come through? Are religious experiences just these little moments that make life worth living, or are they something more? I really wanted to know."

When Fishman called on her, Beth began by telling the class that although she was a Baptist, not a Catholic, and had served as an interim youth minister, she too had left the Church. "I realized that I could not, in good conscience, tell young people that if you follow these guidelines, your life will be better. I wasn't sure I believed in them myself. I saw contradictions between them and my own life, and I knew the ministry was not where I belonged." Beth continued, "But my question is this. I understand that Dewey separates religion from religious experience, and I understand that you can have religious experience away from rituals. But how do you know when you have one? What is Dewey describing? I wonder if I've ever really had a religious experience in his sense. Is it just these small moments, or is it something broader, something more special?"

Achieving Greater Personal and Academic Balance   Fishman was delighted by Beth's contribution and said so. "That's a wonderful question, Beth! Yes, let's try to pin some things down here. Let's take a closer look at what Dewey means when he talks about religious experience." When Beth spoke, Fishman recalls, he felt it was, at that moment, a good time to encourage students to go back into Dewey's text. This is because they now had a reason to look more closely at it, a need for clarification that had grown out of their own interests, one that they themselves owned. It was no longer the teacher handing students the answer. It was, rather, a group of inquirers trying to figure things out together.

Fishman began this text-oriented segment of class discussion—one that also lasted about twenty minutes—by crediting Faith Dennison with naming two of Dewey's criteria for religious experience: feelings of security and peace. Fishman then returned to her example of driving and said that whether this is a religious experience for Faith, according to Dewey, depends on how long her sense of security and peace lasts.

Fishman then told the class that in addition to security and peace, there were other criteria for Dewey of a religious experience. Trying to maintain something of the co-inquirer stance, Steve softened his comments with a characteristic disclaimer: "I'm not sure about all this. I'm trying to figure it out myself. I'm trying to piece things together. . . . [But] I think Dewey would say that an experience is 'religious' if it is powerful enough to get us through darkness and despair. That is, if it involves loyalty to ideals—like art, companionship, love, justice, helping others—that are strong enough to unify our life and, despite failures and discouragement, keep us soldiering on." Steve then asked Chris to read aloud the passage in which Dewey discusses these aspects of religious experience.

When Chris finished, Steve thanked him, and, in the final five minutes of this twenty-minute segment, Fishman seemed to lift the veil on his own inquiry process, thinking aloud about the text and its meaning to him. Steve began, "Ah, that phrase, 'darkness and despair.' I love Dewey's words. They mean a lot to me. Devotion to ideals helps me carry on the fight even when things look bleak, and it makes me feel part of a community. Dewey's big on community. His hope is that we'll feel enough part of the world and the human community that we'll continue to work for our ideals despite our setbacks and disappointments." He also responded to Bob: "Yes, Bob, communities can render us sheep, but we have to rely on others. We're creative and unique, but we need others to get where we're going. I know that when I recite prayers, I connect to the past because I think of those who have written and said them before me. Similarly, when I commit to an ideal, one that has been shared by countless others, my sense of fellowship with them helps me go on."

Steve paused and began again. "I go back to a passage in *Human Nature and Conduct* that means a lot to me, and I thank Dewey for writing it. He tells us, there is great wisdom in the old pagan saying that we must be grateful to those who suffered so we could be here today. This also helps me feel part of the human community. It helps me feel connected to Dewey . . . just as it helps me feel connected to everyone present as we break Dewey bread together." Steve then concluded with another typical move: he apologized for speaking so long. "Sorry to go on like that, but I get excited when you all help me pull threads together."[13]

With about fifteen minutes left in the class period, Fishman turned to Lindsey Weston. "Lindsey," Steve said, "you've not spoken yet. Were there puzzling things for you in chapter 1?"

Lindsey responded, "Can you ask me a more specific question?"

"Well, what stands out for you from this chapter? Does anything resonate with you particularly?"

"I don't really know. I don't have any burning comments. Well, I guess there are a couple things, thanks to Faith's homework paper." Lindsey, who had been paired with Faith Dennison at the beginning of the class, asked Faith to hand her homework paper back to her so she could remember exactly what she had been impressed by. Looking at Faith's homework, Lindsey said, "Faith says that, for Dewey, religious experience is not about your sacrifice to an unknown God but about actions that serve the greater good in this world. That reminded me, like you just said, Dr. Fishman, about respecting our ancestors' struggles and building on those. Religious experience and gratitude to our ancestors fit together, I think. Dewey wants us to honor the past, but he also wants us to question it. At first, this seemed inconsistent to me. But I think what Dewey wants is for us to respect what has been passed down to us but not adopt it totally. He also does not want us to reject the past entirely. Instead, you should make adjustments and add your own input. In this way, like we were saying last week, your small actions, your small footprints on earth, can have a big impact." Lindsey paused and looked at Fishman. "Is this any help in our quest for the elusive Deweyan theory of hope?"

Steve responded, "Yes, yes!" As he and I later discussed the videotape of this class, he explained that not only was he thrilled that Lindsey was able to learn from Faith, but he was also gratified by Lindsey's contribution to the ongoing class inquiry into Dewey's theory of hope. First, it showed the long distance Lindsey had come in her understanding of Dewey—in particular, her reading of certain tensions she continued to hear in his work. However, instead of dismissing Dewey as being "inconsistent" and "contradicting himself," as she had done earlier in the semester, Lindsey seemed to be growing more sensitive to the fact that Dewey was trying to reconcile false dualisms. Second, Steve was pleased that Lindsey had, evidently, listened carefully to Bob's position, his extreme rejection of communal traditions, and was able to entertain it but not accept it completely. That is, she was unwilling to throw out all communal traditions and, thereby, overlook what we might learn from them. Finally, Steve was gratified that Lindsey stepped explicitly into the co-inquirer role when she wondered if her interpretation might be important in "our quest for the elusive Deweyan theory of hope." Steve's pleasure with Lindsey's remarks was also accompanied by his satisfaction that his indirect teaching approach had, apparently, been effective with Lindsey. I will explain further Steve's satisfaction and this aspect of Lindsey's achievement when I discuss Lindsey in greater detail in the next chapter.

The end-of-class bell had already rung by the time Lindsey finished speaking. Steve and his students gathered their papers and returned the desks they had arranged in a circle back to their original straight rows. The videotape shows that as Lindsey, Bob, and Carolyn left the room, they were still conversing.

Conclusion

In this chapter, I have described Steve Fishman's Philosophy and Practice of Hope course, offering some sense of the participants, the assignments, Steve's pedagogical approach, and the nature of classroom discussion. In addition to wanting to help teachers who might like to offer such a course, I provide this information so that my readers will understand the context for the student learning that occurred in Fishman's class. In the next chapter, I offer details about the concepts from Dewey and other authors that students reported they found most useful, the ideas that most affected their levels of hope.

SEVEN

Undergraduates in a Course on Hope

Lucille McCarthy

> Every experience lives on in further experiences. Hence the central problem of . . . education . . . is to select the kind of present experiences that live fruitfully and creatively in subsequent experiences.
>
> —John Dewey, *Experience and Education* (*LW* 13:13)

In this chapter, I describe what Steve Fishman's ten students got out of his class, The Philosophy and Practice of Hope. As I tell these students' stories, I focus on the ideas and experiences that were most important to them and that they said they would take with them from the course. These ideas and experiences are the ones they referred to most frequently in their writing, their interviews with me across the semester, and their classroom exchanges.

In the previous chapter, I reported that Fishman's students generally gave me one of two reasons for enrolling. Five of the ten said it was because they "needed more hope." Four said they signed up because they knew Fishman was a good teacher, and one student, the only non-philosophy major, Faith Dennison, said she took the course simply because it fit her schedule and satisfied a graduation requirement. In the first section of this chapter, I report my findings about the five students who said they needed more hope and believed the course might be of personal value. In the second section, I report on the other five pupils, those who came to Fishman's Hope class with less perceived need for the course subject matter.

Five Students Who Enrolled Because They "Needed More Hope"

The five students who had suffered major hardships prior to the course and were attracted to it because of its content all had, by semester's end, gained insights that, they said, had raised their levels of hope. Although these five pupils drew concepts from a number of the authors they read during the semester, four of them said it was Dewey's work that was most important to them.[1] In addition, all five, in varying degrees, credited the collaborative classroom climate with helping them understand the material and explore its possible meaning for their lives.

I start with Shoua Lao and Charles Dautun, two pupils who had suffered personal tragedies just before the course began.

Shoua Lao

Nineteen-year-old sophomore Shoua Lao enrolled in the course because, she told me, she "had to." She saw its title and went to some lengths to rearrange her schedule, believing that the course might help her with the despair she was experiencing. Shoua's hopelessness, as I described in the previous chapter, resulted from three recent deaths of people close to her: her grandfather, her young uncle, and, two months before the course began, her boyfriend, who committed suicide. These tragedies caused Shoua to do poorly in her courses the previous semester, and, as if that were not enough, she told me she had no friends on campus and felt alienated from her family as well.

Because Shoua knew that she was inadequately prepared for Fishman's course—she had previously taken only two philosophy courses—she spoke with him just prior to the initial class meeting. She stopped him in the hallway to explain her situation as he was about to enter the classroom. In that conversation Steve encouraged Shoua to enroll despite her concerns, and she worked hard across the semester to master complicated material. To compensate for the difficulty she had understanding the reading, in her eleven homework papers Shoua either quoted extensively from the text or spent most of her paper talking about her personal experience. Similarly, as I noted earlier, she brought drafts of her essays to the peer-review sessions that were long personal accounts that her classmates tried to help her theorize. Because of Shoua's problems reading the assigned material, she was never successful with constructed knowing.

However, if Shoua profited minimally from her efforts at constructed know-ing, she learned a great deal as a result of the cooperative climate in Fishman's classroom. She was impressed by the fact that other students listened sympa-thetically to her experiences with hope and despair. She was equally struck by the fact that they were willing to share their own stories. In addition, Shoua felt accepted by a group that was open to a variety of points of view. This was in marked contrast with her own Hmong community that, she told me, was extremely rigid, especially with regard to the education and independence of women. "My parents are always worrying that I'll bring shame to them and the ancestors and damage my family's reputation in the community. I argue with my mom because she tells me I am only a girl and girls are expected to obey."

The most dramatic moment of the semester for Shoua—one in which stu-dents' respect for one another played a central role—occurred in a class session in mid-March. Fishman began by asking students to write about the reasons Dewey would give people for going on despite life's calamities. Fishman also asked students, "What would you personally say to the questions 'Why go on? Why not commit suicide?'?" When discussion started and it was Shoua's turn to tell what she had written, she was able, in a halting voice, to read her response to the question about Dewey. However, when she attempted to read her own reasons for going on, she could only choke out, "It affects the people who love you, and I wouldn't want anyone in my family to go through that," before she began to cry. Her classmates responded with obvious sympathy, two of them, Beth Blalock and Lindsey Weston, sharing stories about friends who committed suicide or attempted suicide and the pain they had felt in those instances. Then forty-two-year-old Carolyn Kamionka, who was sitting next to Shoua, turned to her, put her hand on her knee, and made a comment that Shoua told me in an interview two months later meant a great deal to her. Carolyn told the class that although she did not know specifically what Shoua's situation was, she was aware that when she herself gets really down, it is because she forgets that she is not alone. She forgets that others do care and that if she would just reach out and ask for help, someone would take time to listen to her. Carolyn's comment, Shoua recalled, made her feel like she "belonged," and it presented a model of response that, since then, had been helpful to her.

Thanks to Carolyn Kamionka's remark, Shoua told me, she began to see that she was having trouble making friends at UNCC "not because no one wants to be around me, as I used to think, but because I was distancing myself from people. I realized that sometimes I have to be the one who makes the first move." Put differently, Shoua realized that she had to do the same sort of reaching out that Carolyn, Beth, and Lindsey had done for her. In fact, Shoua had actually practiced this, she was pleased to tell me at the end of the semester, with a young woman in another class. This student had spoken to Shoua and seemed to need a friend. "It's like Carolyn did for me," Shoua told me. "By caring about someone else, you can really help them. It makes you both feel like you belong." In this final interview, Shoua also told me that she was working harder to step into her mother's shoes. She was beginning to realize that there were good things about the Hmong community as well as features she did not like, and she vowed to avoid behaving in ways that might cause her mother unnecessary anguish while, at the same time, continuing to defend her independence.

In sum, although Shoua was not particularly successful applying theoretic concepts from the readings to her own life, she did profit from the collaborative climate in Fishman's classroom. In my last interview with her in May, she recalled the first day of the semester when she had spoken with Fishman in the hallway before class began. She said that after she explained to him her worries about her ability to handle the material, he said that when he was a sophomore he too had enrolled in a class that was too difficult for him, and, although he never caught up to the more senior students, he learned some valuable things. Shoua concluded, "Dr. Fishman encouraged me to do the same, saying that I would get something out of it even if, at times, I was frustrated and could not keep up with the others. Him saying that he'd had this experience too and that he was sympathetic with how I felt made me feel that it would be safe to be in the class."

Charles Dautun

Every act is possessed of infinite import.
—John Dewey, *Human Nature and Conduct* (*MW* 14:180)

Like Shoua, twenty-one-year-old junior Charles Dautun enrolled in the Hope class having recently experienced personal tragedies. His best friend had died the previous year, and his girlfriend's brother had just been killed in Iraq. However, unlike Shoua, Charles did not complete the course. Charles dropped out of school for financial reasons about halfway into the semester, shortly after the group completed reading Dewey and writing their first essay. As a result, the data I have about Charles are limited. They include an hourlong mid-February interview and two brief phone interviews, one just after he withdrew and the other at semester's end; his written work, including essay 1 on Dewey; and my observations of his class participation, both in person and on videotape, during the six weeks he attended.

Compared to Shoua, Charles was far more successful with constructed knowing, and he, like the three others I discuss in this group, said Dewey's ideas were helpful to him. This was despite the fact that Charles struggled initially to make sense of Dewey. In fact, on the second day of the semester, he openly admitted to the class that he needed to read the selection from *Human Nature and Conduct* several times to understand it. He then proceeded to mistakenly attribute to Dewey the position that Dewey was actually criticizing. Fishman's response was to thank Charles for his candor about the challenges he faced reading Dewey and to admit that he too sometimes had trouble understanding him. However, Steve then directed Charles and the class back to the passage that Charles had misinterpreted, and they read it together so that Charles and others could become clearer on Dewey's meaning. I cannot say exactly when or how Charles came to grasp and appreciate Dewey's ideas, but I have little doubt that moments in class like the one I have just described, as well as Charles's frequent participation in class discussion, played a role. In any case, at the end of five and a half weeks of reading Dewey, when it came time to write his essay, Charles had come to admire Dewey and was able to apply some Deweyan concepts to his own life.

One of the two ideas in Dewey that "bedazzled" Charles, to use a word from his essay, was Dewey's view that habits change over generations and that they can be intentionally and intelligently shaped over time. In this regard, Charles was very impressed with Dewey's activist efforts and what Charles saw as Dewey's unrelenting confidence that things could be made better. He told me that he loved the positive approach Dewey took. Of all of the philosophers he had read, Charles said, none went beyond his or her critiques of things like Dewey to make suggestions for improvements. According to Charles, "Dewey wasn't just sitting in a classroom declaring what was wrong with the world; he was trying to be part of the solution."

Charles's respect for Dewey's reform efforts was evident on the day the class read aloud Dewey's 1933 *Encyclopedia of Social Science* article recounting his decade-long participation in the "Outlawry of War" movement (*LW* 8:13–18). In this article, Charles heard Dewey's arguments against those who claim that war is inevitable since it is a necessary expression of a fixed part of human nature. Charles admitted that he himself was politically conservative, and, thus, "believing all war will end is a little far-fetched for me." However, Charles was open to Dewey's argument that the practice of war is simply a social habit, and, like all social customs, the impulses behind it can be expressed in more positive ways. He told the class that Dewey's effort to make a difference by working to reduce war "has refreshed me." Although Dewey and the Outlawry of War movement failed, Charles concluded, there was no telling what impact Dewey's efforts might have on future social institutions and customs.

In Charles's essay, he brings to bear on his own life this Deweyan idea that social customs are simply habits and can be, across generations, intentionally redirected. Regarding the death of his best friend, Montrail, Charles found solace in the idea that Montrail's work with disadvantaged children in a YMCA after-school program had positive consequences beyond anything "Trail" could have dreamed of. He writes that at Trail's funeral, many of the kids that Trail worked with, most of whom had behavioral problems, came to pay their respects and reported they were now doing well in their middle and high schools. Charles also, in his essay, draws comfort from Dewey's related idea that all of our actions have infinite import and that small things may add up to surprisingly big things. He writes,

> John Dewey is claiming that if you believe in something and work at it, although you may be the only one, your idea will continue and may, perhaps, one day be realized. Although Trail and I were just two kids with a little hope and a vision of changing some children's lives around, we made a big difference in their lives. On the first day of this Hope class, someone said that hope is contagious. Well, I agree. Dewey has influenced my way of thinking, and even if I'm the only one to think this way, and even if my contributions seem small, I may influence the world.

Thus, although Charles's stay in Fishman's class was limited, he told me soon after dropping out that he had gotten a great deal from it. He said that writing the essay about Dewey and connecting Dewey to his own life had not been easy. However, he also said that when he was able to employ some of Dewey's concepts to help him reconceive the life of his friend Montrail, he was excited. It was the first paper he had written at school, he explained, that he was truly proud of. When I spoke with Charles on the phone at the end of the semester, he told me that he was still using these Deweyan concepts to help him be supportive of his girlfriend and her family. He was hopeful, he remarked, that his small acts of kindness and support toward them, like

Trail's toward the YMCA children, might eventually have equally positive results.

Beth Blalock

> Only when the past ceases to trouble and anticipations of the future
> are not perturbing is a being wholly united with his environment and
> therefore fully alive.
>
> —John Dewey, *Art as Experience* (*LW* 10:24)

Beth Blalock, the thirty-six-year-old senior philosophy major, like Charles Dautun, did not complete the course. She withdrew from school, also for financial reasons, just after the class finished reading Gabriel Marcel, about three-quarters of the way through the semester. I have fuller data on Beth than Charles since she stayed in class longer and, in addition, was employed on campus and agreed to meet me for an hourlong interview at semester's end.

Like many of her classmates, Beth struggled with constructed knowing, and, like Charles, she found Dewey difficult to follow at first. She explained to me that she used a ruler when she read and went line by line, sometimes reading aloud, so she would slow down and focus. She also copied sentences that she understood and liked on three-by-five cards. However, she still had trouble "absorbing the material" and told the class at the beginning of the late-January session when they were about to discuss chapter 2 of *Experience and Nature*, "I have no idea what Dewey's main point is." Although once again I cannot say exactly when and how Beth overcame her early frustration with Dewey, she was, ultimately, able to understand and use some Deweyan concepts to reconceive her experiences. These concepts, she said, helped her put her trials and difficulties in a new light and see that, despite all the troubles she had experienced—including a mentally ill mother, bouts of depression herself, and her recent divorce—there were still reasons to be hopeful.

The Deweyan ideas that Beth said gave her hope and allowed her to find new reasons to go on in hard times were, first, Dewey's claim that our links to the human community mean that we have obligations to act responsibly because our actions affect those who follow us. The second idea that Beth took from Dewey, one that she read aloud in class during a discussion of *Art as Experience*, was that to live in hope is to experience the present without regrets about the past or fears about the future.

Beth expressed the importance of Dewey's notion of the continuity of the human community during the same class period in which Shoua Lao broke down trying to read her answer to the question "Why go on?" When Shoua could not speak, Beth raised her hand and said that not only did she have a close friend who had committed suicide, but she herself had, at times, considered it. She told the class that reading Dewey's comments in *Human Nature and Conduct* about our links to others helped her realize that she could not "opt out" because "my future is someone else's past." In other words, she explained, to take her life would be, potentially, to diminish the lives of others. "If you give up, if you lose hope and don't keep on keeping on, then you're cutting others short of their future. You're denying your responsibility to the rest of society because you're ending a line of circumstances and consequences. . . . Dewey helps me see my life as kind of continual, like I'm part of an ongoing community since what I do affects everyone else."

Beth, thanks to the second Deweyan idea about present experience, also realized that regrets about the past were affecting her self-image and her ability to like herself, her ability to overcome what she described as failures in the past that made her feel that change was impossible. Dewey's point about finding meaning in the present moment came home to Beth in a "huge" way, she told me, on the day the class discussed Marcel's essay "On the Ontological Mystery." As students explored Marcel's criticisms of what he calls a functional, inhuman society in which people are defined by their social roles, Beth's classmate Rebecca Hinson described how she was looked down upon by customers in the bar where she works. Rebecca explained that because she is blonde and wears a bar girl's outfit, customers assume she is uneducated and "loose" and, therefore, treat her with disrespect. Instead of getting to know who Rebecca really is, they assume they know all about her because of her social function. Beth reported to me in an interview that this was like "a lightbulb going off. . . . Rebecca was talking about how people apply stereotypes to you that have nothing to do with who you really are. Hearing her say that helped me because people in my life—and I myself—do the same thing to me. I realized that I don't have to be limited by these definitions; they aren't a life sentence. They are unfortunate things from the past, but they aren't reasons for giving up hope." Beth concluded by saying that Dewey's stress on not letting the past haunt the present had appealed to her when she first read it, but it was not until this classroom exchange about Marcel's essay that she fully understood why.

During my final interview with Beth in May, a month after she dropped the course, she said something that helped me better understand why, earlier in the semester, she had told me she treated parts of Dewey's work "as religious text." It was a comment that I believe would have made Dewey smile. I say this because Dewey notes that the overall purpose of education is to help us become more educable, that is, more willing to further explore interests that we first encounter in the classroom (*LW* 13:13). Beth explained to me that dropping all her classes was the last thing she expected to have to do, but her divorce had made her financial situation desperate. "I'd put off paying my tuition as long as they would let me, and, when I knew I couldn't get the money together, I once again felt the bottom drop out of my life."

However, Beth continued, in the darkest moments of the last month, "I went to my bookshelf and pulled out Dewey and my notes and papers from this class. I reread them, and they renewed my hope." Dewey's words reminded her, she said, that the semester had not been totally wasted because she had been unable to complete her courses. She had had memorable social interactions in the Hope class, ones characterized by mutual support and encouragement, and had come to the valuable realization that many of her classmates were dealing with issues similar to hers. She had also taken important ideas with her. These ideas included, Beth reiterated, her new sense of obligation to future generations and her increased valuing of the present moment and the rich possibilities of meaning it always holds.

Bob Glahn

> We may recognize [the world's defects and excellencies] separately, but we cannot divide them, for unlike wheat and tares they grow from the same root.
>
> —John Dewey, *Experience and Nature* (*LW* 1:47)

Bob Glahn is the first of the students I have considered in this chapter who was successful at constructed knowing and who also stayed in the course for the entire semester. The ideas about hope that he said were most important to him included ones from Dewey as well as concepts he took from Marcel, Freire, and Snyder. I choose to focus on the Deweyan ideas that were fruitful for Bob because they were most prominent in his final essay and in his comments across the semester in class discussions and interviews with me. That it was Dewey's ideas that most helped Bob surprised me, given that he, like Charles and Beth, had serious problems reading Dewey early on. In fact, Bob told Fishman and his classmates on the day they discussed the second chapter of *Experience and Nature* that he needed a "translation" of Dewey and asked Steve if such a thing existed on the Web. Bob's efforts to write his first essay, which focused on Dewey, were so strangled by difficulties reading Dewey and a case of writer's block that what he ultimately turned in was little more than an outline. However, by mid-semester, Bob had—through some combination of rereading, writing his homework papers, and class discussion—mastered enough Dewey that, he told me, he was able to use several of Dewey's ideas in his own life.

The Deweyan concepts that Bob most profited from and could best apply to his friends' and own lives were closely related. The first has to do with Dewey's remark that "the longest lane turns sometime" (*LW* 1:64), that is, that failures and successes, the precarious and stable, are intimately related, or, as Dewey puts it, they come "come from the same root." The second and closely related idea that Bob seized upon was Dewey's notion that organic life is marked by rhythms of harmony and disturbance and that as we work to recover harmony, we grow.

At the beginning of the semester, Bob, like Beth, seemed to be weighed down by past failures. He was, as he recalled in his final paper, "wrapped in a cocoon of despair . . . believing that all hope was lost." He said that this was because of his unsuccessful courtship of a girl he liked very much, poor grades in several of his courses the previous semester, and a general "self-inflicted sense of worthlessness." What Bob took from Dewey gave him fresh hope about his life because he realized that a person's failures should be no more of a surprise than their successes. He was particularly impressed with Dewey's references to Jack Horner in the children's rhyme (*MW* 14:174; *LW* 1:380). Dewey says that Jack Horner seems to feel that getting a plum because he is a good boy is the normal way of things. By contrast, when misfortune occurs, it is seen as a violation of the natural order. Many of us share Jack Horner's belief, although, according to Dewey, we should expect and anticipate failure as much as success because it is just as much a part of life. Bob, in applying this idea to his own experience, began to see his failures of the previous semester as less earthshaking than they had previously appeared, as "momentary set-backs," he said, "rather than sure signs I was stuck in an unfixable life." Bob told me that he discovered powerful solace not only in Dewey's reminder that "the longest lane turns sometime" but also in Dewey's claim that "it is darkest just before dawn" (*LW* 1:64, 43).

The strength that Bob took from Dewey's comments about life's mixture of success and failure, good fortune and bad, was supplemented by the second idea he took from Dewey, namely, Dewey's suggestion that we should see our setbacks as opportunities to exercise our creative abilities and grow. Bob was so taken with the idea that failure is never a total loss but an opportunity for growth that, in class and in interviews with me, he said that on at least three occasions he had passed this idea on to friends who were living in low hope. "I have a friend who was mistreated and abandoned at an early age, and she has always had the sorrow of the world on her shoulders. The other day she snapped and ran to my door in the rain, begging God to strike her dead. She said life sucked and she was going to kill herself. I'm going like, 'No, you're only twenty years old. You have time ahead of you. Yes, things are bad now, but they will get better if you can just keep your chin up and work to find solutions.'"

Bob's application of Dewey's notion that misfortune can be a "stepping-stone" to growth benefited not only his friend, he told me. It also had an immediate payoff for Bob himself in his schoolwork. Bob, who had serious writer's block not only on the first essay in the Hope class but on the second as well, told me in our end-of-semester interview that constructed knowing was helping him get over this block. He was realizing that what he learned in a class was more important than the grade he got. He said he now believed the reason he had so much trouble writing the first two essays, and the reason he was having trouble in his other classes, was that he was so afraid of getting poor grades that he could not even start his work. He explained:

> After I turned in my first disastrous paper to Dr. Fishman, I went home and picked up my tape recorder and taped my own little personal journal about how I totally gave up. I screwed up because I didn't look at it from the perspective that I've gotten some ideas from Dewey that I can actually use and writing this essay is going to be helpful. I looked at it from the perspective of "Holy crap, I have to say something smart about Dewey that will get me an A." This [final] essay was so much easier for me because I discussed the readings in terms of what they meant to me.

Thus, what Bob took from Dewey and the Hope course helped him see his non-school failures of the previous semester in a new perspective: as opportunities for growth rather than pure disasters. In addition, his positive experience with constructed knowing helped him revise his attitude toward schoolwork. Paying more attention to what he could apply to his life than to grades freed him from the sort of writing paralysis that overemphasis on grades often engenders. As we ended our final interview, Bob said he would miss the course—"the atmosphere, the people, the personal stories, and Dr. Fishman's helping us get the author's points but allowing us to arrive at them in our own ways. I'm amazed at what we managed to do." Bob added that the class's timing had been perfect for him. "If I had not come to the class in despair, Dewey's and others' ideas would not have meant as much to me."

Lindsey Weston

There is sound sense in the old pagan notion that gratitude is the root of all virtue.

—John Dewey, *Human Nature and Conduct* (*MW* 14:19)

Twenty-one-year-old Lindsey Weston, the last of the five students who enrolled because they were low in hope, had been negatively affected, as I mentioned earlier, by her experiences the previous summer in the Air National Guard in Kuwait. In her interviews with me, Lindsey said that she had given up on people and the world. While working in the military as an airplane mechanic, she had done everything anyone asked of her. She had followed the rules. She had never harmed anyone. Yet the world, she said, had been cruel to her. She had lived through a three-month nightmare in which unfounded, ugly rumors about her, including some circulated by people she considered friends, were passed around the group. In addition, Lindsey mentioned to me in an interview and, later, to her classmates in class discussion that during this time there was also a boyfriend at home who turned out to be untrustworthy. "When I came back from overseas last September," she said, "I felt that the universe had screwed me, and it owed me some sort of compensation. I should get a break of some kind to restore the balance of good and bad in my life."

Lindsey, like Charles, Beth, and Bob, found in Dewey's work the ideas that were most helpful to her. However, unlike the other three, Lindsey was not so much perplexed by Dewey at the start of the semester as she was critical of him. On the second day of the semester when the class discussed *Human Nature and Conduct*—the day that Charles Dautun admitted he was lost—Lindsey seemed less confused by Dewey than dismissive of him. He was, she told the class, "contradictory" and "inconsistent." For example, Dewey's saying that habits are both individual and social made him seem like "he's talking out of both sides of his mouth," she said. Lindsey added that, overall, Dewey's writing seemed poor in contrast to that of the psychologists in her second major who seemed "very precise."

Steve listened to Lindsey's criticisms and said nothing. Trying to teach indirectly, Steve deemed it too soon to respond to Lindsey by telling her about Dewey's efforts to resolve what Dewey considers false dualisms. Instead, Fishman accepted her remarks and moved on, trusting that, over time, she would recognize this Deweyan pattern for herself. That Lindsey did indeed do this was evident a month later when the class discussed chapter 1 of *A Common Faith*. As I showed when I described that class session in the previous chapter, Lindsey's comment at the close of that discussion—her recognition that Dewey wants us both to be grateful to our ancestors and, at the same time, look critically at their legacy—really pleased Steve. He was excited not only for Lindsey's sake but also because her comment testified, in his mind, to the power of indirect teaching. This pedagogy had allowed Lindsey to come to this insight about Dewey through her own reading, writing, and conversing, and, thus, in Fishman's view, she was now in a better position to make use of this insight than if he had tried handing it to her on the second day of class.

The Deweyan concepts that ultimately helped Lindsey are similar to those that influenced Bob Glahn. Like Bob, central to Lindsey's experience was Dewey's notion that failure and success are intimately intertwined because they come from the same root. Both students came to see that misfortune and disappointment—things we cannot control despite our best-laid plans—are to be expected. As a consequence, Lindsey began to reconstruct her experiences in Kuwait, and, as she told me in our May interview, she had gradually let go of her anger. She began to see that she needed to change her view of the world, to understand that when things go badly, it is neither a sign that the universe is punishing her or a sign that she has been singled out for bad luck. "When I used to tell people about Kuwait, I would get all worked up because I felt a type of injustice that the good things I hoped for didn't turn out. I was like, 'I'm a good person, and I'm smart, and I can make things happen. So why didn't this or that materialize?' . . . Now when bad things happen, I don't feel so much like I'm being picked on."

Lindsey told me she also profited from a second idea she took from Dewey, namely, that gratitude is the root of all virtue. Giving up her focus on the world's injustice and what the universe did not give her enabled Lindsey to recognize what the world *had* given her. This led her to feel some responsibility, she said, to pay back. Instead of believing that the universe owed her a debt, Lindsey said, "if anything, I owe the world something."

This position, which Lindsey articulated in our May interview, had been tested and shaped during the semester. In late March, Lindsey learned that her parents, who had been married twenty-five years, had decided to divorce. Her father was devastated, and she told me that instead of feeling sorry for herself because of her parents' divorce, she was able to respond to it in a more productive way. She said that she felt grateful she was in college and could take courses in psychology and philosophy, especially this course on Hope, and she wanted to pass along to her father some of the ideas she had learned in an effort to help him. Like Bob, Beth, and Charles, who profited from constructed knowing, Lindsey commented that this was the first time a course had directly affected her life. She said that although she had faced many difficult situations in the past, this was the first time she had some useful tools with which to respond.

Bringing in a third Dewey idea, and again echoing Bob Glahn, Lindsey said that one of the things she discussed with her father was that he might consider the divorce, despite the sadness associated with it, as an opportunity for growth. In effect, she was developing what might be called a corollary to the notion that misfortune and success are intimately connected, namely, that it is *only* in a world where failure is possible are there chances for success. She concluded, "I have tried to offer my dad some of what I've realized this semester, describing for him some of the ideas that helped me feel less angry and victimized. But I never said to him, 'Here's what you should do, or here's how you should see the world, or here's what you should hope for.' I just provided him some ideas, like Dr. Fishman does with us, and he'll have to decide which, if any, of these pieces of theory make sense to him."

Reflections on the Five Students Who Came to Class Saying They "Needed Hope"

On the one hand, it is not so surprising to me that the students who came to Fishman's course needing hope were able get something positive from it. After all, they were highly motivated, hungry for ways to reduce the loneliness, disappointment, and despair that they described. On the other hand, given the difficulty most of them had, at least initially, reading Dewey, I am surprised at the significant understanding of the literature that these students took with them from the course. Without meaning to be critical of them, and certainly without wanting to imply they are unintelligent, it was obvious to me that this was a group of students whose school records were not, on the whole, that impressive. Of the five of them, only Lindsey Weston did not complain about the challenges of the reading, and, of the five, only she did not come to the course with a checkered academic history. By contrast, Shoua Lao was on academic probation because of her grades the previous semester; Beth Blalock rightly described her academic record as a "disaster"; Charles Dautun not only dropped out of school halfway through the semester he took the Hope class but also did the same thing the previous term; and, finally, Bob Glahn, as I have already noted, told me that he had done very poorly in his classes the semester prior to Fishman's course.

Nevertheless, as I have explained, four of these students responded to Dewey, and all five said they profited from the collaborative and supportive spirit in the classroom. It was as if they watched Fishman being an active inquirer into hope, and, for what are certainly numerous and diverse reasons, they all accepted his invitation to join him. A centrally important reason they became co-inquirers is, of course, that they were highly motivated to learn about hope. Other reasons they mentioned to me were that they felt "safe" in this classroom, they wanted to "belong" to the group, and they found solace or encouragement in the class. I also credit Fishman's indirect pedagogy for these students' positive experiences in the Hope course—a point to which I return in the next chapter. As I have shown, although Steve valued critical knowing, and although he frequently took students back into assigned texts for closer reading, he never declared students' interpretations wrong or gave them answers before he felt they were ready.

Five Students Who Enrolled without
Specific Concerns about Hope

In the second section of this chapter, I report on the five remaining students in Fishman's Hope class, those who came with less perceived need for the course subject matter. These students enrolled because they knew Fishman or, simply, because the class fit their schedule. Not surprisingly, because these five pupils came to the course with very different needs, their responses were more mixed than those of the group I have just described.

Three of the five students in this second group—Rebecca Hinson, Chris Vernarsky, and Faith Dennison—did not indicate that the course had the sort of dramatic effect on them that it had on students in the previous group. That is, when these three students talked about the course, they tended to speak in more academic and general terms. This may be the result of a myriad of reasons, including, certainly, the fact that they came to the course without any pressing concerns about hope. In addition, other reasons may include these students' inexperience with constructed knowing and, in some cases, their sense that it was inappropriate or not what they wanted to do in an academic setting. Finally, these pupils may have had less time in which to do the reading and writing that the course required. The three who describe the least impact of the course upon their lives were all working thirty to forty hours per week in addition to taking a full course load. One of these students, Rebecca Hinson, regularly left class early, explaining to Fishman that her work schedule made it impossible for her to stay for the entire session.

The other two students in this group, like the five in section 1, described significant effects from the course upon their lives. Carolyn Kamionka claimed to have derived a great deal, noting that several concepts, the most important of which were from Marcel, helped raise her level of hope. Stan Lefcoski, like Carolyn, also said that his experiences in the Hope course had influenced his life. However, Stan, unlike all the other students, said that these experiences—coupled with other life events—had actually caused him to lose hope and that he was now dealing with personal issues he found very disheartening. I begin with Carolyn Kamionka's story because, of those in this second group, it most resembles the positive stories I have told above.

Carolyn Kamionka

> There are some people who reveal themselves as "present"—that is to say, at our disposal—when we are in pain or need to confide in someone. . . . [T]he person who is [present] is the one who is capable of being with me with the whole of himself.
>
> —Gabriel Marcel, "On the Ontological Mystery" (OMM 39–40)

Carolyn Kamionka, the forty-two-year-old returning student and mother of Bob Glahn, was as positively affected by the Hope course as any of the five students I have already described. Although she said on numerous occasions that she was a big fan of Dewey—and she never complained of difficulties reading his work—the most valuable ideas, the ones that resulted in what she called "bolt of lightning" insights, came from Marcel. Early in the semester, Carolyn revealed to the class and to me that she was a person who often felt down about herself and her situation. She said she believed that people were not open to her or interested in her. "Sometimes I think that no one is on my side, and I'm alone in this miserable world. I get angrier and angrier, thinking that life is way too hard, there's no pleasant place to rest, and tomorrow will be no better." By semester's end, in a way that resembles Lindsey Weston's shift in worldview, Carolyn came to see herself and the world in new ways. In her final essay, she wrote, "In my search for hope, I have found out some things about myself that bothered me, and I have developed ways to correct them."

One of the ideas in Marcel that helped Carolyn "find out about herself" was his suggestion, in line with Josef Pieper, that despair is something we bring on ourselves. It is not something the world does to us but is, rather, a decision we make about how we are going to view the world. Carolyn was especially taken with Marcel's image of despair in "Sketch of a Phenomenology and a Metaphysic of Hope" in which he describes despair as a kind of witchcraft that takes over one's life (SK 42). In one of the four class discussions devoted to Marcel's work, Carolyn related that in "a moment of clarity" the previous day, it hit her that the despair she was experiencing was like Marcel's witchcraft, and it was she herself who was casting the spell. This realization was freeing, according to Carolyn, because if she was responsible for her own despair, she could do something about it. The following week, Carolyn described this "bolt-of-lighting" moment in her second essay for the course.

> I was walking on campus, and it was raining. I needed to complete some homework, I had three more classes to attend, and my pager was vibrating in my pocket with someone calling from my office. My teeth were grinding. Who wanted me now? Why couldn't everyone just leave me alone? I was, for lack of a better term, miserable. Then it hit me. "Carolyn, you fool! Stop! You, my dear, are doing this to yourself." I then felt guilty for the short answers I had spewed out to everyone that morning, for the cold demeanor I had displayed to my family when they went out the door. . . . Life's ups and downs are to be expected, according to Dewey. But what Marcel teaches me is that my responses to these natural rhythms are my choice, and the choices I make profoundly affect my thinking and my behavior toward others.

Like Lindsey Weston, Carolyn was able to change her worldview so as to no longer blame the world for her low hope. However, Carolyn's emphasis was somewhat different from Lindsey's. For Lindsey, her reconstruction involved seeing misfortune as a necessary part of life and an opportunity for growth, whereas for Carolyn it was a matter of her relation to other people. Carolyn's understanding of her hopelessness as affecting—and affected by—her interactions with others came from her coupling of Marcel's notion of despair as something we choose with his concept of "presence." To be present, or "spiritually available," for Marcel, is to be open to others, somehow encouraging them to take best advantage of their divine gifts without demanding in advance or having a clear conception of what that other person should be (OMM 38). Carolyn was excited when she realized that, for her, Marcel's notion of presence could be an important remedy for the witchcraft of despair.

Carolyn expressed her initial excitement about Marcel's concept of presence later in the same class discussion in which she spoke about realizing her own role in her despair. Fishman had begun that session, in which students were to discuss "On the Ontological Mystery," with a freewrite that gave them a chance to do some constructed knowing; that is, Fishman asked students to consider possible connections between their own lives and Marcel's concept of presence. Carolyn was among the students who, later in the class period, read aloud what they had written. What she said was, "I chose to write not about presence but about non-presence. I wrote about my mother, who I now realize has never been present to me. She was never available. But she's not the only one. I also realize that I sometimes do the same thing, that I sometimes am not present to my husband and kids." The videotape then shows Carolyn vowing to discuss the notion of presence with her husband and look for ways they could be more open and present to one another.

In Carolyn's second essay, she explicitly links the two Marcellian ideas that meant so much to her. In her final paragraph, she writes, "Presence is, for me, the key to hopeful living. To really be available to another with the whole of myself, as Marcel says, might be all that I need to reverse the spell of despair that I have cast on myself. And, similarly, a smile or nod from me to another person might be all they need to overcome their despair."

That Carolyn Kamionka took a lot from the course, most important her application of Marcel's conceptions of despair and presence, was evident in her closing words to me in an interview on the day the semester ended. She said, "I feel like I see myself differently now than I did at the beginning of this class. When I sense the danger of my self-imposed witchcraft, I now step back and question my patterns of behavior to determine what role I am playing in the scene. This has been very helpful to me, not only because I realize my role in all this but also because I have the capacity to change the situation. . . . I now understand how important it is for me to be present to others if I am to maintain my own hope and help others keep theirs."

Rebecca Hinson: "Dewey Speaks for Me"

Rebecca Hinson was very taken with Dewey. She told me on several occasions that "Dewey speaks for me." Of all the students who took Fishman's class, Rebecca was, as I have said, the most academically skilled. In fact, in her homework papers that focused on Dewey, she had so mastered Dewey's style that she almost sounded like him. However, unlike the six students I have discussed to this point, Rebecca described no dramatic changes in either her worldview or her view of hope as a result of taking the course. Nevertheless, she said that the class had, at least, helped her sharpen her understanding of hope. She no longer thought of it as just a vague emotion but now saw it as the motivation, the energy, that helps us work hard and figure out ways to achieve our goals.

With regard to Dewey, Rebecca, like several others in the class, wrote in her first essay that he helped her see her defeats as less devastating because she could reconceive them as challenges. She also wrote in her third and final essay that she took from Dewey the idea that the present moment is important, and with this idea, she seemed to come closest to the sort of constructed knowing that Steve wanted for his students. She said that Dewey helped her see that all of her "stressing" about deadlines and grades—she told me that she considered anything less than an A a failure—drained all joy from the process of learning. However, Rebecca did not take her insight as far as Bob Glahn did by discussing ways she might lessen her attention to grades.

In addition to appreciating some of Dewey's ideas, Rebecca also wrote about the importance for her of Marcel's notion of presence. She said that she often becomes impatient with other people's behavior and closes down on further exchanges with them. Rebecca's appreciation of Marcel's notion of presence was evident in the class session in which Carolyn Kamionka talked dramatically about her mother's failure to be present to her. After Carolyn spoke that day, Rebecca told the class a similar story. She too, she said, had written not about presence in her life but about non-presence. She summarized her freewrite for the class in the following way:

> I wrote about my grandmother. I've lived with her since I was ten, and Marcel gives me a word and a concept to capture her attitude toward me. I get so frustrated with her because she doesn't take in the words I am saying. Instead, she's just waiting for her chance to speak, and I know she isn't listening to me because her reactions are often either wholly irrelevant or a restatement of what I have just said. She's set in her ways and won't hear any evidence I give her. My grandmother, I'm sorry to say, is simply not present to me, and it drives me up the wall.

Once again, however, for whatever reasons, Rebecca did not take this insight as far as Carolyn did—at least not in what she said or wrote during Steve's course. In Rebecca's final essay, other than a general remark about wanting to be more open and patient with others, she says nothing about particular steps she might take to bring this about.

Stan Lefcoski

A mystery [is] a problem which encroaches on its own data: I who
inquire into the meaning . . . cannot place myself outside it or before
it; I am engaged in this encounter . . . I am inside it.
　　　—Gabriel Marcel, "On the Ontological Mystery" (OMM 22)

Stan Lefcoski was one of the students who, like Rebecca Hinson, worked at
a job outside school thirty to forty hours per week, Stan as a waiter and cook
in a restaurant. Sometimes, he told me, he didn't get home until two or three
in the morning, and then he had to get up at eight to make his nine o'clock
classes (although he sometimes overslept, he said, and, indeed, he did miss
four weeks of meetings of the Hope class). Getting so little sleep and taking
a full load of courses meant that Stan was not doing well in school, and, he
told me, he expected to get poor grades. In fact, in watching the videotapes,
I noticed that he frequently had, sitting on his desk, a can of high-caffeine,
high-energy drink. At the close of our mid-semester interview, he said with
a sigh, "I'm going through a time that has been deadening to my soul."

Like a number of students in Fishman's class, Stan indicated in his final
essay that he was buoyed somewhat by Dewey's view that life is marked by
·a rhythm of disturbance and harmony. He said that the idea that "life is a
constant recovery" helped him try to enjoy the present moment even when
things looked bleak. Despite this positive note in Stan's last paper, however,
he admitted that it was as if a "sink hole opened up and swallowed me this
semester." He also said that "the person I am now seems to me to have less
meaning than the person I used to think I was." Stan's dejection resulted from
a job that both exhausted and demeaned him, he said, a place where his co-
workers were dismissive of his philosophic knowledge. In addition, the Hope
course had caused Stan to question the value of detached argument and his
own self-image as a philosopher.

I speculate that two factors in the Hope course led Stan to fall into "the sink
hole" he described. The first of these was Fishman's valuing of constructed
knowing and his indirect teaching approach in which he allowed a variety of
personally based interpretations to be placed on the classroom discussion table
before encouraging critical, separate knowing. This is the pattern I illustrated
in the previous chapter on the day the class discussed the first chapter of *A
Common Faith*. In that session, Chris, Carolyn, Faith, and Bob each told what
the reading meant to them before Fishman welcomed Beth's question about
the adequacy of her classmates' reading of Dewey's text. Fishman's entertain-

ing students' experiences and positions rather than, as Bob Glahn put it to me, immediately "poking holes" in their arguments seemed to shake Stan's confidence in his view of philosophy. He no longer saw it as primarily about sharpness in critical separate knowing or about mastery of classic philosophic positions. Stan explained to me in an April interview, "As I heard others in the class say what they thought hope was and what it meant to them, I felt I knew less and less myself. When they read their papers, I thought, 'I don't know if I can say anything like that.' I felt like I had no ideas of my own. It was at this point that something in me switched off. I felt like a kindergartner in a calculus class."

The second factor that I believe may have brought Stan to his "sink hole," calling into question his self-image as a competent critical knower, was a notion he took from Marcel. The Marcellian concept that shook Stan is that much of life is a mystery and defies the sort of thorough explication that analytic philosophy—the sort that I speculate was most familiar to Stan—promises. According to Marcel, life needs to be lived and experienced from the inside, and to make all of our trials into problems we can solve by adopting a neutral, scientific, outside-observer approach is a mistake. Although for Marcel the idea of mystery is a comfort, since it means that there is always hope no matter how discouraging scientists or outside observers may tell us our situation is, it brought Stan no such consolation. Toward the close of his final essay, Stan writes that when he began the class, he thought he would come to a clear view of the nature of hope, but now, affected by Marcel's idea that life and hope are, ultimately, inexplicable mysteries, he concludes that he cannot reach his original objective.

In looking back over Stan's story, there are some silver linings. As I noted above, he said that he found Dewey's view of life as a constant effort to recover harmony helpful, and, after not doing so in his first two essays, he was able, in his final essay, to engage in some constructed knowing. In addition, in his April interview, Stan said he actually admired Marcel, in particular his openness to alternative ways of doing philosophy, and he believed Marcel might even tell him that he was on the right path "because I am confused and I actually don't know." Despite these comments and achievements, however, I believe Stan left Fishman's class with less hope than when he began.

When the semester was over and Fishman and I discussed my findings about Stan's experiences in the Hope class, Steve was, understandably, saddened. Causing a student to become less hopeful was, he said, the last thing he wanted. As Steve had repeatedly told me, his goal was to help students increase, not lessen, their levels of hope. However, Steve said, he saw some positive things in Lefcoski's experience. He was pleased that Stan could find solace in Dewey's view that life is a mix of loss and gain. He was even more pleased that Stan could take a relatively difficult and sophisticated concept from Marcel and apply it to his own life, a wonderful example, Steve said, of constructed knowing. Perhaps, Fishman concluded, Stan found some satisfaction in being able to use philosophy in his third essay to unburden himself and better understand his own situation.

Chris Vernarsky

> Men have never fully used the powers they possess to advance the good in life, because they have waited on some power external to themselves and to nature to do the work they are responsible for doing.
>
> —John Dewey, *A Common Faith* (*LW* 9:31)

Chris Vernarsky played a major role in the class discussion of *A Common Faith* that I described in the preceding chapter. In that session, he said he had read this book in a previous course and loved it. Chris explained that what most appealed to him was Dewey's view that to be religious or have a religious experience did not require membership in an organized religion. Another reason, and perhaps a more powerful one, that Chris gave for admiring Dewey's book was that he agreed with Dewey that organized religion, with its emphasis on a non-earthly heaven, often leads to a dismissal of efforts to reform our this-worldly existence. Not surprisingly, in Chris's final essay he devoted most of his paper to elaborating upon Dewey's claim that it is best to focus on this world rather than on a transcendent one. Chris writes,

> Dewey holds that claiming that the source for all progress and hope for the future lies external to the natural conditions of the world implies a pessimistic attitude toward the natural state of the world. He says that the fault with supernaturalism, as he sees it, "is that it stands in the way of an effective realization of the sweep and depths of the implications of natural human relations." To rely solely on the supernatural, as Dewey says, leaves us vulnerable to a state in which the natural is distrusted or ignored in favor of the supernatural.

As Steve and I discussed Chris's final essay, Steve told me he was impressed with Chris's discussion of this Deweyan principle. Steve said that it was clear to him that Chris had truly mastered this idea by the fluent way in which he wrote about it. Steve also told me that he was impressed with Chris's response to even the slightest hint of criticism of this idea across the semester. During a class period devoted to giving feedback to students' drafts of the second essay, Steve told me that he mentioned to Chris's group that someone like the theologian Josef Pieper might view Dewey's efforts at social reform as working with one hand behind his back. That is, someone like Pieper, a committed Thomist, might argue that Dewey, in rejecting the idea of a divine being, had only his own and his fellow creatures' resources to draw upon. Steve was impressed, he said, that although Chris had been relatively quiet prior to Steve's remark, he suddenly become animated and said, "No, I disagree. It's Pieper who is operating with one hand behind his back and Dewey who is working with two hands."

Chris's strong commitment to Dewey's naturalism is certainly positive. In addition, in the final paragraph of his last essay, Chris says that the Hope course was, of all his courses that semester, the one he enjoyed the most. He concludes by saying that his classmates' determination to make sense of challenging philosophic material, and their willingness to share their efforts with one another, was something that gave him hope that people can work together productively to solve difficult problems.

So far, I have told a very positive story about Chris. However, the thing that stands out for me as I reflect on the class videotapes and other data I reviewed is Chris's apparent disinterest in the authors other than Dewey that Fishman assigned in the Hope course. When Steve, as was his usual practice, asked students to do in-class writing about these other authors, I noted that whereas other students spent ten minutes filling three-quarters of a page, Chris wrote for a minute or two, a couple of sentences, and then looked bored as he waited for his classmates to finish. Fishman must have been aware of Chris's demeanor too because I observed a pattern in which Fishman would call on Chris first as if to bring him back into the group. It got so that it was a class joke, with Fishman wondering aloud, "Who can I ask to start class discussion?" followed by a pause and then a turn toward Chris, who would laugh, shake his head, and say, "I tried to avoid eye contact, but he got me anyway."

In sum, Chris, somewhat like Rebecca Hinson, took some ideas from Steve's course, but he never did the sort of constructed knowing that characterized the experiences of the first six students I have described in this chapter. In Chris's final essay, he speaks in very general terms about the value of Dewey's ideas. He sometimes discusses the implications of these ideas for "people," using impersonal pronouns, and when he examines their application to his own life, he writes in a way that suggests he did not really gain much from Steve's course. For example, when discussing the meaning of the Deweyan principle that Chris was so taken with—Dewey's emphasis on this-worldly rather than other-worldly sources of hope and reform—he stays on the surface, going little beyond what he would certainly have known coming into the class. Chris writes,

> I agree with Dewey that we no longer need to look externally to find a source of hope but can, rather, find it in our natural human relations with one another. In my own life, rather than wait for some external force to grant me my desires and goals, I can now take an active path towards their realization by utilizing the natural powers that are inherent in the world. For example, if I have a desire for world peace, instead of waiting for my desire to be imposed upon the natural world by an external power, I can recognize that the power to turn this ideal into the actual lies within the scope of natural conditions. It may not be within my power alone to make world peace an actuality, but it is within my power to live my life in accordance with this ideal.

When I try to account for Chris's responses to Fishman's pedagogy and assignments, I hit upon explanations similar to those I suggested for Stan Lefcoski. Like Lefcoski, who, except for his final essay, did not attempt constructed knowing, Chris's writing and classroom contributions suggested that he too was comfortable only in the critical separate-knower stance. I say this because when the class discussed Pieper and Marcel, Chris dismissed them as being irrelevant because their theories included a belief in God. When the class discussed Paulo Freire who, as a South American revolutionary and Marxist, criticizes the conservative role that the Catholic Church has historically played in Latin America, Chris suddenly defended the Church and became extremely critical of Freire. He said he thought it unfair of Freire to ask the Church to question its wealthy congregants about their responsibility to take a vow of solidarity with the poor. The same critical reaction occurred when the class considered its final author, psychologist C. R. Snyder. Chris said Snyder's book read like a motivational speech to a bunch of salesmen.

Right or wrong in his responses to Pieper, Marcel, Freire, and Snyder, Chris shows no more inclination to attempt constructed knowing with these authors than he makes in his own essays. Although Steve urged him to step into the shoes and contexts of people like Marcel and Freire to see if he could find something valuable for himself in their texts, Chris never succeeded in doing this. It was as if he was so comfortable as a critical knower, so familiar with "the doubting game," that he could not accept Fishman's invitation.[2] I saw similar resistance to constructed knowing in Chris's reactions to the in-class freewrites, nearly all of which asked students to apply the theory they had read that day to their personal experiences.

Thus, I conclude that Fishman's effort to counter the usual classroom emphasis on received and separate, critical knowing worked no better for Chris Vernarsky than it did for Stan Lefcoski. In fact, it may have led him to get less from the course than if Fishman had spent more time with criti-cal exposition and analysis, the sort of classroom approach that was more familiar to Chris. Chris's inability or unwillingness to take the authors that were discussed in the class other than Dewey seriously may well have resulted from Chris's sense that Steve's pedagogy was inappropriate in an upper-divi-sion philosophy class. The upshot of Chris's story is that Fishman's approach is one that, understandably, has limitations. As I cautioned in Chapter 6, instructors who attempt to borrow from Fishman's pedagogy need to be aware that students like Stan Lefcoski and Chris Vernarsky may find it dif-ficult to see the benefits of constructed knowing.

Faith Dennison

> The fire isn't there. . . . I'm only going through the motions, and I'm not doing anywhere near what I could do if my heart were in it.
> —C. R. Snyder, quoting "Anne," in *The Psychology of Hope* (PH 38)

I have left Faith Dennison until last because, among the ten students in Fish-man's Hope course, she was in a category of her own regarding her reasons for enrolling. As I have noted, Faith took Steve's class because its meeting time fit into her busy schedule and she thought it would be an easy A. As I also have mentioned, Faith was surprised by the difficulty she had reading the assigned texts, and she found the homework assignments too time consuming because of the challenges the reading posed for her. In the end, she said, she really did not like philosophy, a vague discourse about "ethereal issues that often seems to go nowhere." Faith told the class at the close of the semester when several of her classmates, including Chris Vernarsky, were criticizing C. R. Snyder for giving too simple answers about hope, "I like Snyder. I like getting the answers. I feel like we're finally reading someone who tells us exactly what hope is."

Although the course made more demands on Faith than she expected, and although she never really liked philosophy, she indicated at semester's end that she had gotten something from the course. In her final essay she specifies which concepts caught her attention. First, Marcel's notion of presence was important to Faith, as it was to Carolyn and Rebecca, because, Faith said, she realized that being present to others has double significance. Although she does not mention Dewey, she seems to supplement Marcel's notion of presence with Dewey's notion of the infinite consequences of our actions. In her final paper, she writes that her being present to others might not only help them. It might also cause them to be present to their friends and, thus, extend her act of kindness beyond her own purview. In the end, Faith says, her kindness might even return to her. She writes, "There was a movie about this called *Pay It Forward* in which if someone performed three acts of kindness to others, then those who benefited had but one responsibility: to pass it forward to another. In this way, if you are present to one person, then another and another, quickly this idea spreads and rejuvenates the lives of all those it inhabits. Before you realize it, it may come full circle back to you on a day you desperately need it and from an unlikely source."

Another residue from the course that Faith mentioned in her final essay was the impact that Snyder's work had on her. Not only did he offer clear answers about the nature of hope; he also helped her enrich the way in which she sets her goals. In both class discussion and her essay, Faith said that she loves to make lists of objectives, and she feels great when she reaches them and can check them off. In Snyder's *Psychology of Hope*, he suggests that people complexify their to-do lists by categorizing them according to work, family, recreation, and so on and create weekly rather than daily lists. By the time the course ended, Faith said she had begun this practice and found it very satisfying. "I saw that if I wrote my lists out for the entire week, I was better at finding time to finish all I wanted to accomplish. I actually had some of the little moments of joy that Snyder speaks of when I achieved certain goals."

Although Fishman had heard Faith's negative responses to the assigned philosophic texts throughout the course, he became optimistic late in the semester about what she might take from her experience. During her in-class recounting of her appreciation of Snyder, Faith touched on something that Steve believed might lead to some rich constructed knowing. This occurred during the next to last week of the semester when Faith informed the class that when she filled out Snyder's hope scale she was not surprised to find that, according to Snyder's criteria, she was a person of high hope. Faith is someone with a lot of energy and a commanding presence, and she beamed as she looked around the circle at her classmates and Fishman. She said, "I'm the sort of high-hope person Snyder describes. I set my goals, I go after them, and I succeed. I'm a get-things-done sort of person." Then Faith added what Steve considered the most interesting thing she said the entire semester: "But, then, I was reading along in Snyder, feeling good, when he introduces a woman named Anne. This woman told Snyder that although she is clear about her goals and has enough motivation and smarts to reach them, there is no zest, no fire, in her life." Faith continued, "When I read that, I stopped in my tracks. I said to myself, 'That's me! I'm working hard, and I'm succeeding, but it's no fun.' I really don't enjoy being in school, and I really don't like my job much, although it pays very well and I'm scheduled for a promotion when I graduate."

Fishman told me that when Faith said this he was excited. Not only was he pleased about the potential value this discovery might have for Faith. He was also excited because it was the very development he most wanted to happen when he included authors in the course whose work he believed would contextualize a Deweyan theory of hope. Using Faith's comments as a springboard, he asked the class what might be missing in Snyder's approach to hope if someone like Anne, and now Faith, has plenty of Snyder's three elements of hope—clear goals, willpower, and waypower—but still feels that her life is empty or leaves a lot to be desired. Pushing further, Steve asked the class, "What do you believe Dewey would say about Snyder's analysis of hope?" After some back-and-forth, several students suggested that the problem is that no matter how many goals you achieve, if you are not wholehearted about them, your life will seem unfulfilled.

Before the class period ended that day, a number of students said they felt as Faith did, especially about their schoolwork. So much of it, they agreed, seemed "beside the point" or "irrelevant." As students filed out after their discussion of Snyder, Fishman stopped Faith and urged her to think further about her identification with Anne in Snyder's case study. In addition, in the peer-response groups on the drafts of essay 3 that took place a week later, Fishman again encouraged Faith to explore how Dewey's notion of wholeheartedness might help her reexamine not only the goals she had set for herself but also the ways she was going about achieving them. Faith agreed she would do this and said that, in fact, her current job—in a company overseeing the delivery of freight—was not one she had chosen for herself but one that her sister had gotten for her. She explained, "It pays so well I can't easily give it up. In my family, a good salary is all that matters."

However, when Faith's final paper came in, she made no mention of Anne or her discovery while reading Snyder. I suspect that there are several reasons Faith did not pursue her discovery about "zest" being absent from her life despite her being successful in reaching her goals. First, like Chris Vernarsky, Faith may have found constructed knowing outside the bounds of academic thinking and writing. At least, it certainly was outside her own educational experience and interests. As she made clear in our first interview, the sort of course she expected, and the kind she liked best, presented facts she could memorize and give back. Although Faith shared her personal experiences in class discussions and listened with interest as others did the same, it seems likely to me that, in this instance, Steve failed to show her the potential reward of constructed knowing. Second, Fishman did not offer the sort of motivation that might have impressed Faith, a student who was extraordinarily concerned with grades. Although he encouraged and repeatedly made constructed knowing a high priority, he never threatened students that he would penalize them if they did not engage in it. A final possibility is that, for Faith, this idea was just too hot to handle. Accepting Fishman's invitation to further investigate the lack of wholeheartedness in her school and work lives would have meant making the sort of major life adjustments that, at this juncture, may have seemed to her totally impracticable.

The lesson I draw for teachers from my analysis of Faith is that instructors who want to bring constructed knowing into their classroom need to be aware that some of the discoveries students make may be so threatening to their present ways of seeing themselves and their major activities that pursuing constructed knowing may be too painful. As the story I have told about Stan Lefcoski suggests, had Faith followed up on Fishman's recommendation, it is possible that she might also have left the class with less hope than when she started. By backing away from doing this, Faith may have gotten less from the course than Fishman would have wished, but backing away may have helped her avoid the "sink hole" that Stan's pursuit of constructed knowing led him to face.

Reflections on the Five Students Who Came to the Course without Specific Concerns about Hope

In this section, I have reported the impact upon the five students who came to Fishman's Hope course without specific concerns about hope. Evaluation of what Dewey calls the "residue" of an educational experience is, he argues, extremely important because, as he says in the epigraph to this chapter, "every experience lives on in further experiences. Hence the central problem of . . . education . . . is to select the kind of present experiences that live fruitfully and creatively in subsequent experiences" (*LW* 13:13). It is very difficult, however, to judge the long-term effects of a particular course on any student. As teachers, we have all had the experience of meeting a student many years later, one whom we hardly recall or whom we even remember as seeming indifferent, who surprises us by recounting the ways our class has helped him across the years. Thus, when I claim that three of the five students in this group (Rebecca Hinson, Chris Vernarsky, and Faith Dennison) seemed unaffected by the course whereas the other two (Carolyn Kamionka and Stan Lefcoski) were changed by it, I obviously cannot be sure how, in the long run, their stories will play out.

Neither can I be certain why three students in this group seemed not to respond to Fishman's invitation to engage in constructed knowing whereas two were willing to attempt it. Although I have posited some causal factors in individual students' cases, the reasons for their experiences are certainly myriad, more extensive and complicated than I can know. Nevertheless, I have focused on one possible causal factor: student's initial attitudes toward the course subject matter. Common sense suggests that pupils with greater personal need for the course material will take more from it. This turned out to be the case, generally, with Carolyn Kamionka being the lone exception.

EIGHT

Conclusion to Part II:
Highlights of the Classroom Study

Lucille McCarthy

In this chapter, I reflect on the things that stand out for me from my collaborative study with Steve Fishman of his course, The Philosophy and Practice of Hope. I divide my reflections into two categories. First, I present what are, for me, the pedagogical highlights, that is, the aspects of the teaching/learning situation that most impressed me. Second, I comment on the ideas from the assigned literature that students most gravitated to, the ones they said they found most helpful in rekindling and maintaining their hope.

Pedagogical Highlights

SIX OF TEN STUDENTS' SUCCESS WITH CONSTRUCTED KNOWING

First, what impressed me was that although all of Fishman's ten students had trouble with constructed knowing—applying philosophy to their lives—six eventually succeeded. As I have shown, these six had something akin to what Carolyn Kamionka called a "bolt of lightening" experience, moments in which a theoretic concept from the literature led them to reconceive some aspect of their lives. Five of these six claimed that, as a result of bringing their school and non-school lives together at these moments, they became more hopeful. By contrast, the sixth student, Stan Lefcoski, found himself less hopeful. Stan was, however, despite his self-doubts and confusions, facing up to painful questions about himself and his life trajectory that, I believe, may well lead him, in time, to positive new adjustments and growth. Although the remaining four students attended regularly and completed all assignments, and although all four claimed to appreciate at least some of the readings, for whatever reasons—they were too busy, too focused on trying to understand the reading, or had some sense that constructed knowing was inappropriate—they appeared not to apply course ideas to their lives in significant ways.

NINE OF THE TEN STUDENTS' APPRECIATION OF THE COLLABORATIVE CLASSROOM CLIMATE

In addition to being impressed by the majority of students taking advantage of the opportunity to do constructed knowing, a second pedagogical highlight for me is that nine of the ten pupils responded favorably to the collaborative climate in the classroom. The one exception was Stan Lefcoski who expressed discomfort with Fishman's willingness to allow multiple points of view to accumulate before asking students to engage in critical analysis. Among the nine students who said they enjoyed or benefited from this aspect of Steve's teaching approach was Bob Glahn. According to Bob, "Students in this class listen to each other's ideas" rather than "chew each other up" by debating and disagreeing with one another. My observations corroborated Bob's. In Fishman's classroom I saw students who seemed genuinely interested in each others' perspectives and experiences.

In fact, in interviews with me, students frequently tied their learning in the class to their exchanges with peers. For example, as I report in Chapter 7, it was a "huge" moment for Beth Blalock, she told me, when she heard Rebecca Hinson recount the demeaning experiences and stereotyping she had put up with as a bar maid. Other students mentioned profiting from watching their classmates trying to interpret challenging literature. For example, Shoua Lao repeatedly said that she understood very little when she read the material by herself, but when she came to class and listened to her peers, things became clearer. Finally, Chris Vernarsky, a student who did not report significant growth as a result of the course, surprised me when, in the conclusion of his final essay, as I report in the previous chapter, he too praises the cooperative climate in the classroom. Chris writes, "Seeing the determination of every-one to try to understand, and help each other understand, this complicated material has given me hope. Maybe if people work together as we were able to do in this class, they can find solutions to problems which otherwise might seem unmanageable." Chris concludes his essay by remarking, "Although I have never considered myself to be short on hope, I *do* think our classroom community has had a positive impact on my own level of hope."

LUCILLE MCCARTHY

The Ideas That Students Found Most Useful

In addition to describing the highlights for me of Fishman's pedagogy, I summarize the ideas in the literature that students found most personally valuable. I also review concepts that were useful because they helped students contextualize Dewey's work and, thus, see it in a new and clearer light. In the previous chapter, I spoke about these ideas as I narrated students' stories. In this chapter, I organize my discussion of these ideas by author, beginning with the writer who affected students least, Paulo Freire, and progressing up the ladder to Dewey, who affected them most.

IDEAS FROM PAULO FREIRE THAT HELPED STUDENTS CONTEXTUALIZE DEWEY

It is not surprising that none of Fishman's students said they were powerfully affected by the writings of Paulo Freire. Although Fishman knows Freire's work well and is enthusiastic about it, Steve says that, in retrospect, he believes he assigned too little of it. Students discussed Freire for only two class days during the third to last week of the semester, and they simply did not read enough to understand some of Freire's key concepts like *conscientizacao*, our ontological need to become more human, and the Easter experience. Nevertheless, Fishman was pleased that several students said they appreciated Freire's work and, equally important in Fishman's mind, connected it to Dewey in ways that led to better understanding of Dewey.

The first connection students pointed out between Freire and Dewey was that both were men of action. Their social activism, these students also noted, contrasted with the lives of Pieper, Marcel, and Snyder who were not activists. A second Freirian idea that students connected to Dewey was that if one does not help others, one cannot be fully human. These pupils noted that Freire, like Dewey, believes that people who have hope have an obligation to those who are in despair to help them recover hope.

IDEAS FROM C. R. SNYDER THAT HELPED STUDENTS CONTEXTUALIZE DEWEY

As with the case of Freire, none of Fishman's students applied ideas from C. R. Snyder to their lives in significant ways, although several mentioned that they took some tips from Snyder about how to better reach their goals. The reasons that Snyder's *Psychology of Hope* did not provoke major insights for students may be similar to the causes for Freire's work failing to do so. Only two class days were devoted to Snyder's work, and these came at the very end of the semester. Nevertheless, Fishman, looking back, concluded that he was glad he had assigned Snyder for the same reason he was glad he had assigned Freire: Snyder's work provided valuable contextualization for Dewey.

The connections students made between Snyder's work and Dewey's were twofold. First, although pupils had complained about the vagueness and complexity of Dewey's work, when they got to Snyder's clearer—and simpler—conception of hope, it, ironically, made them better appreciate Dewey's more complicated, and they said, more perceptive discussion of hope. Second, Dewey's idea of wholeheartedness came into sharper focus as students recognized the lack of any mention in Snyder's work of the importance for hope of wholehearted, intelligent goal selection.

IDEAS FROM GABRIEL MARCEL THAT HELPED STUDENTS RECONCEIVE ASPECTS OF THEIR LIVES

Although Marcel's work is more difficult to understand than either Freire's or Snyder's, and although Fishman said he felt unsure at times of his own command of Marcel, Marcel's ideas were, nevertheless, personally valuable for a number of students. For two of them, his ideas were most important. Marcel's relative significance may result from the fact that the class spent more time discussing his work than that of Freire or Snyder (four class sessions instead of two).

In particular, three Marcellian notions received special attention. First, one student was strongly affected by Marcel's idea that the world is mysterious and much of what goes on in life we cannot explain. Second, another student found especially useful Marcel's notion of despair as a kind of witchcraft, a spell that one casts on oneself. Finally, an idea that several students appreciated was Marcel's concept of presence or spiritual availability.

IDEAS FROM DEWEY THAT HELPED STUDENTS RECONCEIVE ASPECTS OF THEIR LIVES

The author whose ideas had the greatest impact on students was Dewey. Dewey influenced nearly all the students in the class in some way, and for five of the ten, his ideas were most important in their growing understanding and practice of hope. There are, of course, numerous reasons that students found Dewey most helpful—including their devoting most time to him of all the authors (five and a half weeks), Fishman's special appreciation of him, and some students' familiarity with him from earlier philosophy classes. Whatever the reasons were, I was, in the end, impressed with the confidence with which a number of students were able to discuss and apply Dewey's ideas given the challenges of reading and understanding his work. Ultimately, five Deweyan ideas appealed to Fishman's students.

First was Dewey's view that life is a rhythm of disturbance and harmony in which failure and disharmony are to be expected. These latter do not mean that the world is against you or there is something lacking in you. Connected to this idea, and equally attractive to students, was Dewey's contention that the only way to grow is to learn from one's mistakes and life's disasters. Second was Dewey's notion of gratitude, one of the three keys to Deweyan hope that Fishman describes in Chapter 1 of this volume. Dewey's idea that gratitude to our ancestors for the goods we have received means we have an obligation to pass these goods along to future generations was especially important to two of Steve's students. Third, Dewey's notion of engrossed present experience, another of Fishman's three keys to Deweyan hope, received significant attention from three of Fishman's students. Fourth, students took to heart Dewey's faith that people can work together to change things and make them better. Three students gave this idea special attention when they discussed the concepts that most helped them recover or increase their hope. Finally, Dewey's faith that little acts can have large consequences was mentioned as a cause for hope by five of the ten students in Fishman's class.

In conclusion, as I look back over my semester-long study of Fishman's Hope course, I am impressed that the majority of this group of ten undergraduates, many of whom were not well prepared for the class or particularly academically resourceful, got as much from the class as they did. The combination of the high motivation of many of them and the cooperative classroom climate allowed at least six of the ten to internalize some ideas from the hope literature and use these ideas to recover or increase their levels of hope.

Final Reflections

Steve Fishman and Lucille McCarthy

Ours is the responsibility of conserving, transmitting, rectifying and expanding the heritage of values we have received that those who come after us may receive it more solid and secure, more widely accessible and more generously shared than we have received it.

—John Dewey, *A Common Faith* (*LW* 9:57–58)

In this final chapter, we come full circle. It is not a typical conclusion in that we neither summarize Steve's philosophic findings about hope—he did that in Chapter 5—or Lucille's findings about Fishman's course on hope—she did that in Chapter 8. Rather, we reflect on what we said in the Prologue where each of us described our reasons for undertaking this project. Although we recounted different histories and paths leading each of us to this work, our stories were similar insofar as we each came to this research needing, like five of Fishman's ten students, more hope. We both told how the events of the past few years, coupled with our own aging, have rendered us less hopeful than we have ever been. In these final reflections, each of us describes what we take from this study and if and how it has raised our levels of hope.

Understanding Hope and Connecting Philosophy to the "Problems of Men"
Steve Fishman

The first positive residue that I take from this joint project with Lucille McCarthy is a better understanding of the issues and ongoing conversation about hope. Second, I also understand better my own struggles to live in hope. As I noted in Part I of this book, my habits lead me to emphasize the perils of life rather than its stabilities and good fortunes. I tend to believe that famine and failure are around the corner more often than festival and song (*LW* 1:43). However, learning about the keys to Deweyan hope—gratitude, intelligent wholeheartedness, and rich present experience—helps me be clearer about the moments I have felt most comfortable in the world, most fully alive, most able to lose myself in the present moment, that is, most hopeful.

In addition, thanks to this study, I am better able to recognize the ways in which nature does cooperate with me—for example, the ways in which nature has permitted me the experience of carrying out this project. I also, like several of my students, profit from Dewey's reminder that defeat and success come from the same root. This helps me put my failures and misfortunes in better perspective and take them a little more in stride. I can see them as part of the necessary rhythm of a living world, what Dewey, borrowing from William James, calls our constant "flights and perchings" (*MW* 14:125). In fact, these flights and perchings mark my experiences with hope. My ability to live in hope—to feel grateful, wholehearted, and engrossed in the present—is something I have to continually work at. It is for me, again to borrow from Dewey, a constant effort to use my intelligence to build new hope in the face of fresh temptations to despair.

Besides what I take from this study about the hope literature and my own struggles to live in hope, I am, as this project closes, certainly grateful that the majority of the students in my Hope class reported to McCarthy that they found ideas and had experiences that they could apply to their lives and use to rekindle hope. These reports by my students are especially satisfying because I have been trying to find ways to use philosophic theory to make a difference, in my own and others' lives, ever since I decided to major in philosophy as a college sophomore almost fifty years ago. However, faced with a field dominated by ordinary language analysis and logical positivism, I have often felt, because of this desire to make philosophy hit the ground, a stranger in the discipline. Somehow, I seem always to be asking the wrong question by continually wondering, "Why in the world are we, as philosophers, spending most of our time talking to one another about meta-issues concerning truth, mind, and language while the world is burning and we seem to be doing so little about it?"

This collaborative inquiry—researching, teaching, and writing about hope—has been my modest way of trying to do something about it, my way of avoiding what Dewey warned his philosopher colleagues against: "chewing a historic cud long since reduced to woody fibre" (*MW* 10:47). Instead, with McCarthy's help, I have tried to do what John Herman Randall Jr. suggests we do in one of the epigraphs we chose for this book. I have tried to see a little further than Dewey saw by building on his insights, by constructing a theory of hope that Dewey himself hints at but never explicitly develops. Further, in writing about loss of hope and how to restore and maintain it in dark times, I have also tried to face one of the issues that confronts society at large. I have attempted to avoid "chewing on a historic cud," or focusing only on the problems of philosophers by dealing, instead, with what I believe Dewey would have called one of "the problems of men" (*MW* 10:46).

Collaborative Teacher Research and Hope
Lucille McCarthy

Steve Fishman has just described how he benefited from our joint project. I want now to explore its outcomes for me. Has it raised my level of hope? In the Prologue, I explained that, after initially refusing Steve's invitation to participate in this study, I ultimately changed my mind and joined him because of its focus on hope, something I had to admit I was low on given the world situation and my own lessened enthusiasm in several areas of my life. I also recounted that my reason for refusing at first to be part of this inquiry was that Steve and I had been doing collaborative teacher research for some thirteen years, and I was weary of it. In particular, I felt we had exhausted our pedagogical focus, one in which we had, in numerous studies over the years, explicated and tested various educational theories—Deweyan, Freirian, liberal, communitarian, and so on—and various approaches to the teaching of writing. My refusal to go on with this sort of research did not mean that I believed any less passionately in its benefits for both teachers and their pupils when teachers join with outside researchers, as Steve had done with me, to study their own classrooms. Steve and I had, in fact, witnessed those benefits as he and I reinvigorated our interest in and approaches to teaching as a result of our findings. Nevertheless, I was tired of the collaboration, and I wanted to call it quits.

However, as I also said, after a few weeks of "retirement," a period during which I felt at sea and quite useless, I talked further with Fishman to see if his offer still stood. It did, and after hearing more about the literature he proposed to explore, I decided to come aboard. In the end, I am glad I did because I have indeed taken hope from our work. For me, however, unlike Steve, my increased hopefulness is not, primarily, the result of reading Dewey or Marcel or Freire or Snyder, although I appreciate these men's visions. That is, I did not, like Steve, find concepts in the literature that helped me revise my worldview. Rather, my increased hopefulness results from my classroom inquiry.

First, I am more hopeful as a researcher. I come away with a new vision of classroom research because this project was different from anything I had ever done (and, as far as I know, different from anything any other educational researcher has done). Although, in this project, I continue to discuss pedagogy—for example, the challenges of featuring indirect teaching and constructed knowing—this is the first time I have tried to figure out which ideas students take with them from a course and how they apply them to their lives. This was a daunting task because it involved not only understanding students' personal issues and classroom learning experiences but also knowing the literature students were reading and their perceptions of that literature. At times, I thought I would not be able to do it. However, the fact that I could, ultimately, with Steve's assistance, explore what I see as a central educational question—What residues live on in students from a classroom experience?—gives me hope for my own research future. That is, I see possible sequels to this study, including following Hope course students across time and watching what happens to the ideas that seemed to them, at the end of the semester, to have been so personally valuable.

Second, like student Chris Vernarsky, I am more hopeful as a result of watching these undergraduates' seriousness. More specifically, I was impressed both by students' sincere efforts to understand and cope with their personal problems as well as by their determination to understand—and help each other understand—difficult reading material. Regarding their efforts to understand their personal challenges, I particularly recall my initial interview with Charles Dautun. At first I did not want to speak with Charles, preferring to focus on other students, because Charles had been absent a good deal and spoke so quietly in class that the videotape record was incomplete. Yet when one of the students with whom I did want to talk accidentally handed Charles the interview schedule, he signed up to meet with me, and, despite my reluctance to add Charles to my list, I agreed to do so at Fishman's urging. I left that hour-long interview moved by Charles's story and impressed with his articulateness and the amount of help he was getting from the course. Despite Charles's difficulties reading Dewey, and despite his working two jobs, having an injured back, and spending enormous amounts of time and energy trying to support his bereaved girlfriend and her family, he spoke of ideas in Dewey's work that were sustaining him. I had similarly moving interviews with Beth, Shoua, Bob, Lindsey, and others, most of whom were working as hard as Charles to use course material to make sense of their lives and climb out of despair.

Regarding these pupils' determination to understand—and help each other understand—the assigned reading, I was, as I said, impressed by how diligently students worked together in small groups and in whole-class discussion to figure out what writers like Dewey and Marcel, who are often far from clear, were saying. They seemed to put their heads together, listening carefully to one another, often quoting each other, and nearly all of them telling me in interviews that they learned from their classmates. Of course, in my own classroom, I see young people whom I admire, but I never get to know my own students as intimately as I do my research informants. What I learned about these undergraduates, or at least the majority of them, is that they were not in school just to get a degree so they could go out and make money. They were, rather, committed to figuring out how to live meaningful lives, ones that, if not trouble-free, as they realized full well they could not be, were at least "on a plain of okayness," to use Lindsey Weston's words.

Finally, I derive hope from Fishman's and my having been able to complete this research. As I have said, when we finished our previous book, I believed that our collaboration was over. Yet after I reluctantly agreed to join Steve in an exploration of hope, we managed to negotiate our differences and help each other as we designed, carried out, and wrote up this four-year project. In fact, at various times we achieved harmonies of the sort Dewey describes as life's "intensest" moments, and this has given me great satisfaction. I come away with hope that I can, in the future, overcome obstacles similar to the ones I overcame in this research and experience similar joys.

Last Words

Steve Fishman

Dewey teaches that we are not just in our environment; the environment is also in us. The air we breathe, the food we eat are all part of a process in which we, as live creatures, are constantly transacting with our environment. Where we begin and where our environment ends is not clear. Further, Dewey points out that this environment is unstable. Although all processes do not change at the same speed, some being more or less stable than others, change is inevitable and never fully predictable. Thus, Dewey cautions, we can never be sure of the outcome of our efforts; there are no guarantees. Applying these Deweyan ideas to our inquiry, Lucille and I are in no way sure that our efforts to research, teach, and write about hope, as well as to study student responses to a course on hope, will have long-term positive consequences.

Admittedly, Lucille's and my project does very little to solve the global problems of war, ecological destruction, and increasing poverty that, as we said at the opening of this book, gnaw at our social and personal hopes. However, as Dewey also teaches, we must trust that if we have labored intelligently and wholeheartedly, our work will do something to pass on what we find excellent in our culture in a form, "more solid and secure, more widely accessible than we have received it" (*LW* 9:57–58). More specifically, we must trust that our efforts will increase the hope not only of a few students but also, perhaps, of some of our readers and even a few of the people with whom these students and readers come into contact. Finally, we must have faith that the shared student investigations in my classroom, as well as Lucille's and my collaboration, will, in some small way, further Dewey's ultimate hope: the extension to all people of democratic living and the cooperative, respectful, and ongoing inquiry that characterizes it.

Lucille McCarthy

In order to construct my findings about student and teacher experiences in Steve Fishman's Philosophy and Practice of Hope course, I joined with Steve to conduct a qualitative classroom study of the sort we have done frequently across our thirteen-year collaboration. During the semester, Steve, as inside teacher, and I, as outside researcher, collected a wide range of data offering multiple perspectives on the classroom.

Data Gathered in the Philosophy and Practice of Hope Course, Spring 2005

CLASSROOM AND OTHER OBSERVATIONS

Teacher-researcher-insider Fishman observed all classes and recorded notes after each session.

Outside composition researcher McCarthy observed seven classes and took notes during and after each session.

Videotapes of all classes were made for later study.

McCarthy observed and audiotaped Fishman in his office as he wrote and recorded responses to the three sets of student essays.

TEACHER LOG

Fishman wrote his impressions of class events and their meaning in frequent log entries that came to just under one hundred typed pages by the end of the semester.

INTERVIEWS

Four thirty- to sixty-minute interviews were conducted by McCarthy at regular intervals with nine of the ten students (the tenth, Charles Dautun, had three interviews). Three of the four interviews with each student were done in person and audiotaped for later transcription, and one was conducted on the telephone with McCarthy taking notes. (Charles Dautun's interviews included one hour-long face-to-face interview and two fifteen-minute ones on the phone.)

TEXTS

All of our ten informants' in-class and out-of-class assignments were collected for analysis.

Data-analysis Procedures

Early in the spring of 2005, I began reading and rereading the data we were collecting from the Hope course, looking for themes and patterns.[1] As salient themes and patterns emerged, and as Steve and I collected further data and conversed across the semester, I narrowed my focus to two areas: (1) Fishman's pedagogy, more specifically, the ways of knowing he was trying to balance and the effects upon classroom interaction of his teacher-as-inquirer stance and (2) the philosophic concepts—from Dewey and other authors—that students gravitated to and said were useful to them personally.

In this kind of qualitative research, the researcher makes no claims to objectivity, nor does he or she claim to have controlled variables in ways that render the study replicable or findings generalizable to other classrooms. In fact, no such control is possible in classrooms where, as language researcher James Britton puts it, "every variable is actively varying."[2] Rather, as a researcher engaged in qualitative inquiry, I acknowledge my situated perspective and claim the benefits of it: the insights that come from intimate knowledge of the local context and from collaborating with "native-speaker" participants in this context. My goal is to construct findings about a small number of participants in the local setting—in this case, Fishman and his ten students. That is, I intend to create a "thick description" of events, one that results from my triangulating among multiple data sources and investigators.[3] If the research report I present in Chapters 6 and 7 is successful, my readers will be able to step into Fishman's classroom and into his and his students' experiences and recognize issues that resonate with their own. Readers may, then, transfer findings from my study of Fishman's class to their own settings in ways that inform both their teaching and their understanding of hope.[4]

APPENDIX B:
CREATING A SYLLABUS FOR A COURSE
ON HOPE

Steve Fishman

John Dewey

I chose the Dewey books and their chapters for my course based on passages that I believed were relevant to constructing a theory of hope for him. For example, in the first chapter of *Human Nature and Conduct,* I thought passages were relevant in which Dewey talks about gratitude being the root of all virtue and loyalty to what is excellent being the start of progress. I also saw as relevant some passages in the later chapters of *Human Nature and Conduct* in which Dewey refers to the importance of our sense of the enveloping whole (chapters 21, 22, 23, and 26). When I say these passages seemed important to me, I mean that I thought they were significant for a Deweyan theory of hope yet difficult for me to fully understand. In assigning them in my course, I figured they would provide some clues to my students about developing a theory of hope for Dewey, as they did for me. More than that, however, I also wanted to understand them better myself as a result of preparing to discuss them with my students and hearing what they had to say.

Similar thinking lay behind my choice of other Dewey books and specific chapters. For example, chapter 2, "Experience as Precarious and Stable," of *Experience and Nature* is extremely relevant to a Deweyan theory of hope since only in a world that is precarious and uncertain can there be hope. In other words, in a world of sure things, it would make sense to say that we know about future successes, but it would not make sense to say that we hope for them. In my syllabus, I also included the final chapter from *Experience and*

Nature because of Dewey's echo of Job 13:15—that we must trust although the world slay us—because I was not sure exactly what to make of it.

Regarding the chapters I assigned from *Art as Experience*, I assigned chapter 1 primarily because I wanted to learn more about Dewey's comment that a primordial sense of harmony haunts human life like something founded on a rock. I was also puzzled and eager to discuss with my students Dewey's references, in chapter 2, to Keats, Emerson, and the novelist William Henry Hudson, passages in which Dewey says that the aesthetic in nature and art can provide intense mystical moments akin to religious communion. In addition, I wanted to see what my students could help me figure out about Dewey's claim, in chapter 9, that in art we somehow lose ourselves to find ourselves. We leave our present world to find another world on which the present world is founded.

We read Dewey for the first five weeks of the course, and for the final Dewey readings I assigned the first two chapters of *A Common Faith*. I did so because of the passages in these chapters in which Dewey talks about religious experiences and adjustments that are so pervasive that they yield an enduring sense of peace and stability. I also assigned these chapters because I wanted a chance to explore more fully Dewey's reconstruction of God as the dynamic relation between the ideal—the possibilities that call to us from the dark and unknown future—and the actual.

Josef Pieper

In planning the course, as well as my study of Dewey and hope, I wanted to contextualize Dewey. I wanted to compare the theory I construct for him with theories by researchers who explicitly discuss hope. I decided on Pieper for three reasons. First, he is one of the twentieth century's best-known Thomistic scholars, so his relatively detailed analysis of hope reflects one of the classic approaches to the topic. Second, I suspected that my students would find Pieper accessible, his writing style clear and easy to follow despite his many references to Saint Thomas's work. Third, I believed that Pieper would serve as something of an introduction to Marcel, with whom I also wanted to compare or contextualize Dewey. Although I realize that Marcel did not like being called a Christian existentialist, I expected that my students would find some common ground between Pieper and Marcel. Thus, if things worked out well, Pieper would be both a chance to learn more about Dewey as we compared Dewey and Pieper and something of a bridge to Marcel, whose style is much less accessible than Pieper's.

I chose to have my students read Pieper's 1935 essay "On Hope," because it is his best-known and most definitive exploration of the subject. I also, as a prelude to my students reading "On Hope," assigned the first of Pieper's five 1967 lectures, collected in *Hope and History*, because, in this lecture, Pieper relates his view of hope to the use of "hope" in ordinary language. My thinking was that Pieper's study of ordinary language as a way to begin an exploration of hope would be a good introduction for my students to his earlier, and better-known, 1935 essay.

Gabriel Marcel

I decided to include selections from Marcel in the course because, of all contemporary philosophers, his work comes up most often in philosophic discussions of hope. Further, Marcel himself says that hope is at the center of his philosophy.[1] So, as I planned my course on hope, I decided to devote four classes and four reading assignments to Marcel. For the first reading assignment, I chose his 1943 lecture "A Sketch of a Phenomenology and a Metaphysic of Hope," later published as chapter 2 in *Homo Viator: Introduction to a Metaphysic of Hope*. Marcel saw this lecture as one of the watersheds of his mature philosophy.

For the second Marcel reading, I chose his 1963 talk "Desire and Hope," because in this later address Marcel reflects on his earlier, 1943, lecture. I also chose "Desire and Hope" because I believe it is a less difficult piece, considerably shorter and more focused, than "A Sketch of a Phenomenology and a Metaphysic of Hope."

For the third Marcel reading, I selected his 1933 lecture "On the Ontological Mystery." This lecture provides additional background to Marcel's approach to hope. It presents his view of contemporary society and how it promotes despair by convincing us that we are nothing more than cogs in a social machine. I also chose "On the Ontological Mystery" because Marcel appended it to his stage play *The Broken World*, and, thus, I believed it might provide a good bridge to the fourth and final Marcel reading of the course: the last act of his four-act play, "The Broken World."

Paulo Freire

As I planned the course on hope, my thinking was that Freire would be interesting to read after Dewey, Pieper, and Marcel. More specifically, I thought students might find new viewpoints on our earlier readings by seeing how the democratic and pragmatic traditions of Dewey, the Catholicism of Pieper, and the phenomenology and existentialism of Marcel are combined and transformed in Freire. The image I have of Freire is of a prism through which Catholicism, existentialism, Marxism, and neocolonialism flow to form a challenging, revolutionary hue.

Although there are some passages in Freire's work in which he explicitly discusses hope, these passages are few and far between. This is true, although Freire calls one of his books *Pedagogy of Hope.* This volume, however, despite its title, does not systematically discuss hope but is primarily Freire's recollection of the events and intellectual movements that led him to write *Pedagogy of the Oppressed.* Thus, somewhat like my Dewey selections, the Freire readings I assigned were passages I found scattered throughout Freire's work. These included two sections explicitly focused on hope from his book *Pedagogy of the Heart* (42–51, 101–7), his preface to *Pedagogy of Hope,* several pages from chapter 3 of *Pedagogy of the Oppressed* in which Freire talks about dialogue, and his 1973 essay "Education, Liberation, and the Church."

As a companion piece to these selections from Freire, I also assigned a recent article by the psychologist Richard S. Lazarus, late emeritus professor from the University of California at Berkeley, titled, "Hope: An Emotion and a Vital Coping Resource against Despair." I included the Lazarus article for two reasons. One, I wanted to introduce a voice from the discipline of psychology, a field that has recently begun to devote increasing attention to hope, and, two, I thought my students might find parallels in Freire to Lazarus's claim that hope is an important coping mechanism and requires action to be sustained. I also included as a second companion piece to the Freire readings an article by Randolph Nesse, a professor of psychiatry at the University of Michigan, titled "The Evolution of Hope and Despair." I included this piece because Nesse, like Freire, addresses the politics of hope, in particular what Nesse sees as the conservative way in which much religion and, now, modern psychotherapy function.

C. R. Snyder

A clinical psychologist and professor of psychology at the University of Kansas, Snyder began his research on hope in the early 1990s. Snyder and the so-called positive psychologists, a movement organized by Martin E. P. Seligman at the University of Pennsylvania in the late 1990s, have conducted the most systematic studies of hope in the social sciences. I included chapters from

Snyder's *Psychology of Hope* as a final unit in my course to further contextualize the theory of hope I construct for Dewey. My thinking was that Snyder's language and approach would give my students yet another angle from which to view a Deweyan theory of hope, the theory—or, better yet, its construction—that I thought of as the centerpiece or unifying theme of the course.

APPENDIX C:
SYLLABUS, ESSAY GUIDELINES, AND HOMEWORK ASSIGNMENTS

Steve Fishman

Syllabus—The Philosophy and Practice of Hope

REQUIRED TEXTS

John Dewey, *Experience and Nature* (Open Court)
John Dewey, *Art as Experience* (Perigee Books)
Josef Pieper, *On Hope* (Ignatius Press)
Katharine Rose Hanley, *Gabriel Marcel's Perspectives on "The Broken World"* (Marquette)
C. R. Snyder, *The Psychology of Hope* (Free Press)

Please purchase these books as soon as possible at the University Bookstore.

In addition, handouts of required readings will be distributed by the instructor during the semester. These will include excerpts from the following texts:

John Dewey, *Human Nature and Conduct*
John Dewey, *A Common Faith*
Paulo Freire, *Pedagogy of the Oppressed*
Paulo Preire, *Pedagogy of Hope*
Paulo Freire, *Pedagogy of the Heart*
Gabriel Marcel, *Homo Viator: Introduction to a Metaphysic of Hope*
Gabriel Marcel, *The Philosophy of Existentialism*
Josef Pieper, *Hope and History*

Thich Nhat Hanh, *Touching Peace* (Parallax Press)

COURSE REQUIREMENTS

Attendance—Because this course involves numerous interactive, in-class assignments, as opposed to lectures, attendance is required. Without your attendance and participation, class is diminished. As a result, the course grades of students with more than three absences will be lowered by one half-grade for each absence beyond three.

In-class Writing—Most class periods will begin with five to ten minutes of informal writing. For example, I might ask you to write about what stands out for you from the most recent reading assignment or I might ask you to turn to a specific passage in the assigned text, take notes, and then write a brief response to the author. I call this work "informal" writing because I would like you to compose without concern for grammar and syntax. I would like you to write spontaneously, to use this in-class work as a way of learning and discovering rather than reporting. That is, the main purpose of these in-class assignments is to get us thinking about various issues before we talk about them, a type of "jump-start" for our class discussions. I will collect all of your in-class writing at the end of each period so that I can read it, although I will not grade it.

Homework Writing Assignments—Homework writing assignments will accompany many course readings. Each of these assignments needs to be typed and ready for use at the start of class. No late or untyped papers will be accepted. If you miss class and do not get the assignment, please email me or a classmate so you can get the assignment and complete it on time. If you are unable to attend class on a day when a written assignment is due, please paste your homework into an email and send it to me before the start of class on the day the assignment is due. Completion of these assignments is required, and I will read and respond to them but not grade them. If you fail to hand in two on time, your final grade will drop one grade; if you fail to hand in four on time, your final grade will drop two grades, etc.

Three Essays—You will be required to write three essays across the semester. These must be typed and will be graded, and each will count as one-third of your course grade. Each essay must answer three questions:
　(1) What have you learned about hope from the readings preceding the essay (Dewey for essay 1; Pieper and Marcel for essay 2; and Freire, Snyder, Lazarus, and Nesse for essay 3)?

(2) Discuss your own evolving theory of hope and relate it to the figures you've discussed in part 1.

(3) Describe how your personal theory of hope influences your everyday life.

There will be a class session set aside for peer review and discussion of drafts of all three essays. Five copies of these drafts, of which I will collect one, are due February 22, April 5, and May 3, respectively. Final drafts of the essays are due February 24, April 7, and May 5. Please mark these dates, as no late drafts or essays will be accepted. Failure to turn in a draft or essay on time will result in an F for that assignment. In addition to the written comments I make to your essays, I will respond orally and at greater length on a cassette tape that I will provide for each student when I return your essays.

[Note: Fishman changed the third essay topic and gave the new topic to students two weeks before it was due. This assignment is appended at the bottom of the syllabus.]

ACADEMIC INTEGRITY

Please note that students have the responsibility to know and observe "The UNC Charlotte Student Code of Responsibility." Copies of the code, which appears in the UNC Charlotte catalog, are available at the Dean of Student's Office in 217 King Building. Concern for academic integrity, especially regarding plagiarism, has become increasingly important with material so easily copied off the Internet, so please be aware of the content of UNC Charlotte's Student code of responsibility.

COURSE SCHEDULE

January 11: Course introduction
January 13: Dewey, *Human Nature and Conduct*, chapters 1, 5, and 7
   [Homework Assignment 1]
January 18: Dewey, *Human Nature and Conduct*, chapters 8, 9, and 10
   [Homework Assignment 2]
January 20: Dewey, *Human Nature and Conduct*, chapters 14 and 16
January 25: Dewey, *Human Nature and Conduct*, chapters 21, 22, 23, and 26 (pp. 225–27)
   [Homework Assignment 3]
January 27: Dewey, *Experience and Nature*, chapter 2
February 1: Dewey, *Experience and Nature*, chapter 10
   [Homework Assignment 4]

February 3: Dewey, *Art as Experience*, chapter 1
February 8: Dewey, *Art as Experience*, chapter 2

[Homework Assignment 5]
February 10: Dewey, *Art as Experience*, chapters 3 and 9 (pp. 187–95)
February 15: Dewey, *A Common Faith*, chapter 1

[Homework Assignment 6]
February 17: Dewey, *A Common Faith*, chapter 2
February 22: Draft of essay 1 due
February 24: Essay 1 due
March 1 and 3 No class
March 8 and 10 Spring break
March 15: Pieper, *Hope and History*, pp. 13–31; Pieper, *On Hope*, chapters 1 and 2

[Homework Assignment 7]
March 17: Pieper, *On Hope*, chapters 3, 4, and 5
March 22: Marcel, "A Sketch of a Phenomenology and a Metaphysic of Hope"

[Homework Assignment 8]
March 24: Marcel, "Desire and Hope"
March 29: Marcel, "On the Ontological Mystery"

[Homework Assignment 9]
March 31: Marcel, from *Perspectives on "The Broken World,"* Katharine Hanley's introduction, pp. 13–27, act 4 of *A Broken World*
April 5: Draft of essay 2 due
April 7: Essay 2 due
April 12 and 14: No class
April 19: Freire, *Pedagogy of Hope*, "Opening Words"; *Pedagogy of the Heart*, pp. 42–51, 101–7; *Pedagogy of the Oppressed*, pp. 87–95; Lazarus, "Hope: An Emotion and a Vital Coping Resource against Despair"

[Homework Assignment 10]
April 21: Freire, "Education, Liberation, and the Church"; Nesse, "The Evolution of Hope and Despair"
April 26: Snyder, *The Psychology of Hope*, chapters 1 and 2

[Homework Assignment 11]
April 28: Snyder, *The Psychology of Hope*, chapter 6
May 3: Draft of essay 3 due
May 5: Essay 3 due

Appendage to the Hope Course Syllabus
(added April 21)

When Fishman changed the assignment for essay 3, he handed his students the following guidelines sheet:

ESSAY 3—HOW THIS COURSE HAS AFFECTED MY LIFE

I have changed the focus for the third essay, a draft of which is due Tuesday, May 3—and since you will be sharing your draft with classmates, please bring three copies with you to class.

Instead of focusing on just our two most recent authors, Freire and Snyder, in essay 3, please focus on the entire course. Please choose the principles that have affected your behavior or your ways of thinking or perceiving. You may choose as many principles/ideas as you like, ones that really have made you think and/or change, and they may come from the readings, the teacher, or your classmates. Essay 3, like essays 1 and 2, will be graded.

Organization of the essay: For each principle or idea that has affected you,

(1) describe the principle or idea and its source and explain its meaning; quote the written and oral sources wherever possible

(2) show how each idea has affected your behavior, thinking, or feeling; give examples, please, so I can better see and understand this change

(3) finally, please describe how these ideas have influenced your conception of the nature of hope, your views about why you (and others) might be short on hope, and your thinking about what you (and others) might do to maintain or recover hope

The Eleven Homework Assignments

One written assignment was required each week, usually on the Tuesday class (of the Tuesday-Thursday schedule). The assignment was handed to students at the end of the class period before it was due. They then brought their answers, typed, to the subsequent class period. On several occasions, Fishman had students trade their homework papers and comment in writing about each others' answers at the beginning of class. He then built class discussion around students' homework answers. These homework papers were required, and Fishman responded to them with comments, but he did not grade them.

After reading chapters 1, 5, and 7 of *Human Nature and Conduct* (from the handout), please type answers to the following four questions.

1. What stands out for you from your reading of chapters 1, 5, and 7 of *Human Nature and Conduct*?
2. Dewey writes, "There is sound sense in the old pagan notion that gratitude is the root of all virtue" (p. 19).
   a. What does Dewey mean by this?
   b. What, if anything, does this quote tell you about the nature of Dewey's highest hopes?
3. Dewey also writes, "Individuals with their exhortations, their preachings and scoldings, their inner aspirations and sentiments have disappeared, but their habits endure, because their habits incorporate objective conditions in themselves. So it will be with *our* activities" (p. 19).
   a. What does he mean by this?
   b. What, if anything, does this quote tell you about the way Dewey expects to work toward achieving his highest hopes?
4. What clues do chapters 5 and 7 provide about Dewey's view of the causes of hopelessness or low hope?

Please type answers to the following three questions about chapters 8, 9, and 10 of *Human Nature and Conduct*. (Note: No handwritten papers will be accepted.)

1. What strikes you in these chapters, and what in them do you see as relevant to constructing a theory of hope for Dewey?
2. Do you agree with Dewey that "original modifiability" is the means to a "better human life" (p. 70)? Or do you believe that Dewey's position reflects a false, overly hopeful view of the young?
3. Dewey claims in chapters 9 and 10 that, given his theory of habit and impulse, war and economic exploitation are preventable.
   a. Please outline his argument.
   b. Please evaluate his hope that both are preventable; that is to say, how reasonable is it to hope for the cessation of war and economic exploitation?

Please type answers to the following questions about chapters 21, 22, 23, and 26 (pp. 225–27) of *Human Nature and Conduct.*

1. In chapters 21, 22, and 23, Dewey tells us that the value of the objects we seek is not their attainment at some future moment but their ability to harmonize our activities in the present moment.
   a. Please outline Dewey's attempt to support his position.
   b. After outlining Dewey's argument, explain why you agree or disagree with Dewey about the function of "ends-in-view."
2. At the close of chapter 21 (pp. 179–81) and in the concluding paragraphs of the book (pp. 225–27), Dewey refers to his sense of "the enveloping whole."
   a. Why is a sense of "the enveloping whole" important for Dewey's hopes?
   b. Have you ever sensed "the enveloping whole"? Please explain.

After reading chapter 10 of *Experience and Nature*, please type answers to the following questions.

1. What additional clues does chapter 10 of *Experience and Nature* offer about the object of Dewey's ultimate hopes?
2. What does Dewey mean when he says philosophy is a criticism of criticisms (p. 322)?
3. Dewey argues that there is no "intrinsic difference between the relation of scientific inquiry to belief values, of esthetic criticism to esthetic values, and of moral judgments to moral goods" (p. 347).
   a. Why is this contention important for Dewey's ultimate hopes?
   b. Do you agree or disagree with Dewey's contention? Please explain.

(The word "hopes" appears three times in chapter 10. See if you can spot the three occasions as you read through the chapter.)

Chapter 2 of *Art as Experience* is an especially interesting chapter with references by Dewey to the romantic poets John Keats and Samuel Coleridge, the transcendentalist Ralph Waldo Emerson, and the British ornithologist and novelist William Henry Hudson. After reading chapter 2, please type answers to the following two questions.

1. Choose the passage in chapter 2 of *Art as Experience* that you find most provocative and indicate why it is important to you.
2. Conclude your homework paper with at least two questions about the passage you have chosen that you would like to raise and discuss with your classmates.

HOMEWORK ASSIGNMENT 6—DUE TUESDAY, FEBRUARY 15

Please read chapter 1 of *A Common Faith* and type answers to the following three questions.

1. Although Dewey denies the existence of a transcendent God in *A Common Faith*, he affirms that certain experiences are dominantly religious. How does Dewey characterize the nature and function of experiences that are dominantly religious?
2. Dewey's view of religious experience leads him to reconstruct the concepts of moral faith, religious faith, and the "unseen power controlling our destiny" (pp. 4, 17). As best you can, please describe Dewey's reconstructions of the concepts of moral faith, religious faith, and the unseen power having control over our destiny.
3. In what ways are these Deweyan reconstructions important for developing a theory of hope for him?

HOMEWORK ASSIGNMENT 7—DUE TUESDAY, MARCH 15

Please read chapter 1 of Pieper's *Hope and History* (pp. 13–31) and chapters 1 and 2 of Pieper's *On Hope* (pp. 11–43) and type answers to the following questions.

1. In *Hope and History*, Josef Pieper writes that "hope per se" or "fundamental existential hope" (pp. 30–31) cannot be disappointed.
   a. How does Pieper arrive at this conclusion from his analysis of the linguistic usage of *hope* or what "people mean when they speak of hope and hoping"?
   b. Do you agree with Pieper's findings about how people use the word "hope"?
2. In chapters 1 and 2 of *On Hope*, Pieper distinguishes between natural and theological or fundamental hope. How, according to Pieper, are these two types of hope related?
3. What does your reading of these three chapters of Pieper's work teach you about your own hopes? What questions, if any, do they raise for you?

Please read Gabriel Marcel's "Sketch of a Phenomenology and a Metaphysic of Hope" (from handout) and type answers to the following questions.

1. In his "Sketch of a Phenomenology and a Metaphysic of Hope," Marcel tells us that despair is identical to solitude (p. 58). He says that it "preys" on one's self (p. 44) and that it is "a kind of witchcraft, whose evil action has a bearing on all which goes to form the very substance of a person's life" (p. 42). Please explain, as best you can and in your own words, what assumptions and beliefs lead Marcel to this characterization of despair.

2. In the same essay, Marcel says that hope is both restoration and renewal (p. 67), both communion and love (p. 60). He says that hope draws upon elements brought to us "along canals, often very badly marked out, from friendly cities, of which however [we] often scarcely know the name or the situation" (p. 61).
   a. What does Marcel mean by these claims?
   b. How does he defend them?

3. Please compare Marcel's and Dewey's theories of hope. In which ways are they similar? In which ways are they different?

4. Please compare Marcel's and Pieper's theories of hope. In which ways are they similar? In which ways are they different?

Please read Marcel's "On the Ontological Mystery" and type answers to the following three questions.

1. In his essay "On the Ontological Mystery," Marcel argues that we live within an "increasingly inhuman social order" (p. 12). Where does Marcel lay the blame for what he calls the "stifling impression of sadness" of the contemporary world (p. 12)?

2. Marcel suggests that contemporary society's problem is that it has lost all sense of the wonder and mystery of life.
   a. Do you agree or disagree with Marcel? Please explain.
   b. If you agree with Marcel, what in your life has led you to neglect or dismiss wonderment and mystery as important characteristics of experience? If you do not agree, please indicate where wonder and mystery are present in your experience.

3. Marcel talks about the importance of presence, availability, and creativity for reclaiming our sense of mystery, wonder, and hope. What clues does he offer

in "On the Ontological Mystery" about ways to be present, available, and creative?

4. Have you ever had an experience of "presence"?

HOMEWORK ASSIGNMENT *10*—DUE TUESDAY, APRIL *19*

Please read Paulo Freire, "Opening Words," in *Pedagogy of Hope* (1992); "Hope" (pp. 42–51) and "My Faith and Hope" (101–7), in *Pedagogy of the Heart* (1997); *Pedagogy of the Oppressed* (1970) (pp. 87–95); Richard S. Lazarus, "Hope: An Emotion and a Vital Coping Resource against Despair" (1999) (handouts). Please type answers to the following questions.

Paulo Freire, a Brazilian educator (1922–1997), and Richard S. Lazarus, late emeritus professor of psychology at the University of California at Berkeley, write out of different social perspectives ("first" world and "third" world) and different cultural and academic traditions (educational philosophy and psychology).

1. After reading the four assigned selections from Freire and the article by Lazarus, please indicate the similarities and differences you see regarding their comments about hope. Which of these similarities and differences strike you as most interesting? Please explain.

2. In *Pedagogy of the Oppressed*, Freire talks about the nature and politics of dialogue.

   a. What is dialogue, for Freire?

   b. Where, if any place, does Freirian dialogue exist in your life?

   c. Does Freirian dialogue ever occur in this class? If so, please give specific examples.

HOMEWORK ASSIGNMENT *11*—DUE TUESDAY, APRIL *26*

Please read C. R. Snyder's *Psychology of Hope*, chapters 1 and 2, and type answers to the following two questions.

1. In the first chapter of *The Psychology of Hope*, Snyder identifies what he believes are the essential elements of hope. He then clarifies what he means by hope by explaining what hope is not.

   a. Please present Snyder's view of the essential elements of hope.

   b. What do you learn about hope as a result of Snyder's discussion of what hope is not?

2. In the second chapter of *The Psychology of Hope*, Snyder presents the psychological characteristics of high-hope people.

a. Which of Snyder's characteristics of high-hope people apply to or are true of you?

b. Please complete Snyder's Hope Scale questionnaire on p. 26. Given your score, how reliable in your own case is Snyder's Hope Scale as a predictor of psychological characteristics?

NOTES

PROLOGUE

1. Richard Rorty, *Philosophy and Social Hope*, 201; Robert Westbrook, "Public Schooling and American Democracy," 125–50; Thomas Jefferson, *The Political Writings of Thomas Jefferson*, 93.

2. Christopher Lasch, *The True and Only Heaven: Progress and Its Critics*, 16.

3. Amy Chua, *World on Fire: How Exporting Free Market Democracy Breeds Ethnic Hatred and Global Instability*.

4. See Zevedei Barbu, *Democracy and Dictatorship: Their Psychology and Patterns of Life;* and Patricia White, *Civic Virtues and Public Schooling*.

5. See Stephen M. Fishman and Lucille McCarthy, *John Dewey and the Challenge of Classroom Practice, Unplayed Tapes: A Personal History of Collaborative Teacher Research,* and *Whose Goals? Whose Aspirations? Learning to Teach Underprepared Students across the Curriculum*.

6. Some commentators view Dewey's recognition that life is characterized by periods of "darkness and despair" and his acknowledgment that decisions in our perilous world are always "a gamble" as evidence of his sensitivity to the "tragic" in life. Others disagree. For debates about this issue, see Raymond Boisvert, "The Nemesis of Necessity: Tragedy's Challenge to Deweyan Pragmatism" and "Updating Dewey: A Reply to Morse"; Sidney Hook, *Pragmatism and the Tragic Sense of Life*, 3–25; Eddie Glaude Jr., "Tragedy and Moral Experience: John Dewey and Toni Morrison's *Beloved*"; David Morse, "Pragmatism and the Tragic Sense of Life"; and Cornel West, *Keeping the Faith: Philosophy and Race in America*, 107–18.

7. *The Progressive* (Madison, Wisc., July 1952). For a similar story about Dewey's emphasis on the importance of "mountain climbing," see John J. McDermott, "The Gamble for Excellence: John Dewey's Pedagogy of Experience," 108.

8. Not only does Dewey not explicitly discuss hope, but very few of his commentators attempt to relate Dewey and hope. Among the few who do are Patrick J. Deneen, "The Politics of Hope and Optimism: Rorty, Havel, and the Democratic Faith of John Dewey"; Horace Kallen, "John Dewey and the Spirit of Pragmatism"; Richard

Rorty, "Truth without Correspondence to Reality"; and Patrick Shade, *Habits of Hope: A Pragmatic Theory*.

9. Richard Rorty, *Consequences of Pragmatism*; Alan Ryan, *John Dewey and the High Tide of American Liberalism*; Robert Westbrook, *John Dewey and American Democracy*; Steven Rockefeller, *John Dewey: Religious Faith and Democratic Humanism*.

10. See Lawrence Cremin, *The Transformation of the School*; Jim Garrison, *Dewey and Eros: Wisdom and Desire in the Art of Teaching*; Philip W. Jackson, *John Dewey and the Lessons of Art*; and Laurel N. Tanner, *Dewey's Laboratory School*.

CHAPTER 1: CONSTRUCTING A DEWEYAN THEORY OF HOPE

1. Gabriel Marcel makes a similar distinction between ultimate and particular hopes when he contrasts hope "in all its strength" with "low order" hope (*HV* 29–30). In parallel ways, theologians have contrasted profound and ordinary hopes or what Josef Pieper, the German theologian, designates as *esperance* as opposed to *espoir* (*Hope and History: Five Salzburg Lectures*, 26). See also Marcel, DH, 279; Joseph J. Godfrey, *A Philosophy of Human Hope*; James L. Muyskens, *The Sufficiency of Hope: Conceptual Foundations of Religion*; and Bernard Schumacher, *A Philosophy of Hope: Josef Pieper and the Contemporary Debate on Hope*.

2. Regarding gratitude, Dewey also writes, "He is a dangerous churl who will not gratefully acknowledge by means of free-will offerings the help that sustains him" (*LW* 1:44). A similar sentiment about gratitude is expressed by William James in his 1895 address "Is Life Worth Living?" James asks, "Are we not bound to take some suffering upon ourselves, to do some self-denying service with our lives, in return for all those lives upon which ours are built?" James answers his own question: "To hear this question is to answer it in but one possible way, if one have a normal constituted heart" (50).

Gabriel Marcel also recognizes the importance of gratitude, although he places it at the core of honor rather than at the core, as Dewey does, of virtue. Marcel asks, "In what sense does the ungrateful man sin against honour? Is it not that he is in some sense a betrayer, that he breaks a certain tie, profiting basely from the fact that his benefactor . . . has carefully avoided asking him for any sort of acknowledgment of his debt?" (*Man against Mass Society*, 191). In addition, Marcel, like Dewey, recognizes a deep sense of connection to the historic, evolving human community. He writes that although he cannot fully explore the infinite "ramifications" of his existence, he can "discern enough . . . to follow this umbilical cord of my temporal antecedents . . . stretching back beyond my life in an indefinite network which, if traced to its limits, would perhaps be co-extensive with the human race itself" (*HV* 71). In this regard, Marcel adds that our predecessors are like a living arch under which we travel and against which we often brush (*The Existential Background of Human Dignity*, 84–85; *The Mystery of Being: II. Faith and Reality*, 209). See also Albert Einstein, "What I Believe."

3. For more on the social gospel movement that was popular at the turn of the twentieth century, see Walter Rauschenbusch, *A Theology for the Social Gospel*; and Edward Alsworth Ross, *Sins and Society: An Analysis of Latter-day Iniquity.*

4. For an approach to hope that echoes Dewey's encouragement to soldier on as links in a chain but without divine support or guarantee of success, see Horace Kallen's "Of Death and the Future." Whereas Dewey uses the chain metaphor for members of the human community, Kallen employs the metaphor of a relay team passing a torch from one runner to the next:

> If all human life be a race coming to a standstill in a little finishing canter ["fin-ishing canter" is an image for death used by Oliver Wendell Holmes Jr. in a 1931 radio broadcast marking his ninetieth birthday], then the life of Progress is a torch race such as the Athenians used to hold in honor of Prometheus. The runners are the mingling generations, and the later receives from the earlier, as that comes to its finishing canter, the fire of the idea which defines the spirit of progress. The fire is a working faith that freedom is the mother of intelligence, intelligence the strength of freedom, and *know-how* the substance of intelligence. Progress is in process wherever new runners lift the torch higher, carry it faster, bring it to a newer brighter flame, until in their turn they hand it over and slow down to their own standstill. Countless are the runners, many colored the flames of their torches, and unendingly different in heat, in brightness; nor can any runner be sure in advance who may carry onward his promethean fire. When he runs in the race called Progress, he runs by his own choice at his own risk in a contest without guarantees, on his own faith that others soon or late will take light from his light, and that, when at last he slows down to the standstill of death, another will have accepted the flame from his hand and be hastening to push back the frontier of darkness and impotence. (79–80)

5. For more on the role of ends-in-view in directing present attention, see Dewey's "Brigham Young Educational Lectures" (*LW* 17:269–83).

6. Erich Fromm calls this phenomenon the "idolatry of the future" (*The Revolution of Hope*, 7).

7. Dewey's use of a biblical allusion, drawing upon a passage from Job, "Though He slay me, yet I will trust in Him" (13:15), is not unusual. Although Dewey explic-itly denies the existence of the God of traditional theism, he frequently uses language that echoes famous passages in Western religious literature. For a brief review of the controversy surrounding Dewey's use of religious language, see Michael Eldridge, *Transforming Experience: Dewey's Cultural Instrumentalism*, 167–69.

8. St. Thomas Aquinas, *Summa Theologica*, "Of the Irascible Passions, and First, of Hope and Despair" and "On Hope, of Hope, Considered in Itself"; David Hume, "Dissertation on the Passions" and *A Treatise of Human Nature*; John Patrick Day, "The Anatomy of Hope and Fear," "Hope," and *Hope: A Philosophical Inquiry*; Shade, *Habits of Hope*; Josef Pieper, *Hope and History* and *On Hope.*

9. For the expression of a view, like Dewey's, that hope is part of nature, part of the plant and animal world that surrounds us and not a special gift to humans, see Samuel Taylor Coleridge, "Work without Hope."

10. I further develop the difference between drawing on natural versus supernatural sources of hope when I compare Dewey and Gabriel Marcel in the next chapter.

11. Dewey's search for the continuities in life is a strong theme in his writing. In fact, Dewey himself views it as a root motivation of his lifework (*LW* 5:153). In addition to his reconciliation of animal and human, human and natural, past and present, failure and success, also relevant to constructing a Deweyan theory of hope is his effort to reconcile youthful dreams and adult skepticism. Dewey tells us that the "juvenile assumption of power and achievement is not a dream to be wholly forgotten." It is, he says, as much a part of nature as skepticism, and he argues that we should draw upon our youthful dreams to inspire "adult thought and struggle" (*LW* 1:313). For a discussion of the importance of childhood memory in promoting virtue for two poets, Coleridge and Wordsworth, whose works were an early influence on Dewey, see Lasch, *True and Only Heaven*, 87–119. For criticisms of Dewey's notion of continuity, see Ernest Nagel, introduction to vol. 12 of *LW*.

12. See Rockefeller, *John Dewey*; and Westbook, *Dewey and American Democracy*.

13. See Richard Hofstadter, *Anti-intellectualism in America*, 368; and Niebuhr, *Moral Man and Immoral Society*, xiii–xv.

14. For a commentator who views this Deweyan approach positively, labeling it "hope without illusion," see Kallen, "Dewey and Pragmatism." For a commentator who views this Deweyan approach negatively, labeling it "optimism without hope," see Deneen, "Politics of Hope and Optimism." See also John J. Stuhr, who, like Kallen, takes a positive view of Dewey's approach, calling it a "tough-minded faith" that is both "strenuous" and "disillusioned" (*Genealogical Pragmatism: Philosophy, Experience, and Community*, 293–94).

15. See George Santayana, *The Life of Reason: Reason in Religion*, 279; and Walter T. Stace, *Mysticism and Philosophy*, 63.

16. Letters 04749 and 04751 in Dewey, *The Correspondence of John Dewey*; see also *MW* 14:181.

17. Letter 04751 in Dewey, *Correspondence of Dewey*.

18. For the parallel concepts of "co-arising" and "interbeing" in Buddhism, see Thich Nhat Hanh, *The Heart of the Buddha's Teaching*.

19. Cited in Edward Waldo Emerson, *Emerson in Concord: A Memoir*, 61.

20. See Robert Williams, ed., *John Dewey: Recollections*, 127.

21. See Fishman and McCarthy, *Dewey and Classroom Practice*.

22. For a distinction similar to the contrast I draw between the "familiar" and the "unfamiliar" Dewey, see Stanley Grean's discussion of the "limited" versus the "extended" Dewey ("Elements of Transcendence in Dewey's Naturalistic Humanism," 280).

CHAPTER 2: DEWEY IN DIALOGUE WITH GABRIEL MARCEL

1. Erich Fromm, *The Heart of Man: Its Genius for Good and Evil*, 40–41.

2. Aquinas, *Summa Theologica*, "Of the Irascible Passions" and "On Hope, of Hope"; Pieper, *On Hope*.

3. Despite Marcel's accuracy about the extreme difficulty of leaving the imperialist world of "having" to enter the spiritual world of absolute presence, most of us have experienced brief moments of connection with others that hint at the possibility of such presence. However, because these moments are so fleeting, we usually do not remark on them. Marcel draws our attention to these moments and invites us to see them in a new way when he describes them as "sparks of spirituality":

> When I stop somebody in the street to ask my way, I do say to him, it is true, "Can you tell me how to get to such-and-such a Square?" but all the same I am making a convenience of him, I am treating him as if he were a signpost. No doubt, even in this limiting case, a touch of genuine subjectivity can break through, thanks to the magical powers of the tone of voice and the glance. If I have really lost my bearings, if it is late, if I fear that I may have to grope my way for hours through some labyrinthine and perhaps even dangerous warren of streets, I may have a fleeting but irresistible impression that the stranger I am appealing to is a brother eager to come to my aid. What happens is, in a word, that the stranger has started off by putting himself, as it were, ideally in my shoes. He has come within my reach as a person. It is no longer a mere matter of his showing me the way as a guide-book or map might, but of his really giving a helping hand to somebody who is alone and in a bewildered state. This is nothing more than a sort of spark of spirituality, out as soon as it is in; the stranger and I are almost certainly never to see each other again, yet for a few minutes, as I trudge homewards, this man's unexpected cordiality makes me feel as if I had stepped out of a wintry day into a warm room. (*The Mystery of Being: I. Reflection and Mystery*, 220–21)

4. Marcel, "An Autobiographical Essay," 11–12.

5. Marcel's worries about what he sees as the leveling effects of contemporary society, a leveling that he blames on democracy's emphasis on individual rights, as well as modern technology and mass production, lead him to urge the reestablishment of "aristocracies of craftsmanship" (*MAH* 201). He believes such groups would counterbalance the impact of focus on personal rights by promoting fraternity and selfless service to others. However, despite Marcel's use of the word "aristocratic," there is something of the spirit of Deweyan (and Jeffersonian) democracy in his proposal. I say that Marcel, notwithstanding his self-proclaimed "bourgeois" status (*Existential Background*, 157), sounds Deweyan in this regard because he echoes the latter's remarks about the importance for democracy of "full and free" interplay among small groups (*MW* 9:89). Using very different language to make a similar point, Marcel says small groups must "remain in a sort of state of active expectation or availability in relation to other groups moved by a differ-

ent inspiration, with whom [they] ought to have fertilizing exchanges of view" (*MAH* 201). In other words, like Dewey, Marcel worries about the negative consequences for our chances for growth in a world of individual competition and mass production. Also like Dewey, Marcel views small groups marked by face-to-face communication that are also open and available to other groups as an antidote to contemporary impediments to the autonomy and creative development of individuals.

6. See Elisabeth Kubler-Ross, *On Death and Dying*.

7. For an example of a terminally ill person's protest against an outside observer's viewing his suffering abstractly rather than with respect for the mystery of his individual uniqueness, see Ted Rosenthal's documentary film *How Could I Not Be among You? A Portrait of Poet Ted Rosenthal*.

8. Dewey's description of the intuitions that reveal our intimate connection with nature reflects features of what has been called "extrovertive mysticism," that is, experiences in which one gains a vivid rapport with the world. See Stace, *Mysticism and Philosophy;* and R. C. Zaehner, *Mysticism, Sacred and Profane*.

9. For criticism of Dewey's problem-solving as neglecting what Marcel views as the mysterious, "inner core" of the self, see Robert J. Roth, S.J., *American Religious Philosophy*, 178–82.

CHAPTER 3: DEWEY IN DIALOGUE WITH PAULO FREIRE

1. For previous comparisons of Dewey and Freire, see Joseph Betz, "John Dewey and Paulo Freire"; George Demetrion, "Adult Literacy and the American Political Culture"; Walter Feinberg and Carlos A. Torres, "Democracy and Education: John Dewey and Paulo Freire"; and Danilo R. Streck, "John Dewey's and Paulo Freire's Views on the Political Function of Education, with Special Emphasis on the Problem of Method."

2. Harry K. Wells, *Pragmatism: Philosophy of Imperialism*, 8. See also George Novack, *Pragmatism and Marxism;* and Dale Riepe, "Critique of Idealistic Naturalism: Methodological Pollution in the Mainstream of American Philosophy."

3. See Freire and Donaldo Macedo, "Rethinking Critical Pedagogy: A Dialogue with Paulo Freire," 188–89; Freire, EDL, 18; and Freire, LNAT, 211.

4. See also Ira Shor and Freire, *A Pedagogy for Liberation: Dialogues on Transforming Education*, 61.

5. Another example of the contrast between Dewey's attention to continuity and Freire's attention to wholesale change is their attitude toward animal life and the role it plays in their respective approaches to hope. Although Dewey and Freire both recognize the importance of belonging and community for living in hope, Dewey sees the animal world as part of this community. Much of our knowledge is, Dewey tells us, based on the animal intelligence embodied in our arms and legs. This knowledge, along with our love of action and native hope, is, as he puts it, part of our animal pluck.

By contrast, Freire does not draw positive attention to our relationship with animals. In fact, Freire takes a position on the relation of animal and human life that is opposite Dewey's. Freire says that when we lose hope, when we believe that our tomorrows are no different from our todays and our yesterdays, we fall to the level of animals (*Pedagogy of the Heart*, 42; *Pedagogy of the Oppressed*, 98–101). We no longer believe we can change the world, and, thereby, our distinctive ontological identity as actors in the world is eclipsed. To the contrary, I believe Dewey would say that when we are without hope, something of our animal nature has gone out of us. We have not so much sunk to an animal level as we have lost our connection to nature, including our animal ancestry and the enveloping whole that sustains us and gives us purpose.

6. See also John L. Elias, *Paulo Freire: Pedagogue of Liberation;* Robert Mackie, "Contributions to the Thought of Paulo Freire"; and Paul V. Taylor, *The Texts of Paulo Freire.*

7. Thomas Carlyle, "Inaugural Address at Edinburgh," para. 42.

8. See Charles S. Peirce, "How to Make Our Ideas Clear."

9. Shor, "What Is Critical Literacy?" 12.

10. See also Freire and Antonio Faundez, *Learning to Question: A Pedagogy of Liberation,* 33, 104.

11. Dewey anticipates Freire's view of the role of political leadership when he insists that even the most benevolent leaders fail to truly help others if their efforts leave their followers passive or without an active share in bringing about reform. Dewey and his coauthor James H. Tufts write, "The social welfare can be advanced only by means which enlist the positive interest and active energy of those to be benefited or 'improved.' . . . It takes time to arouse minds from apathy and lethargy, to get them to thinking for themselves, to share in making plans, to take part in their execution. But without active cooperation both in forming aims and in carrying them out, there is no possibility of a common good" (*LW* 7:347). Not only does Dewey reject rule by benevolent dictatorship. He also rejects rule by "experts" or a "specialized class" of the intellectually elite (*LW* 2:364).

12. See also Frantz Fanon, *The Wretched of the Earth;* and Albert Memmi, *The Colonizer and the Colonized.*

13. Freire and Faundez, *Learning to Question,* 42. See also Karl Marx, *Capital: A Critique of Political Economy.*

14. Shor and Freire, *Pedagogy for Liberation,* 118–19.

15. See ibid., 47–48.

16. See Antonia Darder, *Reinventing Paulo Freire: A Pedagogy of Love,* 4; and Streck, "Toward a Pedagogy of a New Social Contract."

17. For contemporary educators who have undertaken a similar process, see Darder, *Reinventing Freire;* Eileen de los Reyes and Patricia A. Gozemba, *Pockets of Hope: How Students and Teachers Change the World;* bell hooks, *Teaching to Transgress: Education as the Practice of Freedom;* Patrick Shannon, *Becoming Political, Too: New Readings and Writings on the Politics of Literacy Education;* Ira Shor, ed., *Freire for the Classroom: A Sourcebook for Liberatory Teaching;* and Shor and Caroline Pari, *Education Is Politics: Critical Teaching across Differences, K–12.*

18. Benjamin Barber, *Strong Democracy: Participatory Politics for a New Age*. See also Jane J. Mansbridge, *Beyond Adversary Democracy;* and Carol Pateman, *Participation and Democratic Theory*.

19. Freire's bold integration of Marxian and Christian visions of liberation and his literacy education work with Brazilian and Chilean peasants have been important contributions to the liberation theology movement. For the importance of Freire's ideas for liberation theology, see Phillip Berryman, *Liberation Theology;* James H. Cone, *A Black Theology of Liberation;* and Gustavo Gutierrez, *A Theology of Liberation*.

CHAPTER 4: DEWEY IN DIALOGUE WITH POSITIVE PSYCHOLOGY AND C. R. SNYDER

1. Martin E. P. Seligman and Mihaly Csikszentmihalyi, "Positive Psychology," 5. See also Shelly L. Gable and Jonathan Haidt, "What (and Why) Is Positive Psychology?"

2. For a contemporary account of the negative repercussions of the fact/value dichotomy for law, public policy, and economics, an analysis that explicitly builds on Dewey's earlier efforts to reconcile this dualism, see Hilary Putnam, *The Collapse of the Fact/Value Dichotomy, and Other Essays*.

3. Reinhold Neibuhr, *Moral Man and Immoral Society*.

4. Seligman and Csikszentmihalyi, "Positive Psychology," 5.

5. Ibid., 5; Gable and Haidt, "What (and Why)?" 108.

6. Seligman and Csikszentmihalyi, "Positive Psychology," 5.

7. Gable and Haidt, "What (and Why)?" 103.

8. For a recent summary of research on goal setting and task performance, see Edwin A. Locke and Gary P. Latham, "Building a Practically Useful Theory of Goal Setting and Task Motivation: A 35-Year Odyssey."

9. Fromm, *The Revolution of Hope*, 7.

10. For someone who takes a similar position to Dewey about life threats as a condition of hope, see Richard S. Lazarus, "Hope: An Emotion and a Vital Coping Resource against Despair." For a rejoinder by Snyder to Lazarus, see "Hope Theory: Rainbows in the Mind," 250. For a parallel discussion about positive psychology's neglect of the "evils" of life but from the perspective of William James rather than Dewey, see James O. Pawelski, "William James, Positive Psychology, and Healthy Mindedness," 65.

11. For a brief review of the psychological literature that, like Dewey, connects hope to faith and trust in the world, see Howard Tennen, Glenn Affleck, and Ruth Tennen, "Clipped Feathers: The Theory and Measurement of Hope," 312.

12. In chapters 5 and 7 of *The Psychology of Hope*, Snyder does discuss how individuals help each other reach their goals in the context of various sorts of personal and professional relationships, including spouses, parent-child, teacher-student, boss-employee, doctor-patient, psychologist-client, and coach-athlete. However, he does not consider the larger political and moral consequences of the institutional practices within which these relationships occur: the U.S. family and heterosexual

marriage, education, business, medicine, or college and professional athletics. That is, he does not consider the ways these institutions hinder or promote a more equitable allocation of scarce resources, better environment conservation, and more just social relations.

13. For an article in which Snyder, without addressing the relative moral merits of different groups, presents a hope scale more sensitive to the social domain and a much more social view of the individual, see Snyder, Jennifer Cheavens, and Susie C. Sympson, "Hope: An Individual Motive for Social Commerce," 109–10, 112–14.

14. For an example of Snyder reporting on someone struggling to achieve hopes that are more communal than individual, see *The Psychology of Hope*, 40–43. For an example of Snyder considering someone who has pro-social, ultimate hopes that are likely unreachable, see "Hope Theory," 266.

15. See also Susie C. Sympson, "Validation of the Specific Domain Hope Scale."

16. See Christopher Peterson, "The Future of Optimism," 51.

CHAPTER 5: CONCLUSION TO PART I

1. For a penetrating analysis and meditation on a Deweyan response to the "Why go on?" question, see John J. McDermott, "Why Bother? Is Life Worth Living? Experience as Pedagogical."

2. Thomas Jefferson, letter to Samuel Kercheval, 1402.

3. Dewey to Scudder Klyce, October 18, 1927, letter 04749 in *Correspondence of Dewey*.

CHAPTER 6: TEACHING A COURSE ON HOPE

1. See Appendix A for a discussion of my research methods.

2. My subsequent review of research about anxiety and depression among U.S. college students has shown me that I should not have been surprised about the high percentage of Fishman's students who were suffering from low hope. In its annual nationwide survey of first-year college students, UCLA's Higher Education Research Institute reported a strong upward trend between 1985 and 1999 in levels of undergraduate stress and depression. Whereas in 1985 only 16 percent of surveyed freshmen reported being "frequently overwhelmed by all I have to do," in 1999 30 percent reported such feelings. Such stress was cited twice as frequently by women as by men, with 38.8 percent of women feeling frequently overwhelmed, compared to 20.0 percent of men. Students' reasons for high levels of stress include long hours of work at jobs outside school and disengagement with and lack of preparation for assigned college course work. See Linda J. Sax et al., *The American Freshman: National Norms for Fall 1999*, 2–5. Two percent of college students attempt suicide each year, with some 125 undergraduates succeeding every year. See Mary Duenwald, "Students Find Another Staple of Campus Life: Stress," *New York Times*, September 17, 2002.

Fishman's and my work reveals that whereas his and my low hope results primarily from deteriorating social, political, and environmental conditions, his students' low hope is caused by personal disappointments. This difference between the causes of faculty and student low hope may also be a general trend and worthy of further inquiry.

3. In analyzing teacher and student roles and interactions, I draw upon Dewey's notion of teacher-as-learner. In adopting the teacher-as-learner stance, Fishman aligns himself with an important Deweyan educational principle: rather than handing information to students, the teacher must set the conditions so that teacher and students can work together to clarify and explore problems about which they care. Dewey writes:

> No thought, no idea, can possibly be conveyed as an idea from one person to another. When it is told, it is, to the one to whom it is told, another given fact, not an idea. The communication may stimulate the other person to realize the question for himself and to think out a like idea, or it may smother his intellectual interest and suppress his dawning effort at thought. But what he *directly* gets cannot be an idea. Only by wrestling with the conditions of the problem at first hand, seeking and finding his own way out, does he think. When the parent or teacher has provided the conditions which stimulate thinking and has taken a sympathetic attitude toward the activities of the learned by entering into a common or conjoint experience, all has been done which a second party can do to instigate learning. (*MW* 9:167–68)

In analyzing Fishman's teacherly stance, I also draw upon Paulo Freire's conception of teacher as problem poser. Freire argues for a pedagogy in which teacher and students "dialogue" and "problem pose" in a process that involves exchanging teacher-student roles. He writes:

> In the banking concept of education, knowledge is a gift bestowed by [teachers] who consider themselves knowledgeable upon those whom they consider to know nothing. . . . Education must begin with the solution of the teacher-student contradiction, by reconciling the poles of the contradiction so that both are simultaneously teacher *and* students. . . . To resolve the teacher-student contradiction, to exchange the role of depositor, prescriber, domesticator, for the role of student among students would be to undermine the power of oppression and serve the cause of liberation. (*PO* 72, 75; chaps. 2–3)

4. See Appendix C for the course syllabus, the three essay assignments, and the eleven homework assignments. See Appendix B for the rationale behind Fishman's choice of course readings.

5. Mary Belenky et al., *Women's Ways of Knowing: The Development of Self, Voice, and Mind*, 100–154, 35–51, 118.

6. Dewey describes his worries about education that is unconnected to students' lives in *Experience and Education:*

> Almost everyone has had occasion to look back upon his school days and wonder what has become of the knowledge he was supposed to have amassed during his

years of schooling. . . . Indeed, he is lucky who does not find that in order to make progress, in order to go ahead intellectually, he does not have to unlearn much of what he learned in school. These questions cannot be disposed of by saying that the subjects were not actually learned, for they were learned at least sufficiently to enable a pupil to pass examinations in them. One trouble is that the subject-matter in question was learned in isolation; it was put, as it were, in a water-tight compartment. When the question is asked, then, what has become of it, where has it gone to, the right answer is that it is still there in the special compartment in which it was originally stowed away. If exactly the same conditions recurred as those under which it was acquired, it would also recur and be available. But it was segregated when it was acquired and hence is so disconnected from the rest of experience that it is not available under the actual conditions of life. (*LW* 13:28)

7. Students' lack of familiarity with constructed knowing may be partially explained by events in the recent history of American philosophy. According to Richard Rorty, in "After Philosophy, Democracy," Dewey's broad sense of inquiry, a philosophic approach that included focus on political and social issues, gave way, after World War II, to a more limited, technical philosophic orientation in the United States. This new approach focused primarily on issues concerning the nature of language, verification, and scientific truth. It also had a view of inquiry that was narrower than Dewey's, one that emphasized separate, critical knowing. This approach was brought to prominence in the United States by European immigrants, many of them refugees from Nazism and members of the "Vienna Circle" movement in philosophy, a movement also known as "logical positivism." Since this movement's emphasis on language analysis, logic, and formal rigor in argumentation is still highly influential in the United States, Fishman's students are probably not unusual in having had few philosophy courses featuring constructed knowing.

However, the lack of constructed knowing is not limited to philosophy. According to a recent survey of more than two thousand college writing assignments in disciplines across the curriculum, only a handful of instructors require students to relate academic concepts to their nonschool concerns. Instead, most assignments ask students to display information in "short essay exams" and "term papers" where personal experience is rarely encouraged or valued. See Dan Melzer, "Discourse across the Disciplines: A National Study of College Writing Assignments." Earlier studies of large numbers of assignments report similar findings. See Arthur Applebee, *Contexts for Learning to Write: Studies of Secondary School Instruction;* and James N. Britton et al., *The Development of Writing Abilities (11–18).*

8. See Fishman's explanation of this informal, in-class writing in his syllabus in Appendix C. For a full discussion of freewriting, see Peter Elbow, *Writing without Teachers.*

9. See Appendix C for Fishman's essay assignments and ways of responding to student texts.

10. Dewey talked about "indirect education" in a 1904 address at the Frances W. Parker School in Chicago:

> The other day a parent of a little boy who recently entered our elementary school, after having been in a public school, told me that her son came to her and said, "I think we learn almost as much at that school as we did at the John Smith school—I believe, maybe, we learn more, only we have such a good time that we do not stop to think that we are learning anything." This story I tell to help illustrate the meaning of the term "indirect education." We have our choice between two methods. We may shape the conditions and direct the influences of school work so that pupils are forever reminded that they are pupils—that they are there to study lessons and do tasks. We may make the child conscious at every point that he is going to school, and that he goes to school to do something quite different from what he does anywhere else—namely, to learn. This is "direct education." Put in this bald way, however, the idea may well arouse some mental searchings of heart. Are we really willing to admit that the child does not learn anything outside of school—that he is not getting his education all the time by what he is thinking and feeling and doing, and in spite of the fact that his consciousness is not upon the fact that he is learning? This, then, is the other alternative—the child may be given something fixed up for purposes of learning it, and we may trust to the learning, instruction and training which results out of and along with this doing and inquiring for its own sake. This is "indirect education." (*MW* 3:240)

11. For Dewey's comments regarding the challenges of teaching indirectly, where the teacher not only has to know the subject matter but must also be sensitive to students' psychology and the effects of various sorts of group dynamics, see *LW* 13:36–37.

12. For a description of this debate, see Westbrook, *Dewey and American Democracy*, 418–22.

13. This aspect of Fishman's teaching resembles what commentators have said about Dewey's own pedagogy at Columbia University where his students described lectures as resembling "thinking aloud." That is, Dewey came to class and spent the entire period working through a problem that was of concern to him while students listened. This may be said to be a very un-Deweyan pedagogy, one in which Dewey did not try, as he himself recommends, to make students active or to integrate student and curriculum. On the other hand, it did enable students who were already interested in the subject matter to observe an active investigator sharing his thoughts while at work. For more on Dewey as teacher, see Max Eastman, "John Dewey: My Teacher and Friend," 282–84; Irwin Edman, *Philosopher's Holiday*, 140–141; Sidney Hook, *Out of Step*, 82–87; Corliss Lamont, *Dialogue on John Dewey*, 39–43; and Harold A. Larrabee, "John Dewey as Teacher."

CHAPTER 7: UNDERGRADUATES IN A COURSE ON HOPE

1. That so many of Fishman's students (five of the ten overall) told me they found Dewey's ideas most helpful was remarkable because, for most students, reading Dewey

was, initially, a struggle. In fact, two of the ten—Shoua Lao and Faith Dennison—never gained a good understanding of his work. As for the others, they began the semester complaining about Dewey's prose style but seemed to become, as time went on, increasingly comfortable with his texts. The reasons for students' increasing comfort with Dewey's writing include, in Fishman's and my analysis, the following: First, students likely became accustomed to Dewey's style and more confident of their ability to understand him as they gained experience writing and speaking about his work. Second, several pupils noted they profited from hearing Fishman interpret Dewey. In class, Steve described various Deweyan concepts and explained what they meant to him, a process in which he often directed the class back to particular passages that they read aloud and worked together to clarify. Finally, students' increasing understanding of Dewey may be linked to the progression of assigned texts. The first two books from which Fishman required students to read sections deal with relatively vague, complex topics: morality and the habits involved in intelligent moral judgments *(Human Nature and Conduct)* and metaphysics and the generic traits of existence *(Experience and Nature)*. By contrast, the final two books' subject matter was more familiar to students: art and religion. Fishman's students could, thus, as they read *Art and Experience* and *A Common Faith*, more easily engage in constructed knowing.

2. See Elbow, *Writing without Teachers*, 147–92.

APPENDIX A: CLASSROOM RESEARCH METHODS

1. See Yvonna S. Lincoln and Egon G. Guba, *Naturalistic Inquiry*; Matthew B. Miles and A. Michael Huberman, *Qualitative Data Analysis*; and James Spradley, *The Ethnographic Interview* and *Participant Observation*.

2. Britton et al., *Development of Writing Abilities (11–18)*.

3. See Clifford Geertz, *The Interpretation of Cultures*.

4. Dewey appears to favor qualitative educational research of the sort I have conducted over more "scientific," quantitative inquiry. He said in a 1928 address to educators: "[Research in education] requires judgment and art to select from the total circumstances of a case just what elements are the causal conditions of learning. . . . It requires candor and sincerity to keep track of failures as well as successes. . . . It requires trained and acute observation to note the indications of progress in learning . . . a much more highly skilled kind of observation than is needed to note the results of mechanically applied tests" *(LW* 3:268).

APPENDIX B: CREATING A SYLLABUS FOR A COURSE ON HOPE

1. Marcel, *Presence and Immortality*, 231.

WORKS CITED

The works of John Dewey are listed chronologically. All other multiple texts by a single author are listed alphabetically. The abbreviations used throughout this book for the works of Paulo Freire, Gabriel Marcel, and C. R. Snyder follow their citations below.

Applebee, Arthur. *Contexts for Learning to Write: Studies of Secondary School Instruction.* Norwood, N.Y.: Ablex, 1984.

Aquinas, St. Thomas. *Summa Theologica,* First Part of the Second Part, Question 40: "Of the Irascible Passions, and First, of Hope and Despair," and Second Part of the Second Part, Question 17: "On Hope, of Hope, Considered in Itself." Benziger Brothers, 1947. EWTN Online. Hypertext edition, by New Advent staff. Hypertext Version Copyright 1995, 1996, New Advent. http://www.ccel.org/a/acquinas/summa.

Barber, Benjamin. *Strong Democracy: Participatory Politics for a New Age.* Berkeley and Los Angeles: University of California Press, 1984.

Barbu, Zevedei. *Democracy and Dictatorship: Their Psychology and Patterns of Life.* New York: Grove Press, 1956.

Belenky, Mary, Blythe Clinchy, Nancy Goldberger, and Jill Tarule. *Women's Ways of Knowing: The Development of Self, Voice, and Mind.* New York: Basic Books, 1986.

Berryman, Phillip. *Liberation Theology.* Philadelphia: Temple University Press, 1986.

Betz, Joseph. "John Dewey and Paulo Freire." *Transactions of the Charles S. Peirce Society* 27, no. 1 (Winter 1992): 107–26.

Boisvert, Raymond. "The Nemesis of Necessity: Tragedy's Challenge to Deweyan Pragmatism." In *Dewey Reconfigured: Essays on Deweyan Pragmatism,* edited by Casey Haskins and David I. Seiple, 151–68. Albany: SUNY Press, 1999.

———. "Updating Dewey: A Reply to Morse." *Transactions of the Charles S. Peirce Society* 37, no. 4 (Fall 2001): 573–83.

Britton, James N., Tony Burgess, Nancy Martin, Alex McLeod, and Harold Rosen. *The Development of Writing Abilities (11–18).* London: Macmillan, 1975.

Carlyle, Thomas. "Inaugural Address at Edinburgh." In *Harvard Classics,* edited by Charles W. Eliot, vol. 5.4, paras. 1–51. New York: P. F. Collier and Son, 1909. (Original address delivered on April 2, 1866.)

Chua, Amy. *World on Fire: How Exporting Free Market Democracy Breeds Ethnic Hatred and Global Instability.* New York: Random House, 2003.

Coleridge, Samuel Taylor. "Work without Hope." In vol. 1 of *The Complete Works of Samuel Taylor Coleridge,* edited by E. H. Coleridge, 447. Oxford: Clarendon, 1912.

Cone, James H. *A Black Theology of Liberation.* Maryknoll, N.Y.: Orbis Books, 1987.

Cremin, Lawrence. *The Transformation of the School.* New York: Vintage, 1964.

Darder, Antonia. *Reinventing Paulo Freire: A Pedagogy of Love.* Boulder: Westview Press, 2002.

Day, John Patrick. "The Anatomy of Hope and Fear." *Mind* 79 (July 1970): 369–84.

———. "Hope." *American Philosophical Quarterly* 6, no. 2 (April 1969): 89–102.

———. *Hope: A Philosophical Inquiry.* Helsinki: Philosophical Society of Finland, 1991.

de los Reyes, Eileen, and Patricia A. Gozemba. *Pockets of Hope: How Students and Teachers Change the World.* Westport, Conn.: Bergin and Garvey, 2002.

Demetrion, George. "Adult Literacy and the American Political Culture." In *Under Construction: The Role of the Arts and Humanities in Postmodern Schooling,* edited by Donovan R. Walling, 169–92. Bloomington, Ind.: Phi Delta Kappa Educational Foundation, 1997.

Deneen, Patrick J. "The Politics of Hope and Optimism: Rorty, Havel, and the Democratic Faith of John Dewey." *Social Research* 66, no. 2 (Summer 1999): 577–610.

Dewey, John. "Ethical Principles Underlying Education," 1897 (*EW* 5:54–83).

———. "Brigham Young Educational Lectures," 1902 (*LW* 17:269–83).

———. "Logical Conditions of a Scientific Treatment of Morality," 1903 (*MW* 3:3–39).

———. "Religion and Our Schools," 1908 (*MW* 4:165–77).

———. *Ethics,* 1908 (*MW* 5) [Dewey, John, and James H. Tufts].

———. "Education, Direct and Indirect," 1909 (*MW* 3:240–48).

———. "Science as Subject-Matter and as Method," 1909 (*MW* 6:69–79).

———. Contributions to *Cyclopedia of Education,* 1911 (*MW* 6:359–467).

———. *Democracy and Education,* 1916 (*MW* 9).

———. "The Need for a Recovery of Philosophy," 1917 (*MW* 10:3–48).

———. "Freedom of Thought and Work," 1920 (*MW* 12:8–11).

———. *Reconstruction in Philosophy,* 1920 (*MW* 12:77–201).

———. "Events and Meanings," 1922 (*MW* 13:276–80).

———. "Education as Religion," 1922 (*MW* 13:317–22).

———. "Education as Politics," 1922 (*MW* 13:329–34).

———. *Human Nature and Conduct,* 1922 (*MW* 14).

———. *Experience and Nature,* 1925 (*LW* 1).

———. "A Key to the New World," 1926 (*LW* 2:226–30).

———. *The Public and Its Problems,* 1927 (*LW* 2:235–372).

———. "Impressions of Soviet Russia," 1928 (*LW* 3:203–50).

———. "Progressive Education and the Science of Education," 1928 (*LW* 3:257–68).

———. *The Quest for Certainty*, 1929 (*LW* 4).

———. *Individualism, Old and New*, 1930 (*LW* 5:41–123).

———. "Construction and Criticism," 1930 (*LW* 5:127–43).

———. "From Absolutism to Experimentalism," 1930 (*LW* 5:147–60).

———. "What I Believe," 1930 (*LW* 5:267–78).

———. "Three Independent Factors in Morals," 1930 (*LW* 5:279–89).

———. *Ethics*, rev. ed., 1932 (*LW* 7) [Dewey, John, and James H. Tufts].

———. "Outlawry of War," 1933 (*LW* 8:13–18).

———. *How We Think*, rev. ed., 1933 (*LW* 8:105–352).

———. *A Common Faith*, 1934 (*LW* 9:3–58).

———. "Imperative Need: A New Radical Party," 1934 (*LW* 9:76–80).

———. "Intelligence and Power," 1934 (*LW* 9:107–11).

———. "Education for a Changing Social Order," 1934 (*LW* 9:158–68).

———. "Education and the Social Order," 1934 (*LW* 9:175–85).

———. "The Need for a Philosophy of Education," 1934 (*LW* 9:194–204).

———. *Art as Experience*, 1934 (*LW* 10).

———. *Liberalism and Social Action*, 1935 (*LW* 11:1–65).

———. "Toward Administrative Statesmanship," 1935 (*LW* 11:345–47).

———. "The Meaning of Liberalism," 1935 (*LW* 11:364–67).

———. *Logic: The Theory of Inquiry*, 1938 (*LW* 12).

———. *Experience and Education*, 1938 (*LW* 13:1–62).

———. *Freedom and Culture*, 1939 (*LW* 13:65–188).

———. "Time and Individuality," 1940 (*LW* 14:98–114).

———. "Creative Democracy—the Task before Us," 1939 (*LW* 14:224–30).

———. "Reconstruction Seen Twenty-five Years Later," 1948 (*MW* 12:256–77).

———. *The Correspondence of John Dewey* (CD-ROM). Edited by Larry Hickman. Charlottesville, Va.: Intelex Corp.

Eastman, Max. "John Dewey: My Teacher and Friend." In *Great Companions: Critical Memoirs of Some Famous Friends*, 249–98. New York: Farrar, Straus, and Cudahy, 1959.

Edman, Irwin. *Philosopher's Holiday*. New York: Viking Press, 1938.

Einstein, Albert. "What I Believe." In *Living Philosophies: A Series of Intimate Credos*, edited by Clifton Fadiman, 3–7. New York: Simon and Schuster, 1931.

Elbow, Peter. *Writing without Teachers*. New York: Oxford, 1973.

Eldridge, Michael. *Transforming Experience: Dewey's Cultural Instrumentalism*. Nashville: Vanderbilt Press, 1998.

Elias, John L. *Paulo Freire: Pedagogue of Liberation*. Malabar, Fla.: Krieger Publishing, 1994.

Emerson, Edward Waldo. *Emerson in Concord: A Memoir*. Boston: Houghton Mifflin, 1889.

Fanon, Frantz. *The Wretched of the Earth.* Translated by C. Farrington. New York: Grove Press, 1961.

Feinberg, Walter, and Carlos A. Torres. "Democracy and Education: John Dewey and Paulo Freire." *Educational Practice and Theory* 23, no. 1 (2001): 25–37.

Fishman, Stephen M., and Lucille McCarthy. *John Dewey and the Challenge of Classroom Practice.* New York: Teachers College Press, 1998.

———. *Unplayed Tapes: A Personal History of Collaborative Teacher Research.* New York: Teachers College Press, 2000.

———. *Whose Goals? Whose Aspirations? Learning to Teach Underprivileged Students across the Curriculum.* Logan: Utah State University Press, 2002.

Freire, Paulo. "Conscientizing as a Way of Liberating." In *Paulo Freire*, 3–10. Washington, D.C.: U.S. Catholic Conference, 1973. CWL

———. "The Educational Role of Churches in Latin America." In *Paulo Freire*, 15–28. Washington, D.C.: U.S. Catholic Conference, 1973. ERC

———. "Education: Domestication or Liberation?" In *Deschooling: A Reader*, edited by I. Lister, 18–21. Cambridge: Cambridge University Press, 1974. (Original work published 1972.) EDL

———. *Education for Critical Consciousness.* Translated by M. Bergman Ramos. New York: Continuum, 1996. (Original work published 1969.) *ECC*

———. "Education, Liberation, and the Church." In *The Politics of Education*, translated by Donaldo Macedo, 121–42. Westport, Conn.: Bergin and Garvey, 1985. (Original work published 1973.) ELC

———. "Letter to a Young Theology Student." In *Paulo Freire*, 11–12. Washington, D.C.: U.S. Catholic Conference, 1973. LYTS

———. "Letter to North American Teachers." Translated by Carmen Hunter. In *Freire for the Classroom: A Sourcebook for Liberatory Teaching*, edited by Ira Shor, 211–14. Portsmouth, N.H.: Boynton/Cook Heinemann, 1987. LNAT

———. *Pedagogy of Freedom: Ethics, Democracy, and Civic Courage.* Translated by P. Clarke. Lanham, Md.: Rowman and Littlefield, 1998. PF

———. *Pedagogy of Hope.* Translated by Robert R. Barr. New York: Continuum, 1999. (Original work published 1992.) *PHOPE*

———. *Pedagogy of the Heart.* Translated by Donaldo Macedo and Alexandre Oliveira. New York: Continuum, 2000. (Original work published 1997.) *PHEART*

———. *Pedagogy of the Oppressed.* Translated by M. Bergman Ramos. New York: Continuum, 2003. (Original work published 1970.) *PO*

———. "The Process of Political Literacy." In *The Politics of Education*, translated by Donaldo Macedo, 99–108. Westport, Conn.: Bergin and Garvey, 1985. PPL

———. "Response." In *Mentoring the Mentor: A Critical Dialogue with Paulo Freire*, edited by Paulo Freire, J. W. Fraser, Donaldo Macedo, T. McKinnon, and W. T. Stokes, 303–29. New York: Peter Lang, 1997. RES

———. "The Third World and Theology." In *Paulo Freire*, 13–14. Washington, D.C.: U.S. Catholic Conference, 1973. TWT

Freire, Paulo, and Antonio Faundez. *Learning to Question: A Pedagogy of Liberation.* New York: Continuum, 1992. (Original work published 1989.)

Freire, Paulo, and Donaldo Macedo. "Rethinking Critical Pedagogy: A Dialogue with Paulo Freire." In *The Politics of Education*, 175–99. Westport, Conn.: Bergin and Garvey, 1985.

Fromm, Erich. *The Heart of Man: Its Genius for Good and Evil.* New York: Perennial Library, 1971.

———. *The Revolution of Hope.* New York: Bantam, 1968.

Gable, Shelly L., and Jonathan Haidt. "What (and Why) Is Positive Psychology?" *Review of General Psychology* 9, no. 2 (2005): 103–10.

Garrison, Jim. *Dewey and Eros: Wisdom and Desire in the Art of Teaching.* New York: Teachers College Press, 1997.

Geertz, Clifford. *The Interpretation of Cultures.* New York: Basic, 1975.

Glaude, Eddie, Jr. "Tragedy and Moral Experience: John Dewey and Toni Morrison's *Beloved*." In *Pragmatism and the Problem of Race*, edited by Bill Lawson and Donald Koch, 89–121. Bloomington: Indiana University Press, 2004.

Godfrey, Joseph J. *A Philosophy of Human Hope.* Dordrecht: Martinus Nijhoff Publishers, 1987.

Golden, Harry. *Only in America.* Cleveland: World Publishing, 1958.

Grean, Stanley. "Elements of Transcendence in Dewey's Naturalistic Humanism." *Journal of the American Academy of Religion* 52, no. 2 (1984): 263–88.

Gutierrez, Gustavo. *A Theology of Liberation.* Maryknoll, N.Y.: Orbis Books, 1973.

Hanh, Thich Nhat. *The Heart of the Buddha's Teaching.* New York: Broadway Books, 1998.

———. *Touching Peace: Practicing the Art of Mindful Living.* Berkeley: Parallax Press, 1992.

Hofstadter, Richard. *Anti-intellectualism in America.* New York: Vintage, 1963.

Hook, Sidney. *Out of Step.* New York: Harper and Row, 1987.

———. *Pragmatism and the Tragic Sense of Life.* New York: Basic Books, 1974.

hooks, bell. *Teaching to Transgress: Education as the Practice of Freedom.* New York: Routledge, 1994.

Hume, David. "Dissertation on the Passions." In vol. 2 of *The Philosophical Works of David Hume*, edited by T. H. Greene and T. H. Grose, 139–66. London: Longmans, Green, 1898.

———. *A Treatise of Human Nature*, edited by D. F. Norton and M. J. Norton, bk. 2, pt. 3, sec. 9. Oxford: Oxford University Press, 2001.

Jackson, Philip W. *John Dewey and the Lessons of Art.* New Haven: Yale University Press, 1998.

James, William. "Is Life Worth Living?" In *The Will to Believe, and Other Essays in Popular Philosophy*, 32–62. New York: Longmans, Green, 1927.

Jefferson, Thomas. Letter to Samuel Kercheval, Monticello, July 12, 1816. In *Thomas*

Jefferson: Writings, edited by Merrill D. Peterson, 1395–1403. New York: Library of America, 1984.

———. *The Political Writings of Thomas Jefferson*. Edited by Edward Dumbauld. Indianapolis: Bobbs-Merrill, 1955.

Kallen, Horace. "John Dewey and the Spirit of Pragmatism." In *John Dewey: Philosopher of Science and Freedom*, edited by Sidney Hook, 3–46. New York: Dial, 1950.

———. "Of Death and the Future." In *Patterns of Progress*, 53–83. New York: Columbia University Press, 1950.

Kubler-Ross, Elisabeth. *On Death and Dying*. New York: Macmillan, 1968.

Lamont, Corliss. *Dialogue on John Dewey*. New York: Horizon Press, 1959.

Larrabee, Harold A. "John Dewey as Teacher." In *John Dewey: Master Educator*, edited by William W. Brickman and Stanley Lehrer, 93–100. New York: Atherton Press, 1966.

Lasch, Christopher. *The True and Only Heaven: Progress and Its Critics*. New York: W. W. Norton, 1991.

Lazarus, Richard S. "Hope: An Emotion and a Vital Coping Resource against Despair." *Social Research* 66, no. 2 (Summer 1999): 653–78.

Lincoln, Yvonna S., and Egon G. Guba. *Naturalistic Inquiry*. Beverly Hills: Sage, 1984.

Locke, Edwin A., and Gary P. Latham. "Building a Practically Useful Theory of Goal Setting and Task Motivation: A 35-Year Odyssey." *American Psychologist* 57, no. 9 (2002): 705–17.

Mackie, Robert. "Contributions to the Thought of Paulo Freire." In *Literacy and Revolution*, edited by Robert Mackie, 93–119. New York: Continuum, 1981.

Mansbridge, Jane J. *Beyond Adversary Democracy*. Chicago: University of Chicago Press, 1980.

Marcel, Gabriel. "An Autobiographical Essay." In *The Philosophy of Gabriel Marcel*, edited by Paul Schilpp and Lewis Hahn, 3–68. LaSalle, Ill.: Open Court, 1984.

———. *Being and Having: An Existentialist Diary*. Translated by Katharine Farrer. New York: Harper and Row, 1948. BH

———. *The Broken World*. In *Gabriel Marcel's Perspectives on "The Broken World,"* translated by Katherine Rose Hanley, 31–152. Milwaukee: Marquette University Press, 1998.

———. "Concrete Approaches to Investigating the Ontological Mystery." Translated by Katharine Rose Hanley. In *Gabriel Marcel's Perspectives on "The Broken World,"* edited and translated by Katharine Rose Hanley, 172–97. Milwaukee: Marquette University Press, 1998. OM

———. "Desire and Hope." Translated by Nathaniel Lawrence. In *Readings in Existential Phenomenology*, edited by Nathaniel Lawrence and Daniel O'Conner, 277–85. Englewood Cliffs, N.J.: Prentice-Hall, 1967. DH

———. *The Existential Background of Human Dignity*. Cambridge, Mass.: Harvard University Press, 1963.

————. *Homo Viator: Introduction to a Metaphysic of Hope*. Translated by Emma Crau-furd. Gloucester, Mass.: Peter Smith, 1978. *HV*

————. *Man against Humanity*. Translated by G. S. Fraser. London: Harvill Press, 1952. *MAH*

————. *Man against Mass Society*. Translated by G. S. Fraser. London: Harvill Press, 1952.

————. *The Metaphysical Journal*. Translated by Bernard Wall. London: Rockliff Publishing, 1952. *MJ*

————. *The Mystery of Being: I. Reflection and Mystery*. Translated by G. S. Fraser. Chicago: Gateway, 1960.

————. *The Mystery of Being: II. Faith and Reality*. Translated by Rene Hague. Chicago: Gateway, 1960.

————. "On the Ontological Mystery." In *The Philosophy of Existentialism*, translated by Manya Harari, 9–46. New York: Citadel Press, 1970. OMM

————. *Presence and Immortality*. Pittsburgh: Duquesne University Press, 1967.

————. "Sketch of a Phenomenology and a Metaphysic of Hope." In *Homo Viator: Introduction to a Metaphysic of Hope*, translated by Emma Craufurd, 29–67. Gloucester, Mass.: Peter Smith, 1978. SK

Marx, Karl. *Capital: A Critique of Political Economy*. Vol. 1. Translated by S. Moore and E. Aveling. Edited by Frederick Engels. In *The Marx-Engels Reader*, edited by Robert C. Tucker, 294–442. 2d ed. New York: W. W. Norton, 1978. (Original work published 1867.)

McDermott, John J. "The Gamble for Excellence: John Dewey's Pedagogy of Experience." In *Values and Value Theory in Twentieth-Century America*, edited by Murray G. Murphey and Ivar Berg, 101–21. Philadelphia: Temple University Press, 1988.

————. "Why Bother? Is Life Worth Living? Experience as Pedagogical." In *Philosophy and the Reconstruction of Culture*, edited by John J. Stuhr, 273–83. Albany: SUNY Press, 1993.

Melzer, Dan. "Discourse across the Disciplines: A National Study of College Writing Assignments." Unpublished ms., California State University at Sacramento, 2005.

Memmi, Albert. *The Colonizer and the Colonized*. Translated by H. Greenfeld. Boston: Beacon Press, 1967. (Original work published 1957.)

Miles, Matthew B., and A. Michael Huberman. *Qualitative Data Analysis*. Beverly Hills: Sage, 1984.

Morse, Donald. "Pragmatism and the Tragic Sense of Life." *Transactions of the Charles S. Peirce Society* 37, no. 4 (Fall 2001): 555–72.

Muyskens, James L. *The Sufficiency of Hope: Conceptual Foundations of Religion*. Philadelphia: Temple University Press, 1979.

Nagel, Ernest. Introduction to vol. 12 of *The Later Works*, by John Dewey (*LW* 12: xiii–xv).

Neibuhr, Reinhold. *Moral Man and Immoral Society*. New York: Scribners, 1960. (Original work published 1932.)

Nesse, Randolph. "The Evolution of Hope and Despair." *Social Research* 62, no. 2 (Summer 1999): 429–69.

Novack, George. *Pragmatism and Marxism*. New York: Pathfinder Press, 1975.

Otto, Max. *The Progressive* (Madison, Wisc., July 1952). Available online at http://www.harvardsquarelibrary.org/unitarians/dewey.html.

Pateman, Carol. *Participation and Democratic Theory*. New York: Cambridge University Press, 1970.

Pawelski, James O. "William James, Positive Psychology, and Healthy Mindedness." *Journal of Speculative Philosophy* 17, no. 1 (2003): 53–67.

Peirce, Charles S. "How to Make Our Ideas Clear." In *The Essential Writings of C. S. Peirce*, edited by Edward C. Moore, 137–57. Amherst, N.Y.: Prometheus Books, 1998.

Peterson, Christopher. "The Future of Optimism." *American Psychologist* 55, no. 1 (January 2000): 44–55.

Pieper, Josef. *Hope and History: Five Salzburg Lectures*. Translated by David Kipp. San Francisco: Ignatius Press, 1994. (Original work published 1969.)

———. *On Hope*. Translated by Sr. Mary Frances McCarthy. San Francisco: Ignatius Press, 1986. (Original work published 1977.)

Putnam, Hilary. *The Collapse of the Fact/Value Dichotomy, and Other Essays*. Cambridge, Mass.: Harvard University Press, 2002.

Randall, John Herman, Jr. "John Dewey, 1859–1952." *Journal of Philosophy* 50, no. 1 (1953): 5–13.

Rauschenbusch, Walter. *A Theology for the Social Gospel*. Louisville: Westminster John Knox Press, 1997. (Original work published 1917.)

Riepe, Dale. "Critique of Idealistic Naturalism: Methodological Pollution in the Mainstream of American Philosophy." In *Radical Currents in Contemporary Philosophy*, edited by David H. DeGrood, Dale Riepe, and John Somervile, 5–22. St. Louis: Warren H. Green, 1971.

Rockefeller, Steven. *John Dewey: Religious Faith and Democratic Humanism*. New York: Columbia University Press, 1991.

Rorty, Richard. "After Philosophy, Democracy." In *The American Philosopher*, edited by Giovanna Borradori, 103–17. Chicago: University of Chicago Press, 1994.

———. *Consequences of Pragmatism*. Minneapolis: University of Minnesota Press, 1982.

———. *Philosophy and Social Hope*. London: Penguin, 1999.

———. "Truth without Correspondence to Reality." In *Philosophy and Social Hope*, 23–46. New York: Penguin, 1999.

Rosenthal, Ted. *How Could I Not Be among You? A Portrait of Poet Ted Rosenthal*. Produced by Marshall Potamkin. Directed by Thomas Reichman. Briarcliff Manor, N.Y.: Benchmark Films, 1970.

Ross, Edward Alsworth. *Sins and Society: An Analysis of Latter-day Iniquity.* Boston: Houghton Mifflin, 1907.

Roth, Robert J., S.J. *American Religious Philosophy.* New York: Harcourt, Brace, and World, 1967.

Ryan, Alan. *John Dewey and the High Tide of American Liberalism.* New York: W. W. Norton, 1995.

Santayana, George. *The Life of Reason: Reason in Religion.* Vol. 3. New York: Scribner, 1906.

Sax, Linda J., Alexander W. Astin, William S. Korn, and Kathryn M. Mahoney. *The American Freshman: National Norms for Fall 1999.* Los Angeles: Higher Education Research Institute, UCLA, 1999.

Schumacher, Bernard. *A Philosophy of Hope: Josef Pieper and the Contemporary Debate on Hope.* Translated by D. C. Schindler. New York: Fordham University Press, 2003.

Seligman, Martin E. P., and Mihaly Csikszentmihalyi. "Positive Psychology." *American Psychologist* 55, no. 1 (January 2000): 5–14.

Shade, Patrick. *Habits of Hope: A Pragmatic Theory.* Nashville: Vanderbilt University Press, 2001.

Shannon, Patrick. *Becoming Political, Too: New Readings and Writings on the Politics of Literacy Education.* Portsmouth, N.H.: Heinemann, 2001.

Shor, Ira. "What Is Critical Literacy?" In *Critical Literacy in Action,* edited by Ira Shor and Carolyn Pari, 1–30. Portsmouth, N.H.: Boynton/Cook Heinemann, 1999.

———, ed. *Freire for the Classroom: A Sourcebook for Liberatory Teaching.* Portsmouth, N.H.: Boynton/Cook Heinemann, 1987.

Shor, Ira, and Paulo Freire. *A Pedagogy for Liberation: Dialogues on Transforming Education.* Westport, Conn.: Bergin and Garvey, 1987.

Shor, Ira, and Caroline Pari, eds. *Education Is Politics: Critical Teaching across Differences, K–12.* Portsmouth, N.H.: Heinemann, 1999.

Snyder, C. R. "Hope Theory: Rainbows in the Mind." *Psychological Inquiry* 13, no. 4 (2002): 249–75. HT

———. "The Past and Possible Futures of Hope." *Journal of Social and Clinical Psychology* 19, no. 1 (2000): 11–29. PPFH

———. *The Psychology of Hope.* New York: Free Press, 1994. PH

Snyder, C. R., Jennifer Cheavens, and Susie C. Sympson. "Hope: An Individual Motive for Social Commerce." In *Group Dynamics: Theory, Research, and Practice* 1, no. 2 (1997): 107–18. HIM

Snyder, C. R., and Shane J. Lopez. "The Future of Positive Psychology." In *The Handbook of Positive Psychology,* edited by C. R. Snyder and Shane J. Lopez, 751–67. New York: Oxford University Press, 2002. FPP

[Snyder, C. R.], Hal S. Shorey, C. R. Snyder, Kevin L. Rand, Jill R. Hockenmeyer, and David B. Feldman. "Somewhere over the Rainbow: Hope Theory Weathers Its First Decade." *Psychological Inquiry* 13, no. 4 (2002): 322–31. SOR

Snyder, C. R., and Susie C. Sympson. "Development and Initial Validation of the

Domain Specific Hope Scale." Unpublished manuscript. Lawrence, Kans.: University of Kansas Department of Psychology, 1997. DIV

Spradley, James. *The Ethnographic Interview*. New York: Holt, 1979.

———. *Participant Observation*. New York: Holt, 1980.

Stace, Walter T. *Mysticism and Philosophy*. London: Macmillan, 1960.

Streck, Danilo R. "John Dewey's and Paulo Freire's Views on the Political Function of Education, with Special Emphasis on the Problem of Method." Ph.D. diss., Rutgers University, 1977.

———. "Toward a Pedagogy of a New Social Contract." *Globalisation, Societies, and Education* 2, no. 2 (2004): 215–29.

Stuhr, John J. *Genealogical Pragmatism: Philosophy, Experience, and Community*. Albany: SUNY Press, 1997.

Sympson, Susie C. "Validation of the Specific Domain Hope Scale." Ph.D. diss., University of Kansas, 1999.

Tanner, Laurel N. *Dewey's Laboratory School: Lessons for Today*. New York: Teachers College Press, 1997.

Taylor, Paul V. *The Texts of Paulo Freire*. Buckingham: Open University Press, 1993.

Tennen, Howard, Glenn Affleck, and Ruth Tennen. "Clipped Feathers: The Theory and Measurement of Hope." *Psychological Inquiry* 13, no. 4 (2002): 311–17.

Wells, Harry K. *Pragmatism: Philosophy of Imperialism*. New York: International Publisher, 1954.

West, Cornel. *Keeping the Faith: Philosophy and Race in America*. New York: Routledge, 1993.

Westbrook, Robert. *John Dewey and American Democracy*. Ithaca, N.Y.: Cornell University Press, 1991.

———. "Public Schooling and American Democracy." In *Democracy, Education, and the Schools*, edited by Roger Soder, 125–50. San Francisco: Jossey-Bass, 1996.

White, Patricia. *Civic Virtues and Public Schooling*. New York: Teachers College Press, 1996.

Williams, Robert, ed. *John Dewey: Recollections*. Washington, D.C.: University Press of America, 1982.

Zaehner, R. C. *Mysticism, Sacred and Profane*. New York: Oxford, 1957.

INDEX

of ancestry, 7–8; on constructed knowing, 111; on creative moments, 101–2; on education for democracy, 72–76; on intelligent wholeheartedness, 10; on negative capability, 29, 31, 75; reflections on "Philosophy and Practice of Hope" course, 163–65; on ultimate hope, 22
"flickering" of life, 6, 99
Ford, Henry, 41
Freire, Paulo
—personal life: exile from Brazil, 63; experiences with social revolution, 64; lecture on corporal punishment, 68–69
—views: on animal life, 192–93n5; on capitalism, 69–72; on the Catholic Church, 151; on *con-scientizacao*, 55–56, 61–63, 159; contributions to liberation theology, 75, 194n10; on democracy as ultimate hope, 64–72, 99–100; on the Easter experience, 62–63, 159; effects on students, 151, 159; on pedagogical and social reform, 56–64, 72–76, 196n3; on social action, 54–55
—works: *Pedagogy of the Oppressed* (1968), 59, 69, 174; Interview with Donaldo Macedo (1985), 58; *Pedagogy of Hope* (1992), 174; *Pedagogy of the Heart* (1997), 174
Fromm, Erich, 34, 82, 182n6
functional worldview, 34, 39–40, 135

Gable, Shelly L., 80
Garrison, Jim, 188n10
getting-there/being-there balance, 82–83
Glahn, Bob: biographical sketch, 106–8; as discussant for *A Common Faith*, 123, 126; experiences of personal

misfortune, 138; experiences with co-inquiry, 158; experiences with constructed knowing, 112–13, 136, 147–48
goals: animal impulses as, 15–16, 87; cultural values and, 91–93; faith in choices of, 47–49; hope as emotion and, 14–15; integration of goals, 85–86; learning high-hope habits and, 84–86; measurement of progress and, 21–22; particular hopes and, 4, 21–22, 81–84, 88–90, 188n1; personal ownership of, 83–84; positive psychology and, 81–86; self-interest and, 93–95
God: absolute hope and, 51–52, 98; brevity of life and, 3; devotion to God, 36–39; unconditional love and, 47
Golden, Harry, xvi
gratitude: as experience of Deweyan community, 125; as key to Deweyan hope, 4–8, 45–46, 99, 161, 171, 188n2; Marcel on, 188n2
greed. See competition; self-interest

habit, 14, 132–33, 139
Haidt, Jonathan, 80
harmony: cycles of disturbance/harmony, 147–49, 161; as general object of hope, 16–17; limited vs. enduring extent of, 25–26; as pedagogical experience, 110
high-hope personality, 82–88, 91, 96–97, 153–54
Hinson, Rebecca: biographical sketch, 106–7; on course writing assignments, 114; experiences with constructed knowing, 112, 142, 145–46; on present experience, 135, 146
Holmes, Oliver Wendell, Jr., 189n4
honor, 188n2

inquiry approach, 109–10, 113–27, 158–59, 196n3; constructed-knowing approach, 110–13, 116, 157–58, 197n9; data collection and analysis for, 169–70; impact of key ideas, 159–61; impact on students, xxiv, 159–61, 166, 198–99n1; as intelligent wholeheartedness, 10; McCarthy role in course, xx–xxii; profile of students, 106–9, 128–29; reading list, 108, 109; students' engagement of Dewey, xix, 160–61, 198–99n1; syllabus, 171–86; writing assignments, 113–19, 177–78, 180–86

Pieper, Josef, 37, 109, 143–44, 150, 172–73

poetry, 28–29

positive psychology, xxiii, 78, 81–96

pragmatism, 67–68

presence (Marcel), 72, 144–45, 152–53, 160, 191n3. *See also* enriched present experience

progress, xv, 21–22

purposefulness: gratitude as source of, 5; high-hope personality, 82–86, 91, 96–97; nature and, 46

Randall, John Herman, Jr., xii, 165

reasonable hope, 18–20

religion: conscientization as rebirth, 62–63, 159; course writing assignments on, 114–15; Dewey use of religious language, 189n7; fatalism and, 70; Freire critique of Catholic Church, 151; liberation theology, 194n19; Pieper Thomist views, 172–73; religious experiences, 25, 121–25; student reactions to *A Common Faith* and, 120–25, 149–50

Rockefeller, Steven, xix, 190n12

Rorty, Richard, xv, xix, 188n8–9, 197n9

Ryan, Alan, xix

self-interest, 23–24, 93–95. *See also* competition

Seligman, Martin E. P., 78–80, 174

Shor, Ira, 192n4, 193n14, 193n17

Snyder, C. R.
—views: effects on students, 152–55, 159–61, 174–75; on hopelessness, 87–90, 98; on the importance of planning, 18; on moral hope, 90–95; positive psychology study and, xxiii, 95–97; theory of hope, 81–87, 152–54
—works: *Psychology of Hope, The* (1994), 81, 90–91, 93–95, 153; "Hope: An Individual Motive for Social Commerce" (1997), 94–95; "Somewhere over the Rainbow: Hope Theory Weathers Its First Decade" (2002), 92

social gospel, 7

social intelligence, 66

social reform: conscientization (Freire), 61–63; Freire-Dewey views on, 54–55, 192–93n5; intelligent wholeheartedness and, 88–89; "method of intelligence" (Dewey), 59–61; passive vs. active involvement in, 193n11; philosophy and, 164–65, 167; positive psychology and, 91–93, 96–97. *See also* education for democracy

society: benevolent dictatorship and, 193n11; community as object of hope, 49–51; cultural diversity in, 42, 91–93; democracy as social articulation, 56, 64–65; functional worldview and, 34, 39–40, 135; *gesellschaft* societies (Tönnies), 35; instinctive

participation in, 23; I-thou vs. I-it relationships, 56, 67–69. *See also* class
Stoicism, 24
success/failure, 12–13, 137–38, 146, 161, 187n6. *See also* hopelessness

temporal integration. *See* enriched present experience
time: community problem solving and, 50–51, 101–2; idolatry of the future (Fromm), 82; present alertness, 11–12; resolving the particular/infinite dualism, 27; youth-age continuity and, 190n11. *See also* chain of ancestry; enriched present experience
Tönnies, Ferdinand, 35
transcendence. *See* God

ultimate hope (Dewey): defined, 4; comparison of Dewey and Marcel views on, 32, 45–51; Fishman experience of, 22, 31; integration of goals and, 85–86; nature as context for, 6, 24; particular hopes and, 88–90, 188n1; positive psychology and, 95–96; purpose of, 20–21, 51–53; uncertainty of, 24
uncertainty, 24

University of North Carolina at Charlotte (UNCC), 106, 111. *See also* "Philosophy and Practice of Hope"
utopian philosophy, xv, 21–22

Vernarsky, Christopher: biographical sketch, 106–7; on course writing assignments, 115; on Deweyan naturalism, 149–50; as discussant for *A Common Faith*, 120–22, 125; experiences with co-inquiry, 158, 166; experiences with constructed knowing, 142, 150–52, 155

war, xviii, 43, 79, 132–33. *See also* combativeness
Westbrook, Robert, xv, xix
Weston, Lindsey: biographical sketch, 106–8; as discussant for *A Common Faith*, 125–26; experiences of community, 139; experiences of personal misfortune, 130, 140–41, 144; experiences with constructed knowing, 118–19
Wieman, Henry, 120
willpower/waypower, 81, 86–87
wishful hope, 18

STEPHEN M. FISHMAN teaches philosophy at the University of North Carolina at Charlotte. Since attending his first Writing Across the Curriculum workshop in 1983, he has been studying student writing and learning in his classes. He is an alumnus of Camp Rising Sun, Rhinebeck, New York, an international scholarship camp founded in 1930 to promote world peace.

LUCILLE MCCARTHY teaches composition and literature at the University of Maryland, Baltimore County. She is the coauthor of *Thinking and Writing in College* with Barbara Walvoord (1990) and *The Psychiatry of Handicapped Children and Adolescents* with Joan Gerring (1988).

Together, Fishman and McCarthy have conducted a number of theory/practice inquiries. These have appeared in various journals, including *College English*, *Written Communication*, *Transactions of the Charles S. Peirce Society*, and *Philosophy Today*. In addition, they have coauthored three books: *John Dewey and the Challenge of Classroom Practice* (1998), *Unplayed Tapes: A Personal History of Collaborative Teacher Research* (2000), and *Whose Goals? Whose Aspirations? Learning to Teach Underprepared Writers across the Curriculum* (2002). Their work has twice earned them the James N. Britton Award from the National Council of Teachers of English.

The University of Illinois Press
is a founding member of the
Association of American University Presses.

———————————————

Composed in 10 /13 Janson Text
with Type Embellishments Ornaments
by Celia Shapland
at the University of Illinois Press
Manufactured by Thomson-Shore, Inc.

University of Illinois Press
1325 South Oak Street
Champaign, IL 61820-6903
www.press.uillinois.edu